A STRANGE LIBERATION

Tibetan Lives in Chinese Hands

A STRANGE LIBERATION

Tibetan Lives in Chinese Hands

by David Patt

Snow Lion Publications

Ithaca, New York USA

Snow Lion Publications
P.O. Box 6483
Ithaca, New York 14851 USA

Copyright © 1992 David Patt

First Edition USA 1992

Designed and Set in Caslon 11 on 13 point by Gigantic Computing

Printed in USA

ISBN 1-55939-013-1

Library of Congress Cataloging-in-Publication Data

Patt, David.
    A strange liberation: Tibetan lives in Chinese hands / by
David Patt. — 1st ed.
            p.   cm.
    ISBN 1-55939-013-1 :
    1. Tibet (China)—History. 2. Tibet (China) —History—
Uprising of 1959. I. Title. II. Title: Tibetan lives in
Chinese hands.
    DS786.P28 1992
    951'.505—dc20   92-44590
                                                        CIP

Contents

ཁ་བ་བབས་སོང་མ་སྐྱོ་ཨང་།
ཁ་རྒྱབ་ཉི་མ་དྲོ་རྒྱུ་འོང་།།

The snow has fallen, but don't be sad,
After the snowfall, comes the warmth of the sun.

–Traditional Tibetan folk song sung by Ama Adhe

This work is dedicated to the memory of Iryne,
who taught me to care.

PART 1

A STRANGE LIBERATION

Ten Truths About Tibet

A Strange Liberation:
Ten Truths About Tibet

There are places on this planet that are sacred, where the spirit rises and the divine descends to meet the heart of human consciousness. In the natural geography of our world system we look up to find the infinite, to the life-giving sun, the soothing love-light of the moon, the incalculable messages of the constellated stars. We look up to the illuminated mysteries of the heavens, to reawaken a deeply foreshadowed memory of beyond.

We experience our lives as earthbound, weighed down by gravity in a physical form that will in its time betray us, decay from pleasure to pain to leave in the end a spent carcass back in the mud of our beginnings.

To find transcendence from this physical plane of time and death we look up. We look up to the mountains, to the realm of the gods, to the almost unattainable, the snow-fields of cloud, where the material earth reaches out to the ethereal sky.

We look up to cosmic mountains, to Mount Meru, the center of the Hindu and Buddhist universe, the jewel mountain surrounded by seven encircling seas. We imagine mountains as the embodiment of the spirit of our faith, as the four sacred directional mountains of Buddhist China, where the bodhisattvas of each mountain appear to pilgrims as wise and ancient hermits. We look up to mountains of revelation – Mount Sinai, where the Lord was revealed in storm and fire and the ten commandments were delivered to Moses as the moral bedrock of western civilization. From mountains we receive wisdom, as when Jesus, "seeing the multitudes, went up on a mountain" to deliver a sermon of surpassing compassion and peace, and included the words, "Blessed are those who are persecuted for righteousness' sake." We look out from mountains of vision, as Han-shan, the Chinese hermit poet looked out from Cold Mountain and wrote,

> *High, high from the summit of the peak,*
> *Whatever way I look, no limit in sight.*[1]

There, at the top of the world, is the jumping-off point, where the spirit soars, the peak of existence. There, we remember, at the top of the world, is what we always knew. Freedom, peace, light, are high things. They gravitate, they levitate, to high places. To find the sacred places of this world we look up.

Tibet has been called the "Altar of the Earth."[2] It is the highest inhabited plateau in the world, and it contains some of the world's highest mountains. Open your atlas and see. Look at any physical map of central Asia and immediately it is there, its shape clearly defined by the color-code of altitude, a diving swirl of white and mauve set off by the unarguable fact of immoveable mountains from the diminishing browns and mustards and greens of its neighbors below.

The first truth about Tibet: By the hard rocks of geography Tibet is not China, not India, Burma, or Nepal. Those are the lowlands, terrestrial worlds, tapering down from the high altar of the Tibetan peaks, down to touch the outer seas. Tibet stands above. It is a place where the habitable lands lie between 10,000 and 15,000 feet above sea level and the mountain passes rise to 18,000 feet. You can walk through an upland pasture in Kham at the same altitude that you fly in a jet airplane from Chicago to Milwaukee. The sky is an uncanny color of blue; rainbows tumble from mountain mists. And most of Asia's mighty rivers plunge to their distant destinations from the trickling streams of Tibet's melting spring snows.

It is a vast area, half a million square miles, the better part of western Europe. Its population, never accurately counted, was estimated by the Tibetan Government to be about six million. Their early ancestry is obscure but generally traced to nomadic tribes of herders who ranged across the eastern regions of Central Asia. The second truth about Tibet: Racially, Tibetans are not Chinese. They are visibly of a different racial stock, and in fact the Chinese have always recognized them as a separate race. Physically, Tibetans resemble no group more than the Navajo Indians of the American Southwest.

Tibet enters recorded history in the middle of the seventh century when the unstable assortment of clans and localized noble lords unite in support of a unified monarchy in the person of the king of the Yarlung Valley. With astonishing rapidity they forge a political and military entity that expands Tibetan borders in every direction. By 640 C.E. they have taken such a bite out of the western edges of the Empire of the Tang Dynasty that the Chinese find it prudent to make a peace offering of a princess bride to King Songtsen Gampo.

But this was only the beginning of over two hundred years of Tibetan military expansionism. To the north they took control of strategic points on the trade routes, cutting China off from its westerly provinces and establishing Tibet as the dominant force in Central Asia. The Tibetans gobbled up, held and administered the Chinese province of Gansu, large chunks of Sichuan, and Yunnan. The Chinese records show that in the year 763 C.E. they were paying an annual tribute to the Tibetans of 50,000 rolls of silk. At the peak of their power the Tibetans captured Chang'an, the capital of the Chinese Empire, and for a time even placed their own puppet on the throne.

In 821 C.E. a treaty was concluded between the two powers and recorded in both the Tibetan and Chinese languages on a pillar in Lhasa. The text of the treaty begins:

> The Great King of Tibet, the Miraculous Divine Lord, and the Great King of China, the Chinese Ruler Hwang-ti, being in the relationship of nephew and uncle, have conferred together for the alliance of their kingdoms. They have made and ratified a great agreement. Gods and men all know it and bear witness so that it may never be changed....
>
> Tibet and China shall abide by the frontiers of which they are now in occupation. All to the east is the country of Great China; and all to the west is, without question, the country of Great Tibet. Henceforth on neither side shall there be waging of war nor seizing of territory.[3]

The third truth about Tibet: From its inception as a unified state Tibet was a sovereign and independent nation, recognized and treated as such by a respectful – and at times intimidated – neighbor, China.

In the course of their foreign excursions the Tibetans found Buddhist culture flowering in every direction. King Songtsen Gampo's Chinese and Nepalese princess brides each brought – along with their own Buddhist faith – an image of the Buddha. Chapels were built, and these two images became the most holy in all of Tibet. During his reign the King sent his minister, Thonmi Sambhota, to India to devise a script for the Tibetan language, and upon his return he introduced the Tibetan alphabet, based upon the Indian Gupta script. The fourth truth is that the Tibetan language is historically and structurally unrelated to Chinese. The only Chinese to be found in Tibetan is a few loanwords, mainly describing Chinese objects.

So began an extraordinary process of cultural importation

and assimilation that has no apparent counterpart in world history. For the next four hundred years the Tibetans applied their national wealth and energy to the adoption of Buddhism, translating its literature from Indian Sanskrit sources and integrating Buddhist monastic social structures into the socio-economic life of the country.

In its initial phase Buddhism took hold gradually, and under the patronage of the Dharma Kings it was confined to the noble class. By the late eighth century the first monastery had been built at Samye, under the spiritual direction of the Indian sage Shantarakshita. It was at Samye, around 792 C.E., that, according to tradition, a decisive debate was conducted between Shantarakshita's disciple Kamalashila and the Chinese monk Hoshang Mahayana to determine whether Tibet should pursue the Indian system of Buddhist teaching or the Chinese.

According to the Indian scholastic tradition, enlightenment is attained by a gradual process, over many lifetimes, based on a vast accumulation of merit, the cultivation of single-pointed concentration, and the incisive application of analysis to produce insight into the ultimate nature of reality.

The Chinese school emphasized the inherent Buddha-nature alive but dormant in all beings, and based its practice on the possibility of spontaneously and suddenly awakening this natural state. Kamalashila argued for the need to meditate by means of analysis in order to realize the true nature of things – their origination in dependence on causes and conditions, their emptiness of any inherent and independent existence. The Chinese approach rejected analysis, and based its meditative practice on non-conceptuality, a state of actualized emptiness, in which the natural state of Buddhahood could spontaneously arise.

The historical records of this debate are obscure, but the tradition tells us that the judgment went for Kamalashila, and the Indian teaching was declared the orthodox system for the future of Buddhism in Tibet. Although the ideas and practices characteristic of the Chinese tradition were never truly expunged from the diverse lineages of Tibet, the rejection of

Chinese Buddhism was in fact a rejection of Chinese influence on Tibetan culture. From the time of the Samye debate Tibet turned its attention to Indian Buddhism, drawing its religious literature and its lineages of practice almost exclusively from the holy land of the Buddha.

The breakup of a unified Tibet in 842 C.E. seems in part to have stemmed from a reaction by conservative forces opposed to the rising political influence of Buddhist monks, and the increasing displacement of traditional religious practice, called Bon, by the newly imported religion. Whether or not there was an actual suppression of Buddhism at this time, certainly the organized introduction of Buddhism under the patronage of powerful kings came to a halt. For 150 years Buddhism in Tibet must have simmered quietly, based on the foundations laid during the time of the Dharma Kings.

By the end of the tenth century the revival of Buddhism was evident in both Western and Eastern Tibet, and soon activity was apparent in Central Tibet as well. The process of cultural importation reached its peak in 1042 with the arrival of Atisha, perhaps the greatest Indian Buddhist master of his age. This sage was repeatedly invited to Tibet by the kings of Western Tibet and was eventually paid vast sums in gold to come to Tibet and teach. Atisha's authority as an Indian master, his emphasis on the morality of traditional monasticism and the philosophical traditions of Indian Buddhism, gave a solid and orthodox foundation to future developments in Tibet. "From this time on the Tibetans clearly began to subordinate everything else to the propagation of their holy religion."[4]

During the very period when Buddhism was in decline in its native India the Tibetans were translating and absorbing its entire corpus of theory and practice. By the time the Turkic Muslims invading North India delivered the mortal blow to Indian Buddhism by sacking its most important monastic centers, Tibet was well established as a treasure house of Buddhism in Asia, carrying on the lineages of late Indian Buddhism, with the better part of Indian Buddhist canonical literature available in Tibetan translation.

To this huge volume of literature in translation the Tibetans added thousands of volumes of their own, writing in their native language commentaries, manuals, and philosophical works that rose to a level of scholarship and philosophical sophistication equal to any of the great civilizations of world history.

Buddhism provided Tibet not just the dominant religion, but also the fundamental world-view, the unifying cement of the society that pervaded every aspect of the spiritual, cultural, and economic life of the country. The physical isolation and magical land- and sky-scapes created a realm ideal for spiritual endeavor and transformation. Isolated mountain caves offered silence and renunciation to practitioners on extended intensive meditation retreats. And scholarship flourished at the many thousands of monasteries which grew up in towns and villages throughout the country. Some of these monastic centers developed into huge and powerful institutions, dominating the economic life of their communities and wielding great influence in the worldly domain of politics.

The Tibetan people, who during the pre-Buddhist era of military dominance were described in Chinese records as a barbarian tribe of savage warriors who painted their faces red with ocher, became a people permeated with faith and devotion toward the Three Jewels of Buddhism – the three objects of faith to which a Buddhist looks for protection and guidance on the path to becoming a better person, and ultimately a fully enlightened Buddha.

The first of the Three Jewels is the Buddha, the one who succeeded in his own spiritual quest, perfected his qualities of morality and compassion, and applied his powerful meditative concentration to the nature of reality, until he attained the enlightened understanding of its ultimate nature of suffering, impermanence, and interdependent origination.

The second jewel is the Dharma: On one level, Dharma is the religious system, embodied in written texts, that the Buddha taught so that others could follow his method. On a deeper level, Dharma refers to the actual realizations that come in the course of the path, and the cessation of delusion and suffering brought about by these realizations.

The third jewel is the Sangha: On the highest level the Sangha are those who have directly realized the interdependence of existence, which is the true nature of all things. But in its more common usage the Sangha is the community of ordained monks and nuns, as well as highly accomplished lay practitioners, who exemplify the Buddhist path and behave as spiritual friends, accompanying the practitioner along the way. It is estimated that fifteen to twenty percent of the male population of Tibet entered the monasteries. There was no family that did not have a son, a brother, or an uncle who was a monk, and the monks were everywhere venerated. The monasteries were the cultural centers of the society, places where yak-herding peasant boys became literate students, sometimes brilliant scholars, and occasionally highly realized saints.

Religion came to permeate every element of the society, from deciding when to plant the barley in a remote village, to the selection of a new Dalai Lama, the supreme spiritual and temporal leader of the country. Every road was lined with stones carved with the mantra *Om Mani Padme Hum*, the mantra of Avalokiteshvara, the manifestation of the Buddha's compassion and the patron deity of Tibet, incarnating since the fifteenth century in the lineage of Dalai Lamas. It might seem that every peasant, monk and trader walking down those roads was carrying a rosary and peacefully muttering that mantra.

Tibet was certainly one of the most intensely religious countries that the world has ever known, a hidden land, a society uniquely organized to support and benefit those who sought to spend their lives in the spiritual pursuit of mystical self-transformation.

We have lingered in our consideration of the absorption of Buddhism into Tibetan life in order to emphasize the fifth and sixth truths about Tibet: Buddhism flows in the veins of the Tibetan people, and to try to extract Buddhism from Tibetan life is to murder the civilization.

The sixth truth: To the extent that Tibetan culture is Buddhist culture it is Indo-Tibetan Buddhism we refer to. Tibet was influenced only at the margins by Chinese culture. "From the end of the royal period (approximately 842 C.E.) onward Chinese studies were never fostered in Tibet, and the Tibetans have remained to this day as ignorant of Chinese literature and philosophy as of Chinese historical records. Chinese cultural influence has been so slight compared with what it might have been, and is virtually limited to just a few artifacts."[5]

In February, 1949 the Communist army entered Beijing. By the end of the year they were moving into Amdo, in northeastern Tibet, and fervidly declaring their intention to liberate all of Tibet, claiming that, "Tibet is Chinese territory ... and the Tibetan people are an indivisible part of the Chinese people."[6] In January, 1950 the Indian Government formally recognized the Communist Government of China. The Indians urged restraint toward Tibet by the Chinese and in August the Chinese assured the Indians that their intentions toward Tibet were entirely peaceful. On October 7, 1950 the People's Liberation Army (PLA) launched a full-scale attack in Eastern Tibet with 40,000 troops. By October 19 they had captured the provincial capital at Chamdo and its defenders, and were in a position to force a peace settlement on the Tibetans.

In November the sixteen-year-old Dalai Lama was invested with full authority as temporal ruler of Tibet. The Tibetan Government appealed to the United Nations for help. They wrote:

> The attention of the world is riveted on Korea where aggression is being resisted by an international force. Similar happenings in remote Tibet are passing without notice. It is in the belief that aggression will not go unchecked and freedom unprotected in any part of the world that we have assumed the responsibility of re-

porting to the United Nations Organization....

We can assure you, Mr. Secretary-General, that Tibet will not go down without a fight, though there is little hope that a nation dedicated to peace will be able to resist the brutal effort of men trained to war, but we understand that the United Nations has decided to stop aggression whenever it takes place.

The armed invasion of Tibet for the incorporation of Tibet within the fold of Chinese Communism through sheer physical force is a clear case of aggression. As long as the people of Tibet are compelled by force to become a part of China against the will and consent of her people, the present invasion of Tibet will be the grossest instance of the violation of the weak by the strong....

The problem is simple. The Chinese claim Tibet as a part of China. Tibetans feel that racially, culturally, and geographically they are far apart from the Chinese. If the Chinese find the reactions of the Tibetans to their unnatural claim not acceptable, there are other civilized methods by which they could ascertain the views of the people of Tibet....

We Ministers, with the approval of His Holiness the Dalai Lama, entrust the problem of Tibet in this emergency to the ultimate decision of the United Nations, hoping that the conscience of the world will not allow the disruption of our State by methods reminiscent of the jungle.[7]

The Republic of El Salvador urged the General Assembly to consider the Tibetan appeal, stating that the U.N. would be neglecting its responsibility if it failed to condemn the unprovoked aggression that had been committed against Tibet. It was true that the General Assembly was at the time absorbed in the problems in Korea. It had just been confirmed that the Chinese Communists had intervened in the war, and on the day that El Salvador presented its case General

MacArthur launched a major offensive.

The Indian Government suggested that a peaceful resolution in Tibet might still be possible and preferred that the matter not be included on the agenda. This was a shocking reversal, as the Indians had told the Tibetans they would support their appeal on the grounds that the Chinese should not have used force to pursue their aims. But the Indians had apparently been intimidated by a series of angry and uncompromising memoranda from Beijing. They feared that a full airing of the issue in the General Assembly would ruin any hopes of coming to some sort of peaceful resolution in Tibet, and undermine their ongoing efforts to mediate a cease-fire in Korea. There was also a store of good-will toward China within certain elements of the Indian Government, that is, among those who saw China as a sister post-colonial power in Asia. Nehru himself was about to embark on his fanciful dream of "Panchshil," a pan-Asian peace based on non-alignment and led by India and China. The dream was to be shattered in 1962 when the Chinese, having secretly built a network of military roads in Southern and Western Tibet, attacked India and captured territory which they claimed was also "an integral part of China."

As a further slap in the face to the Tibetans from a nation they had long considered a friend, the United Kingdom agreed with the Indian position. Hugh Richardson, with palpable sorrow, noted the events at the U.N. in this way:

> It must be recorded with shame that the United Kingdom delegate, pleading ignorance of the exact course of events and uncertainty about the legal position of Tibet, proposed that the matter be deferred. That was supported by the delegate of India, the country most closely affected and, uniquely, bound to Tibet by treaty obligations, who expressed certainty that the differences could be settled by peaceful means which would safeguard Tibetan autonomy. Both the Soviet and the Chinese Nationalist delegates opposed discussion on the ground that Tibet was an integral part

of China. The United States delegate agreed to an adjournment solely because of the statement by the Indian representative.

The debate was, accordingly, adjourned and the matter not heard of again for nine years. In this way the opportunity was lost of examining the facts when the Chinese were still unsure of world reactions and had not yet proceeded, irrevocably, to extremes. The conduct of the Indian and British Governments amounted to an evasion of their moral duty to make plain what they alone had special reason to know – that there was no legal justification for the Chinese invasion of Tibet.[8]

With the PLA poised to continue its thrust into the Tibetan heartland, the Dalai Lama moved to Dromo, a town just a few miles from the Indian frontier, ready to flee across the border should it become necessary. From Dromo the Dalai Lama, a sixteen-year-old boy with the fate of his nation weighing on his shoulders, chose to send a delegation to Beijing, with the hope of negotiating a peaceful resolution, sparing his people a bloody war with an inevitable outcome.

The delegation was not empowered to conclude any agreements, and was instructed to refer all major issues to the Government residing at Dromo. But the Chinese were not offering the opportunity for a meaningful or prolonged negotiation. The Tibetans were browbeaten, and, in essence, presented with an ultimatum: Either sign the "Agreement on Measures for the Peaceful Liberation of Tibet" which was put before them, or see the PLA resume its march and capture Tibet by force.

The delegates had little choice but to sign what came to be known as the Seventeen-Point Agreement. This Agreement, on the face of it, preserved religious freedom and the Tibetan cultural identity, as well as the traditional Tibetan political system and the powers of the Dalai Lama. But the Seventeen-Point Agreement proved to be a mere facade, behind which

the Chinese, at first gradually, and in the end ruthlessly, un-
dertook to transform – one might more accurately say, to dis-
figure – Tibetan society into an image that conformed to Mao
Zedong's ideological notions of a peasant and workers' paradise.

Liberation is a wonderful word. It carries with it the promise of
release after a prolonged period of suffering and bondage. To
the Tibetans the word carries just this meaning, but in the ultimate sense of final liberation from the sufferings of the eternal cycle of birth and death. This liberation is what constitutes
Buddhahood, and is the spiritual goal of every Buddhist Tibetan.

In the Buddhist view of life, the wheel of birth and death is
always characterized by suffering – sometimes gross, in the
form of physical pain, sickness and death; and sometimes
subtle, as when we feel happy, but are unaware that this very
happiness is pervaded with the tragic reality of our transitory
and ignorant condition. We are in bondage, bound to the inevitable consequences of our own actions in this and previous
lives. There is a way to break free of these chains by means of
the path of morality, loving-kindness, and insight, but due to
our own ignorance we normally act in ways that perpetuate our
own suffering and enslavement within the wheel of life.

It is only with an act of will, which can grow out of faith in the
benefit of the path to enlightenment, the path taught by the
Buddha, that we can bring an end to our beginningless sufferings, achieve the benefit of freeing ourselves from the cycle of
death and rebirth, and benefit others by taking on the responsibility of showing them the way to alleviate their own sufferings. This is the meaning of "liberation" to a Tibetan.

Tibet was, in more ways than one, a place that time forgot.
The economic relationships built into its social structure were
ancient, and had existed, essentially unchanged, for many
centuries. It was a traditional culture, whose patterns had been

left completely undisturbed by the forces of industrial urbanized society.

Unquestionably the political power in the country was held by two major groups: a collection of aristocratic families or clans, and the monastic establishment, led by the three Great Monastic Seats in Lhasa. With a purely agrarian economy, the fundamental source of wealth was the land and the animals that lived on the land. The aristocracy and the monasteries owned huge estates, usually received as patronage from the central government. Many small peasants owned their own plots, but many also worked the land of the great estates, owned by the monasteries and leading families. A taxation system which demanded payment to the local authority, either in grain or free labor, kept such peasant families bound to their estates and often in debt.

It was from this feudal relationship that the Chinese so proudly came to liberate the poor Tibetan serfs. Of course when one class of people holds complete economic domination over another there is bound to be abuse. The peasants were quite simply poor, obliged to work hard on the land, while the aristocrats, high government officials, and monks, did not have to get their hands dirty.

To a Marxist, such a state of affairs is by definition oppressive, and any objective observer would have to admit that Tibet was not an egalitarian society. But, as recent events in Eastern Europe and the Soviet Union have dramatically shown, the Marxist analysis, by which control over the sources of wealth is the only criterion for judging the goodness of a society, is a gross oversimplification of the diversity and complexity of human motivations.

As the Dalai Lama has pointed out, socialism and Buddhism have one important element in common—they are both based on the motivation to make people happy. But they stand on very different assumptions about the meaning and end of happiness. Marxism assumes that happiness is materially based and will be achieved when all people are materially satisfied to an equal degree. Buddhism holds that people can never be materially satisfied, and that people can only become truly happy through peace of mind, which is attained by spiritual paths that cultivate non-attachment to material things and an understanding of one's own inner being.

Nevertheless, Buddhism and Marxism share the goal of making people happy. Any valid use of the term "liberation" as applied to the change in the conditions of the Tibetan peasantry under the Chinese, must mean that their conditions were improved, that their lives, as they experienced them, were made better, that after liberation they were happier people than they were before.

A closer examination of the status of Tibetan "serfs" reveals several important features. First, besides agriculture and herding there was another potential source of income in Tibet, namely trading. Every year in the autumn caravans of yaks and other pack animals crisscrossed the vast country, scaling the high passes to descend into the borderlands of India and Nepal, carrying wool, salt, gold, furs, musk, and yak tails. They returned with tea, tobacco, silk, metal utensils, precious stones, and silver – commodities rare and precious in the hidden kingdom.

Though the large estates, with vast capital at their disposal, were the greatest beneficiaries of this trade, families from every social stratum participated, sending young men with their excess produce to join the great caravans and to return with the profits in the form of foreign goods.

There were several avenues to the achievement of higher social status. One was simply the accumulation of wealth by means of trade, skill in business, and the good old-fashioned virtues of frugality and hard work. This does not mean that there were not structural obstacles making it difficult for the poor to become rich – there were – and such cases were the exception, as they are today in any capitalist country. But it was possible and there were many recorded cases.

Another avenue to status and wealth was through the monasteries themselves. The monasteries were structured somewhat like universities, and they had the means to recognize and reward scholastic talent as well as genuine spiritual attainment. (Sometimes these two have been confused in the Tibetan context, but that is a separate issue.) A poor peasant boy with a good head on his shoulders could enter a monastery as just one more anonymous face among the thousands. If he could withstand the hardships – poor monks could be just as deprived, if not more so, in the monasteries as they were back home – and if he excelled in his studies, showing unusual talent in memorizing texts, and then in the challenging arena of philosophical debate, if he came to be recognized as a great scholar, he could eventually earn all the prestige and wealth that came along with such recognition.

In this way wealth could be accumulated purely on the basis of intellectual merit. Famous teachers gathered students who perpetually made offerings to the Master, while families from far and wide would come to request prayers, advice, and special ceremonies, each request being accompanied by a generous offering of the best one had to give. A popular comedic buffoon in Tibetan literature is the fat and rich lama who has exploited his position for all it is worth, but the Tibetan Buddhist teachings are full of warnings to the student of the dangers of studying, practicing, and teaching with the attainment of worldly wealth as a motivation.

A third and unique avenue to the attainment of wealth and status was the system of *tulkus* or reincarnate lamas. In the Mahayana branch of Buddhism, which Tibet adopted, the practitioner, perceiving that all beings in the world are suffering in the same manner that he or she is, undertakes to attain enlightenment – liberation – not merely for his or her own benefit, but in order to be able to remain in the world to teach and ultimately to lead all other beings to the same happy state.

Given such a motivation, it is a natural step to the assumption that those who have reached advanced attainments on the path will in fact return after death, in life after life, to continue their own spiritual journey and to assist others on theirs. From these premises there grew up in Tibet a common practice of seeking, after the death of a high and important lama, his reincarnation, among boys born at a suitable time. Various oracular means and tests were used to determine the identity of such reincarnations, and once identified, they were invested with the full status, special treatment, and previously accumulated wealth of their predecessors from previous lives.

They would be taken to their respective monasteries and given the best available education and conditions for study, and as reincarnations of previously great lamas they were expected to excel. In fact, some did and some did not. The system had its potential for abuse, but the fact is that tulkus, while often from good families, were also found in the more humble strata of society. Having a high tulku found in one's family could immediately elevate the whole family to a position of wealth and prestige.

Beyond the possibility of social mobility in Tibetan society, it must be remembered that Tibet had a significant middle class, made up of stewards of the large estates, traders, and lower ranking government officials and army officers. Even among the peasants there were many who controlled sufficient family land holdings to prosper. The simplicity of the lifestyle meant that the very rich did not live much differently from the rest of society. Although bound in a feudal relationship to the aristocratic or monastic estates, most families had a modest but decent standard of living. They worked hard, but not too hard, and there was sufficient space in their lives for leisure, rest, and play. Regular religious festivals provided plenty of holidays while famine and widespread economic hardship were unknown. As Hugh Richardson (who lived in Tibet between 1936 and 1950) described it, "Conditions of work were by all appearances easy. The Tibetan, although certainly not an idler, did not give the impression of being overburdened with work or with care."[9]

As long as work obligations – which were considered a form of tax – were fulfilled, people were free to travel, to visit relatives, or go on pilgrimage. The government and landlords did not interfere in the private lives of the citizens, and there were no restrictions on freedom of speech or freedom of association.

This is not to say Tibet was a paradise of libertarianism. Of course options were restricted by built-in social structures – as they are in every society. We might assume that if there ever had been a genuine attempt at a people's revolution – and there never was – the establishment powers would have demonstrated the limits of freedom of speech. But in general, people could do and say what they wanted and go where they pleased. Tibet, though feudal, was a free country.

Now there are some sincere as well as dogmatic individuals of the left who will see the society described here as an archaic and unfair historical anomaly, in which the peasant masses were exploited to the advantage of a ruling elite and an unproductive monastic establishment. They will insist that Tibet was indeed in need of liberation and ask what meaningful freedoms there could be for peasants who were obligated from birth to labor for the enrichment of an elite class of unproductive landowners.

We must return to the fundamental issue: Were the people happy? To answer this question finally we must add the sine qua non of Tibetan society – religious faith. It is indisputable that a large portion of the wealth in Tibet was in the hands of the monasteries, and that many people had to labor on the land in order to support the large segment of the population that lived in the monasteries studying and practicing religion, but doing no productive labor. Was this fair?

I do not think it is possible for any outsider who has not had intimate contact with the Tibetan people to answer this question. Anyone who knows Tibetans knows that they are so utterly and deeply grounded in their faith in the Three Jewels of Buddhism that there can be no question of their wanting to see an end to the monastic system. Every family had a close relative who was a monk or a nun. To the average Tibetan, the monks and the monasteries represented everything that was good in their society. To be able to support institutions and individuals who were actively pursuing enlightenment as a full-time job was the most virtuous possible use of one's life as a layman or laywoman.

Furthermore, the Buddhist doctrines of karma and rebirth, while by no means fatalistic, do provide individuals with a sense of meaning and justice in their current circumstances, along with the unlimited potential to change their circumstances in this and future lives by their own actions. According to the law of karma, by one's previous actions – generosity, patience, and kindness, for example – one will experience good results – prosperity, health, friendship and so on. If one was malicious, a liar, or a thief in past lives, one will be bound to experience their results – poverty, deprivation and misfortune – in this and future lives. There can be no doubt that virtually every Tibetan conceived of his or her circumstances in these terms.

This, the Marxist argues, is precisely the means by which religion creates the theoretical superstructure to pacify and maintain the exploited classes in their oppressed circumstances. Mao Zedong told the young Dalai Lama at one of their meetings in Beijing in 1954 that Buddhism was a good religion – it had been the dominant religion of China for 1500 years – because the Buddha was concerned with the common people. But, he concluded, "Of course, religion is poison."

At this point we come to an impasse. On the one hand is the person of faith, whose world-view, whose entire sense of reality, is grounded in his or her religious assumptions. To a Buddhist, to argue that one can make a better world by dismantling monasteries or disrobing monks and nuns is inherently illogical.

On the other hand there is the Marxist, who puts faith in the very assumption that religion is by nature a useless or even malevolent diversion of peoples' attention to their own material reality. Denying, a priori, any true life of the spirit, such a person interprets all religious beliefs purely in terms of the effects they might have on the social structure and economic relationships of the society.

As the Communist Parties of Eastern Europe and the Soviet Union have learned, human spirituality, the human faculty of religious faith, is a far more dynamic, persistent and meaning-

ful force in the lives of human beings than scientific materialism ever conceived. If Tibet was the most religious society in
the world, then in the equation of happiness that Chinese liberation was intended to solve, the treatment of Tibetan religion by the Communists must stand as the dominant figure.

Whatever economic and political reform the Chinese might
have imposed – for better or for worse – on Tibet, it was the
humiliation, torture, and mass murder of monks and nuns, the
desecration of holy statues and books, and the demolition of
monasteries, that tipped the balance irrevocably in the hearts
and minds of the Tibetan people against the Chinese version
of liberation.

The Chinese Communists have attempted to realize in
body, speech, and mind the claim that Tibet is an integral part
of China. In the beginning they must have believed their own
propaganda, that the Tibetan serfs would rise up to join their
Chinese brothers and sisters to throw off the chains of feudalism. But events proved that the vast chasm that separated
Communist China from Buddhist Tibet – in terms of religion,
culture, language, history and political ethos – was so vast, so
utterly unbridgeable, that in the end the Chinese must have
come to the conclusion that the only way they could liberate
Tibet was to destroy it.

This they proceeded to do. From the middle of the 1950s
until the end of the 1970s, the Chinese used all the tools of the
fascist state – political terror, mass slaughter, concentration
camps, slave labor, and a pervasive atmosphere of fear created
by the omnipresent threat of secret informers linked to an
omnipotent police apparatus unfettered by due process of law.

These are the means that the Chinese have used to make
Tibet a peasant and worker's paradise. The results are a shattered society, a decimated population. Today, forty years after
the first occupation of Tibet, the Tibetan people are more determined than ever to regain their human rights, their fundamental freedoms, and their political identity, while the
Chinese find themselves incapable of abandoning the methods of state terror in their desperate effort to maintain a grasp

on a land and a people over which they have power, but to which they have no right. The seventh truth about Tibet is that the Chinese did not liberate Tibet, they have tried to annihilate it.

When His Holiness the Dalai Lama fled Tibet in 1959 about 100,000 Tibetans followed him into India, where they eventually settled into communities spread along India's mountainous northern frontier, and among the rolling hills of the southern state of Karnataka. Through their adaptability, resourcefulness, intelligence, and hard work they have carved out for themselves a stable life of modest prosperity in their adopted land. But all Tibetans, including those born and raised and schooled in India, wait for the day when they can return to their home on the other side of the Himalayan mountains.

At the time of the Tibetan nation's greatest trial, it has been their great fortune to be blessed with a leader who truly embodies the ideals of wisdom and compassion that are the cornerstones of the Tibetan Buddhist faith. Under the guidance of Tenzin Gyatso, the Fourteenth Dalai Lama, the Tibetan community in exile has managed with singular success to preserve its cultural identity and heritage, its religion, literature and traditional arts. And this at a time when the Chinese in Tibet were ruthlessly and systematically striving to erase any vestige of Tibetan tradition and culture. The eighth truth is that His Holiness the Dalai Lama is the only leader recognized – in fact, adored – by virtually all Tibetans, inside or outside of Tibet.

He embodies the Tibetan nation, and has single-handedly preserved the non-violent nature of the Tibetan struggle. While holding the Tibetan people together and inspiring them to preserve their cultural heritage, he has led them down the road to democracy, abdicating the role as "king" of any future independent Tibet and instituting a democratic constitu-

tion and a popularly elected representative legislature for the
Government-in-Exile.

Sera Monastery was one of the Three Great Seats of monastic
learning that thrived in Lhasa before the Chinese invasion.
According to tradition it housed fifty-five hundred monks, and
it was only the second largest of the three. Out of this population only about three hundred escaped to India in 1959. Today the reconstructed Sera, near Mysore in South India, is
home to fourteen hundred monks, including some four hundred who fled Tibet after 1980 in order to pursue their religious
studies.

I remember one evening in the summer of 1989, sitting in a
room at Sera Monastery, eating my dinner of *thukpa* – Tibetan
noodle soup – while the room darkened and India's early
Western monsoon drizzled rain on the muddy streets outside
the window.

Gen Tenzin Dorje, one of the original three hundred who
had made the trek to India in 1959, was laughing as he recounted the conditions that he, and eventually some fifteen
hundred monks from other monasteries, endured at the Buxa
refugee camp in West Bengal following their flight from Tibet. They were housed in a compound of concrete barracks
surrounded by barbed wire, which had been constructed by
the British as a prisoner-of-war camp during World War II.
Sixty-six monks slept in each of these long huts, on rows of
bamboo beds only six inches apart.

In the summer the humidity and intense heat were intoler-
able to people used to the cool and dry climate of the mountains. Many died. They died of T.B., epidemic among the
Tibetans in India, and they died of all sorts other diseases,
made susceptible by their lack of resistance and inability to
adjust to the torrid climate. During the monsoons the rains
turned the camp into a muddy swamp. The drinking water,
always scarce and never too clean, became a source of disease.

Mosquitoes swarmed, and any blood the mosquitoes didn't take the bedbugs were eager to drink.

The food, India's staples of rice and dal, was supplied by Indian traders under contract to the Government. The contractors were paid a flat fee, negotiated in advance, to supply food to the refugees; and the cheaper the food, the greater their profit. The results, dished out on the tables of the Buxa refugee camp, were rotten rice, mildewed dal, rancid oil, and spoiled vegetables. The monks of Sera Monastery lived under these conditions for ten years.

Gen Tenzin Dorje laughed when he told this story – the rueful laugh of one who has survived adversity. A very Tibetan laugh. In truth, these were the lucky ones. Though they suffered the deprivations of refugees, they had been offered sanctuary by the Indian Government and had escaped their beautiful homeland on the brink of its descent into a cauldron of blood and rubble.

The room was dark. To save money at the monastery no one turns the lights on unless there is something that you specifically want to see. On the altar a butter lamp flickered before a photograph of the Dalai Lama surrounded by a colorful assortment of Buddhas, Bodhisattvas and protector deities – each one manifesting a particular aspect of the enlightened qualities of a Buddha.

At that moment I suddenly felt the great distance, the loneliness and isolation of the Tibetan people. I was sitting in a Tibetan monastery, rising incongruously amidst cornfields in South India, at the verge of a forest that had once been the game preserve of the Maharajah of Mysore. A Tibetan monk in his early fifties was laughing as he recounted the trials of his first ten years in India, living in the middle of an inhospitable jungle, in a POW camp built by the British Raj. No one in the world outside of this remote Indian district would ever know the names of the monks who died of T.B. and malaria and dysentery in Buxa.

From the world outside, the BBC brought us news of oppressive regimes crumbling from East Germany to Bulgaria. In

South Africa apartheid was dissolving under the pressure of historical inevitability and a world-wide boycott. But what about Tibet?

No one boycotts apartheid in Tibet, where imported Chinese cadres manage every aspect of the economic and political life, while Tibetans are relegated to menial labor; where Tibetan children are taught in school that they are intellectually inferior to the Chinese because the high altitude has starved their brains of oxygen.

There is no question of the world forgetting the atrocities that were committed in Tibet over a forty-year period – and still continue today – because most of the world has not heard and does not know of these atrocities. And in the interests of maintaining good relations with China, most of the world's governments do not want to know.

Tibet has been known for centuries as the land of mystery. Its geographic and linguistic isolation, the very features that served as its best protection throughout its history, and allowed it to cultivate Buddhist philosophy and practice with such single-pointed devotion, are the same barriers that today serve to obscure the world's scrutiny and to obstruct the Tibetans' own efforts to tell the world the truth.

Today the younger generation of exile Tibetans, trained in schools financed by the Indian Government or by the Tibetan Government-in-Exile, do speak English. They are as familiar as anyone in India with the political forces operating in the world around them. But the older generation, the witnesses, those who survived the Chinese concentration camps of the 1960s and 1970s, are without a voice, cut off, without the means of telling their stories. Not only cut off by the language they speak, but by a lack of education, as in the case of Ama Adhe. Or, like Tenpa Soepa, who received the best education, by being grounded in a culture that has no literary tradition of personal memoirs or autobiography.

In Tibet, the very act of writing was a special skill, taught separately from reading as "the art of grammar," and not necessarily mastered by the average educated and literate person.

Tenpa Soepa, trained as a government servant, does know the art of grammar and composition. Urged by others to recount his story he has made extensive notes toward the eventual publication of his autobiography in Tibetan. But, having come out of Tibet only in 1980, he does not speak any English. When his autobiography is finally published it will be in Tibetan, and inaccessible to most of the citizens of the world. And it is only world public opinion, coming to recognize what has happened and is still happening in Tibet that can save it from its nightmare.

A Strange Liberation tells the stories of two survivors of the Chinese "liberation" of Tibet. It is an attempt to give a voice to those who previously had no means and no forum to tell their story. It is an effort to bring into the community of world literature, and into the body of world history, full and detailed accounts of events that have up until now been told in generalized and brief summaries.

There is today no shortage of Tibetan concentration camp survivors living in India. Every Tibetan who remained in Tibet after 1959 has terrible stories to tell of their own sufferings, those of their families, their monasteries, their villages. I did not make any effort to find the "worst cases" in order to present a loaded picture of the historical events. The cases of Ama Adhe and Tenpa Soepa were suggested to me by Tibetan acquaintances, and presented themselves for the obvious reason that they are people willing and able to speak of their lives.

Ama Adhe decided early on in her captivity that if she lived, she would live to tell her story. Throughout her captivity she watched carefully and as she says, "engraved the memories on my heart." She is so determined to tell her story to the world that she has earned the Tibetan nickname of "Rangzen Ama-la," "Freedom Mama." Here, in her own words, she remembers her life, from her youth in the pure and fresh highland pastures of Kham, in Eastern Tibet, through her arrest and the twenty years she spent as a prisoner in nine different Chinese camps and prisons.

Tenpa Soepa was trained to be a civil servant. For the first nine years of the Chinese occupation of Tibet he worked in the Potala, the great palace of the Dalai Lama and the seat of the Tibetan Government. He was intimately involved in the flight of the Dalai Lama from Lhasa on March 17, 1959, and was himself in the party that crossed the Kyichu River to accompany the Dalai Lama on that fateful night. The dramatic story of his escape and eventual capture presents a vivid picture of the final fall of Tibet into Chinese hands. After his twenty years behind barbed wire Tenpa Soepa is today a reserved and cautious man. He is not a survivor eagerly seeking every opportunity to tell his story. But he was trained to be a leader, and he has lived his life bearing the responsibility of serving the people. His colleagues in the Tibetan Government have urged him to tell his story, and he sees the value and usefulness of doing so.

Together these two stories provide a balance of gender as well as a geographical balance, with Ama Adhe recounting events in Kham, where Chinese depredations and Tibetan resistance to them began five years earlier than in Central Tibet, where Tenpa Soepa lived and worked.

The facts presented here are the facts as they exist in the memories of the narrators. The stories are as the subjects told them, although some editing and rearranging has been done for the sake of clarity. The selective process of human memory has been discussed at length by Primo Levi in *The Drowned and the Saved*. It is an elusive and undependable thing, memory, and all the more so in the face of the kind of trauma described on these pages. As an outsider, as an interviewer, I had no access to the events I was aiming to uncover other than the memory of my informants and their willingness to speak.

I make no pretense to judge or to verify the facts presented in these cases. It was evident to me, and I hope it will be to the reader, that there has been no effort to over-dramatize the case or dress up the horror. My goal was to give voice to the witnesses, and as far as it is possible within the bounds of translating between two utterly different languages, the stories are told by the survivors themselves.

If it is true that we look up to find the sacred spaces of this earth, then we can easily see in Tibet a sacred land; at the top of the world, where a peaceful people lived simple lives in pursuit of a spiritual ideal. The great global paradigm shift that began with the industrial revolution – away from spiritual metaphysics, faith in unseen forces, and an unconscious integration of human culture with its natural environment, toward faith in science, materialism, and the conscious effort by man to dominate and exploit his realm – reached a symbolic, dramatic, and violent climax in the Communist conquest of Tibet.

But in the heart of the human consciousness the seeds of the ninth truth about Tibet are awakening: Scientism and materialism cannot bring human happiness, and they certainly cannot bring liberation. In the end they leave the human heart untouched, alienated and confused. Science and economic theories offer models for managing our material world, but when we place our ultimate faith in that power to manipulate, we displace our sense of the transcendent with a fixation on the tangible. Whether it takes the form of Maoist communism or technological corporate capitalism, when we seek happiness in what we have instead of who we are, we are doomed to disappointment. At the extreme this dehumanizing process leads to fascist totalitarianism. Less pernicious, but in the long term no less destructive, is the laissez faire exploitation, pollution, and degradation of our common human home, the planet Earth.

Today humanity stands at the moment of return in the arc of the pendulum, or rather at the curve in the spiral of the evolution of human consciousness. We live in a world traumatic with change; a world struggling, slowly and reluctantly to awaken from the deadening destructiveness of colonialism, failed ideologies and material obsession. A world tentatively but hopefully reaching out for the support of eternal human values – freedom, peace, compassion, and the perfection of undisturbed nature.

If we seek an exemplar of this ancient and yet new paradigm, we should look up, and we will see it in Tibet – a spiritual people, living in peace, in harmony with their natural environment. Tibet is a living world treasure. A world peace-park of the mind. The struggle of Tibet to emerge from its dark night is the struggle of the people of the earth to liberate themselves from the distortions and excesses of the past. Tibet is the top of the world, the ultimate symbol, the paradigm of the new paradigm. Insofar as we are human beings, we are all Tibetans. We all want to live in peace in our homes. We all want to pursue our personal and spiritual quests. We all want to be free.

The Buddha said, "All beings want happiness, and do not want suffering." It is based on this ancient truth that the Tibetan people want to build their new society, reviving the eternal values of the old, and integrating it with the dynamic energy of the new. Opposed by the huge power of a ruthless regime that has harnessed the world's most populous nation to its service, the only countervailing force that can save Tibet is the sympathy, compassion, and wise support of the rest of the world.

The tenth truth about Tibet is that the survival of Tibet, the altar of the earth, the living world treasure, depends on you and me.

NOTES

[1] Burton Watson, tr., *Cold Mountain, 100 Poems by the T'ang Poet Han-shan* (New York: Grove Press, 1962), p. 80.

[2] Peter Gold, *Altar of the Earth* (Ithaca: Snow Lion, 1988).

[3] Hugh E. Richardson, *Tibet and Its History* (Boston: Shambhala, 1984), p. 259.

[4] D. Snellgrove and H.E. Richardson, *A Cultural History of Tibet* (Boulder: Prajna Press, 1980), p. 129.

[5] *Ibid.*, p. 64.

[6] Political & Secret files of the India Office, London, 12/4232, Foreign Office to Singapore, quoting Beijing Radio Broadcast. Quoted in Michael C. van Walt van Praag, *The Status of Tibet* (London: Wisdom, 1987), p. 89.

[7] U.N. Document A/1549, 11 November 1950, "Appeal by His Holiness the Dalai Lama of Tibet to the United Nations."

[8] Richardson, *Tibet and Its History*, p. 186.

[9] *Ibid.*, p. 16.

PART 2

AFTER THE SNOWFALL

Ama Adhe's Story

*Ama Adhe in her room at the Hostel for Recent Arrivals,
Dharamsala, India. Photo by Lois Raimondo.*

After the Snowfall:
Ama Adhe's Story

1

I was born in Nyarong, in Gotsa, in Kham, in 1934. Right after I was born my father named me Adhe. Tapey is my family name. My father was known as Dorje Rabten. He was married to two women – we Tibetans sometimes do that – and his elder wife was named Bochuma. I was the daughter of the younger wife. My mother's name was Sonam Drolma.

My father was a very honest and straightforward man. The people of our area selected him to be a leader – a kind of magistrate, and he would be called upon to settle disputes between people when they could not agree. He was so honest – sometimes one person in a dispute would offer him a lump of gold, and the other person couldn't offer anything, but he would still make his judgment impartially and fairly.

There was a chieftain in the District of Nyarong named Dorje Norgyal, and my father became one of his ministers. After he became a minister of Dorje Norgyal he was chosen by the people themselves to be appointed as a judge. They said that because he was such an honest and straightforward man, they wanted him to be the magistrate.

That was the situation for our family in Nyarong. But actually, although I was born there, the whole family left that area shortly after my birth, and I grew up in Kanze, so I don't remember that much about the region where I was born.

In Kanze there was another chieftain named Zhipatso. Since my father had such a good reputation from his previous work in Nyarong, the people and the chieftain again asked him to be the magistrate in Kanze.

In Kanze, as I remember it, our family was always a self-sufficient family, so we always had enough to live well. My family was what we call *sa ma drog*, people who both tend cattle in the open grazing lands and also have settled property where they grow grain. In the summer we would drive our livestock up into the nomadic highland regions where there were many nomads with their yaks. And in the winter we would come back down to work in our fields, where we had quite a bit of land for cultivation.

From our house you could see a very high rocky mountain, a snowcapped mountain touching the sky. It is called Nyate Khalori. The mountain is encircled by lakes and surrounded by rich forests. These forests were full of all kinds of wildlife – tigers, brown bear, deer, many different kinds of animals lived in those forests. It was such a beautiful country, but nowadays this region is closed to foreign travellers and no one is allowed to visit.

My native land in Kanze is called Lobasha. For me, having been in other areas of Kham, I find Lobasha to be the most beautiful land to live in. In this region, on the plains and in the passes you would see nomadic people living with their herds of goats and sheep and other livestock. And there was such natural beauty, the forests full of wildlife, and especially the meadows full of flowers – when you walked in these mountains, when you came home you would find flowers between your toes.

I remember in the summer when we used to go up to live

among the nomads. In the fourth Tibetan month, in the spring, when you looked around you, there were red, white, blue, yellow, so many different flowers you couldn't even name them all.

So people would go up into these hills and pitch their tents. In one tent there would be monks performing *pujas*. There would be the nomads, and we *sa ma drog*. And when I was in my teens, we young people would put on our best clothes, our ornaments – our earrings and bracelets – and we would dance. And we would sing a kind of musical question and answer back and forth between the boys and the girls.

My father would always have a very good time. They would drink beer, what we call *chang*, and sometimes my father would sing songs. In our land the breed of horses is very good, and the men would have horse races and special sporting contests. One of the games was to race as fast as you can toward a *khata* – a white scarf – that would be placed on the ground. With the horses running at full gallop the riders would swoop down and with one hand try to snatch the khata from the ground. Another game – and not many could do this – while they were galloping they would jump down from the horse and then jump back up into the saddle. My brother, Juguma, who is now eighty-two and lives in Nepal, he used to do that. After the horse races they would have shooting competition, and whoever could hit the bull's-eye would be considered the sharpest shooter.

Now, when I recall these moments, the beautiful scenes, the snowcapped mountains with the slopes covered with sheep and goats and yaks, the different people, the flowers and the horses, I consider them the happiest moments of my life. And as I am telling you this today, it is as if I am seeing them again.

In those summers, when the people would come together for picnics and drinking and dancing and games, the main thing was that there was inner peace for everyone. There was freedom for everyone to do what they wished. In our land, we consider killing people as dirty, so people respected each other's life, and there wasn't any kind of crime like that. And the area was full of monasteries, temples, and hermitages.

In the morning we would send all the cattle, the yak and *dri*, the *dzo* and *dzomo*, up to graze in the hills. And in the evening we would go up to the high meadows or forests to collect them. Most of my work was early in the morning. I would milk the dri, and then I would help with boiling the milk, churning the butter, making the yoghurt, and so forth. During the day it was the time for games and good food and fun, a time for people to enjoy themselves.

A little bit about my mother, Ama Sonam Drolma. She was like a woman who never gets angry. You see, my father had two wives. Now normally, if the two wives are sisters, they will be compatible, and there will be no problems. But in my mother's case, she and the first wife did not know each other. But after my mother joined the family they became so compatible, such good friends, that people would say that their friendship was better than sisters. They were so close that when they both had babies, whenever one of them was looking after the children she would breast-feed both of the babies at the same time. They would just nurse each other's children.

I remember how, when my father's first wife was getting older, my mother would keep her comfortable by not letting her work, and just make her sit on the bed and play with the kids while my mother did all the housework.

In the family, I was the youngest child. Bochuma, my elder mother – we can call her my stepmother – she would always say about me, "Oh she is my daughter. She should come and sleep with me tonight. I will breast-feed her." Like that, we were so close. And I remember thinking then that my stepmother was my real mother. It was only a bit later, when I got older that I learned that my real mother was Sonam Drolma.

Then, at the age of eighteen, I got married. The marriage was arranged by our parents. Although my husband and I never saw each other before our marriage, these arrangements were discussed among the family. Someone might say, "Your daughter ought to get married to the son of this family." Then my parents would have discussions with the other family, and then they would decide.

Was I consulted? In my region, when our parents said, "We have decided this, and we have promised this," there was no thought of denying the wish of your parents. I remember both my mothers advising me, "Now you should get married and go and live with your husband's family, because you can't stay here forever. There is your older brother and his wife and they have so many kids. If you don't get married you will have to become a nun, then you can stay here." In those days I used to think, if I become a nun I can stay in my own family, but if I am a nun I won't be able to wear all these nice clothes or any jewelry or ornaments in my hair.

As is the tradition with Tibetans, at the time of my wedding I was adorned with all sorts of jewelry, beautiful clothing and elaborate ornamental hats, and we had to ride on horses to go to my husband's home. first we stayed there for three days during which there were a lot of festivities and dances. And after three days we returned to our family's home, and the marriage ceremony continued there. After the wedding, a bride may stay back with her own family for six months or a year, and then she will go to live permanently at her husband's home. After that your home is considered to be with your husband's family.

My husband came from a reputable family, and he was a very handsome man. But for me, I was thinking, "These family members, they are not like my father, they are not like my two mothers." So I was feeling a bit doubtful about my life with them.

The family was of similar status to my own – not very rich but having both cattle and land – as far as wealth was concerned, the same as my family. So I went off to my husband's family's home. The first year was not a very happy one, because I didn't know anyone in this new place. Sometimes I had to cry, thinking of my family, my mother and father, and the happy times we had in our land.

My husband's name was Pachen. He was a very handsome man, and he was very considerate. Whenever he found me crying he would comfort me and tell me, "Don't be sad. If you are missing your family you can visit them for a month, make frequent visits to them."

My husband's home was also in the Lobasha region. Not very far from my family, on horse perhaps two hours' ride. In the summers the two families would join together with our herds, camping and picnicking. And during the winter we would spend time with my family, or my mother would visit me, my stepmother or my father would visit. So our two families lived very closely. There were never any difficulties between our people.

2

When the Chinese first arrived in Lobasha I was just a teenager. Until then I had never even seen a Chinese face. I was always frightened that they would carry me away. They would come marching in lines, the leader might be on horseback, and as a child, every time I saw them I was scared. I would hide behind my mother or my father. Sometimes the grown-ups would tease us, saying, "If you don't behave yourselves we will give you to these Chinese and they will take you away." And we kids really believed them, so whenever the Chinese appeared we would run and hide wherever we could.

At that time the Chinese had a silver coin which was known as *Da Yang*. Sometimes they would bring these coins and tell us kids, "Don't be scared. Go ahead and take one." But I was always too scared, I never had the guts to take a coin. Then they would give them to the parents, telling them, "Buy the children some sweets."

Sometimes the Chinese would come into our house and they would see my parents in a prayer session, counting their rosaries or turning prayer wheels. Then the Chinese would act as if they respected religion very much. They would ask questions, and say, "Your religious practice is very good. We also love religion."

Sometimes they would take the prayer wheel and spin it, or touch sacred statues to their head – a sign of respect. Or they would come into our shrine room, they would see all the statues on the altar and all the religious murals on the walls and the *thankas*, and there, where we would prostrate, they would do the same thing. While we were watching them they would try to prostrate to the Buddhas on our altar.

We were very surprised when we saw this, and we said, "Oh, these Chinese, they like religion." But I remember my father telling me, "No, no, no. These people don't like religion. They are acting. Just putting on a show to satisfy us." When I look back at this now, I think it was all done just to get our trust.

The Chinese would also talk about Mao Zedong, saying, "He is the leader of the people. He is the father of the people. He is here to liberate everybody's suffering." So slowly they started trying to plant these ideas into Tibetan minds. They said, "We, the People's Liberation Army, have been sent here by Mao Zedong to see if people have problems and to solve the problems of the people." They told us, "We are just visitors." And they went to such an extent that they would help Tibetans who were carrying water, help them with their harvesting and making hay.

And then they started giving these silver coins to the monasteries, and telling the monks, "We like Buddhism. Chairman Mao loves religion. This money is for the monasteries." And they gave them many many of these silver coins.

One of my brothers had both a pistol and a rifle, an old musket of that period. And the Chinese soldiers would tell him, "That's very good. You are well-armed." And they would even give him bullets. All to win his favor.

But my father was an intelligent and shrewd man. He said, "Believe me, they are no good. It is all a swindle. They are just trying to make us happy in order to win our trust. I don't think they have any good intentions for us."

My father was among the group of leaders from our region that the Chinese selected to visit China. At that time they would lead delegations of Tibetans to China to show how developed and prosperous their country was. When my father came back from his visit he was very angry. He said he saw nothing good. He said, "I have found that these Chinese do not have any good intentions for the Tibetans. They are just giving donations to the monasteries to win peoples' hearts. But basically, they are lying to us."

He told us that he saw many Nationalist Chinese – *Kuomintang* – being arrested and taken away in trucks. He also witnessed many people being executed by machine guns. Once there was a truckload of women prisoners – Kuomintang Chinese, and these women, when they were about to be shot they were so scared that they fell down on the ground, and they were just shot there on the ground.

In the markets in China they were already selling many of the Buddha images, thankas, and religious articles that were plundered from the Chinese monasteries. A lot of Tibetans were going into areas of Western China to buy these religious articles. My father was against that. He said there was no use in going there to buy these things because in the end they will wind up in the Chinese hands anyway. But some business people would go and buy these things to bring back and sell in Tibet. Some just bought things for their own altars. These people wouldn't listen to my father. They believed that the Chinese had no intentions of looting the Tibetan monasteries the way they had already done to the Chinese temples. And afterward, when the Chinese actually started plundering our shrines, then many of them said, "Oh yes. We should have listened to Dorje Rabten when he warned us."

So, based on this experience, he never felt happy about the Chinese coming into Tibet. All the Tibetans who went to China in his group, when they came back they had portraits of Mao Zedong and of Joseph Stalin – the one with the big moustache. The Chinese gave these to people to put up in their houses. My father said, "There is no need for us to hang these portraits in our house. Because these are not good people, they don't have good intentions. It is better if we burn them." So he just threw them in the fireplace.

But after he returned from this trip my father's health went downhill. I don't know if it was because of the heat in China, or whether they had given him something, but he became very weak and he started having diarrhea, non-stop diarrhea. And somehow, although the Chinese tried to treat him in their hospital, he passed away.

When we went to the hospital, we saw that my father was not taking any pills. The Chinese gave him tablets but he didn't want to take them. Sometimes while we were there with him in the hospital, the Chinese doctor would come to give him medication, or some concoction to drink, but he would never touch it.

At the time of his death – though I was not there, my brother tells me now – his last words were, "Don't trust the Chinese. They are here to eliminate us. To spoil the whole country. So you should find whatever means you can to try and save our land from destruction." This was his last advice to our family at the time of his death. I was twenty years old.

After my father's death, after all that was happening, we were not comfortable with the Chinese anymore. My husband had many friends in Lhasa, so he decided to go to Lhasa to inform the Tibetan Government of the Chinese intentions and activities. We thought that eventually we might leave our homeland and go to stay in Lhasa. But to everyone we just said he was going to Lhasa for a pilgrimage to seek the blessing of the Buddha in the Jokhang Temple.

Before he left we decided to have a sendoff party, so we hosted a banquet. But at that party somehow my husband got poisoned. It is very difficult to say who did it, there were so many people attending the party – we just don't know how it happened but he got some kind of poison from the food.

Everyone suspected the Chinese, but we don't know for sure. All we know is that after the meal he had pain, and even before we could take him to a doctor he died, right there at the party. I myself believe that the Chinese were able to plant someone at the party to put poison in his food during the banquet. But as I said, no one knew for sure how it happened.

That was 1957 when my husband died. I had a two-year-old son, and I was two months pregnant with my daughter.

3

The Chinese started to set up some kind of committee. They invited all the well-off families, the elders and nobles, the senior lamas and monk officials from the monasteries, and they said they wanted to set up a political committee. But when they started meeting we discovered there were sentries guarding the entrance to the Kanze District Headquarters, where this group was supposed to work. And whenever we went there to bring them meals, these sentries would not allow us to go inside.

It was then that we Tibetans began growing seriously suspicious – began forming the impression that these Chinese really meant to make trouble for us. Because what was actually happening with this "committee" was that the community leaders were virtually under house arrest. And during the meetings they were being indoctrinated, with the Chinese saying, "The Communist Party is great. Mao Zedong is great. Our policy is right."

Then one day they started collecting all the silver coins! Going around to the monasteries asking them to give back all the silver coins they had given to them. They said, "If you don't return the coins you will be imprisoned." I think this was done to convert the currency. Because they were exchanging the coins for Chinese currency, for paper money. They even said that if anyone shops with the silver coins they would be punished.

After that, they started ordering the people to hand over their weapons and any ammunition that they had. "Because," they said, "if you keep these you will fight among yourselves. We are here to protect you. If there is a danger from outside we will defend you, so there is no need for you to keep any weapons or ammunition. They will only produce fights among yourselves."

Of course the Tibetans were never too happy about these developments. First they saw all their capable men, all the leaders, put under house arrest. And then they saw all this exchange of paper currency for the silver coins. And then they were told to hand over their guns and ammunition, and even their traditional knives. So with all of this, many of the men really got wind of the Chinese intentions, and instead of handing over their weapons, they went up into the mountains, to begin to fight.

Eventually half the population, nearly all the men, were hiding off in the mountains with their weapons. They said, "We are not going to hand over our weapons, we are going to fight with them."

Then, what the Chinese did is they brought out some of the community leaders who were under house arrest – one man might be escorted by ten armed soldiers – and they made these Tibetans speak out and tell the men up in the mountains to come down. They had to say, "There is no use in fighting. You should hand over your weapons. We have no external enemies. It is better to come down and turn in your guns." So at first the Chinese tried to calm the men in the mountains and win them over by using these Tibetan leaders, the figures who the people would normally listen to.

But that had no effect on the men in the mountains. So in the next stage the Chinese began to use the Tibetans who were under house arrest as bargaining chips with the people in the mountains. They started harassing them in public, putting them through struggle sessions, what we call *thamzing*. These were like public trials, public meetings, where you would be disgraced. You would be beaten and tortured. They would call the Tibetans from the whole area, maybe there would be thousands of them assembled, and in front of the people these lamas would be molested.

They tied them up with rope, put cloth gags in their mouths, made them kneel, then they started accusing the lamas, saying, "You have been practicing religion. You have been using religion to cheat the people." They tried to force them to drink urine from the female Chinese soldiers. When the lamas refused to drink it they would just splash it in their face.

And in this way the Chinese would threaten the people in the mountains, "If you don't come down and surrender we are going to kill these lamas."

But of course the people in the crowd would be wondering, "What's happening to our lamas? Why are they doing such things?" People would stand up and shout and protest. Every Tibetan who shouted, who showed unhappiness with what was going on, he or she would be arrested and imprisoned immediately.

By this time the Tibetans, seeing these things happening, had become very sad. They started crying at these public humiliations. This was the first really violent action that the people could actually witness. In the evening the Tibetans from the villages would go up into the hills and tell all the men up there, "Never surrender. Now that we know what the Chinese want to do, it is better to die than to surrender." And then the people in the villages started working together with the men who were hiding in the mountains.

At night the men in the hills would raid the Chinese offices. They would find out where the various offices were, and what the Chinese were doing. Then they would come down and attack these Chinese facilities. In the morning, after these raids we would hear that maybe ten Chinese were killed last night, maybe twenty Chinese were killed. Or ten Tibetans had died. And it went on like this for two or three years, beginning about 1955.

There is a huge field in the region known as Bo Na Tho. Above this plain the men were hiding in the mountain forests.

Then the Chinese started using airplanes to fight the guerrillas, and they started bombing them in the forest. They bombed the forest heavily and indiscriminately, it was very effective, almost half of the men hiding up there were killed. Eventually the Tibetans began running out of ammunition. When they ran out of bullets there was no use in keeping the gun, so they would throw it away. They destroyed their guns so that the Chinese could not use them.

Then they resorted to the traditional Khampa way of fighting, carrying your long sword and charging the enemy. And that field of Bo Na Tho became a famous battlefield where many many Tibetans died. Because they ran out of ammunition and they began fighting with knives against guns. These traditional swords are one meter long or even longer, and in many cases, where Tibetans were killed with their swords in their hands, the grip around the sword was so strong that when they died their hands and the swords were sealed together with blood. They found many Tibetans in that state.

Almost all the Tibetans in that battle were killed. Only those who were wounded survived. Many Tibetans did not want to be arrested. They thought it was better to fight and die than to suffer under the Chinese. Afterward, when you looked up into the hills where the battlefield was, it was surrounded by hundreds of vultures circling over the corpses. In Kanze region that battle, in 1957, was considered one of the biggest, a decisive battle.

And among many of the injured, the Chinese started giving them good medication in the hospital, bandaging their wounds, and so forth. But their main intention was to extract information from them, to find out who came from the villages up to the mountains to give information, who brought the food, and who was helping the guerrillas. Even if a prisoner was about to die they would try to make him live so that they could interrogate him. And finally, after they got all their information, then this wounded Tibetan would die.

In this way the population in our region dramatically decreased. So many of the men who had been fighting in the mountains were killed, and those who were left were imprisoned. Many were arrested from the civilian population as well, because these wounded Tibetans had given their names.

The Chinese collected all the beggars in our region, and they started giving them lots of money, giving them good food, giving them good clothes, titles, pistols to carry around. They indoctrinated them, telling them, "You became poor because these monasteries and these noble estate-holders took your property. Otherwise you are a human being just like them. Now you have Mao Zedong as your father, and we are behind you, so you must take revenge."

Among these beggars, there were two types. There was one group who knew, "Now Tibet is going to disappear. I am a Tibetan. I am not Chinese. Their policy is totally against Tibetan nationalism, Tibetan identity." So this group would merely wear the clothes and carry guns and titles, but inside they never liked it. They just pretended that they liked it.

There was another group who were really converted by the Chinese ideas. Previously in their lives they were always beggars, begging for their food. Now they thought, "Now I am a big person. I have a title. I have good clothes and good food. I carry a gun." So they would do exactly as the Chinese told them.

And then the Chinese started having more public "parades." This time they started saying, "Religion is of no use. From today onward you are not supposed to involve yourselves in Buddhist practices. You are not allowed to carry rosaries or recite mantras."

The monks and nuns of our region were the main targets of these parades. What they did was they compelled the monks and nuns to get married. They were told that, "From today onward you are not supposed to wear monastic robes. You have to wear ordinary clothes and you have to get married."

Some of the younger monks and nuns did get married at that

time. But in general most of them didn't, they just began to wear ordinary clothes. The Chinese picked up a few boys and girls, made them shave their heads, dressed them up and brought them in front of the monks and nuns as examples. They said, "Look. These two used to be monks and nuns, but now they have gotten married. This is the way to do it. So why have you not married? If you don't marry you will either be imprisoned, or you will be executed." This was the threat.

I remember one elderly monk committed suicide by hanging himself. He left a note in which he said, "Now they are not allowing us to do religious practices, which was what I wanted to do in my life. So for me it is better to take my life than to get married." And in this note he also asked for a blessing from His Holiness the Dalai Lama.

Then things became completely abnormal. It was strange, not seeing even a single Tibetan dressed in the robes of a monk or a nun. The monasteries were completely emptied. All the statues and thankas were transported to China. And some monasteries were converted into prisons.

So, among the small number of Tibetans who were left, everyone became very sad and depressed. For them there was nothing to do except to cry. And by that time the people who were left were mostly either children or old people. Everyone else was either killed or imprisoned.

4

At that time, when the Chinese were committing these atrocities, there was a group of Tibetan women who were trying to inform people what was going on and what the Chinese were doing, so that once everyone knew what was happening they would rise up against the Chinese. I myself was involved in planning this opposition movement. We would tell people, "Our religion is being destroyed. Our race, our

nationality is being destroyed. With so many Chinese inter-
fering in our lives, their ultimate aim is to undermine the Tibetan identity."

We met in various places to plan strategy. Many times in the
night, without anyone knowing, we would hold meetings. We
set up the delivery of food rations to the guerrillas in the
mountains. We sent them information about what was happening on the Chinese side. And for ourselves, we had to go
on living, planning what to do next, making decisions about
our own lives.

The Women's Committee was a group that grew up spontaneously, among friends. Whoever I was closest to, I would tell
her, and she would talk to her most trusted friends. And one
by one it grew. If something important happened, or we got
some information, one woman might come and tell me. Then
I would immediately spread word to the other ladies, asking
them to come to a meeting.

It was a group of perhaps fifty or sixty women. The most
trustworthy women. We had to scrutinize them well before we
accepted anyone in the group. Someone might be too talk-
ative, and something might leak out, so we had to be careful.
Most of the women were farmers. In the nomadic regions the
Chinese had already clamped down. Most of our members
were farmers and farmer-nomads, mostly middle-class women.

I myself could not actively work out in the open, because my
family was too well-known, so they would suspect me. But the
other women worked as spies. They would go around and
look to see where the prisons are, how many prisoners are inside; to locate the main Chinese offices, how many staff were
working in each one. Also to find out where the main military
installations are, and to see what kind of equipment they had.
So the women in the group were constantly monitoring the
Chinese activities. Then, at night we would gather together
and collect all this information.

How often we met depended on developments. If there was
some special activity that we came to know about, something
sensitive and urgent that the Chinese were doing, then we

would meet immediately. If there was nothing like that, we might not meet for a week or more.

By 1956 they had already tortured to death many Tibetan lamas. All the lamas who were arrested, the Chinese tortured them by hanging them from the ceiling with their hands tied behind their backs. The victim died choking on his own mucus and vomit.

And by 1957 they had transported all the religious objects to China, everything from the smallest implements to the biggest statues. All the monasteries were locked up and some were turned into prisons. Many Tibetans had already been killed, and many imprisoned.

So we in the Women's Committee wanted to know who was the Chinese officer ordering these atrocities. Who had the final authority, who was in command. So we investigated, and found out who was the head man, and we discovered where he lived. After finding out everything we sent a message up to the mountains, to Pema Gyaltsen, my brother-in-law, who was a leader of the guerrillas. Then one night the guerrillas surrounded this Chinese leader's house with three rings of men. And they began firing on his house from the main entrance. He was a *Xianzhang*, a County Commissioner – a civilian administrator for the region. In this attack he and two of his staff were killed.

After that the Chinese atrocities decreased somewhat. The local people were glad to hear that this particular Chinese leader had been killed.

Of course our work in the Women's Committee was very dangerous. If one person was caught, it became a very dangerous situation for everyone. The arrested woman would be tortured and questioned and the Chinese would ultimately make her talk. And then a second would be arrested, then the third, and so on.

When we met, women would be posted on all four sides as lookouts, to watch for the Chinese who had night patrols in the village. In a Tibetan house the ground floor is where we keep the cattle, above that are the living quarters. When the night

58 A Strange Liberation

patrols came by everyone would quickly hide, and keep absolutely silent. We had black curtains across the windows, and just the dim light of a few small lamps lit the room.

Eventually, I suspected the Chinese were becoming aware of my activities. By that time, every night, every day, people were getting arrested. And in the mountains, more and more people were getting killed in the fighting. And of course it did cross my mind, "Now they might come and arrest me."

I was not really worried about my own well-being, but the one thing that really concerned me was my children. My son was very young, and my daughter was just a baby. Sometimes I had dreams of the Chinese arresting me, and then I would realize, "Oh! My two children are left behind." I thought if it was just me, there would be nothing to worry about. But if I am taken away, my two children will be left alone. So I was always thinking about them. What will happen to them if I am arrested?

Under those circumstances, I remember telling my friends in the Women's Committee, "If you get arrested, you must take the responsibility. You should never give the names of others to them. Because if you do, all of us will suffer." We discussed the present situation, the killings, imprisonment, the torture, and I told them that I myself, if I am arrested, I will take the entire responsibility myself. And there is no need for me to give information about other Tibetans to the Chinese. This generated a lot of encouragement and determination in my friends. In the end we all cried.

My brother's name is Ucho. He was one of the leaders who the Chinese put on their original political committee, and he was held with the others under house arrest. Then one day they announced that they were going to execute my brother Ucho. He was charged with having a connection with the assassination of the Chinese County Commissioner. The death sentence came to be known by my brother-in-law, Pema Gyaltsen, up in the mountains. Ucho Tapey was a very capable, intelligent man. When Pema Gyaltsen found out that there was danger to the life of Ucho Tapey, he came down from the mountains with four of his men, all well-armed with rifles and knives. He went to the Chinese police, and he said, "I am the one who assassinated the Chinese leader. I am the one who has been fighting battles with you. This fellow Ucho Tapey, he is not involved in any of this, he doesn't know anything about it. If you want to punish someone, if you want to execute someone, you have to execute me, not Ucho Tapey."

Of course the Chinese were very happy with this surrender. They immediately handcuffed him and took him away. Then they started announcing to the Tibetans in the mountains, "Now your leader Pema Gyaltsen has surrendered, so you too should give yourselves up." My brother Ucho was not executed, but they continued to keep him with the others under house arrest.

By early 1958 the Tibetans had lost their fight with the Chinese. Those left fighting in the mountains were fewer and fewer, most were already killed, others were arrested. Tibetans in the villages were also arrested, along with the lamas and family members of the fighters. In our region only old people, women, and children were left.

So this was the situation. It was 1958, I was staying in the nomadic uplands near Dri Tse Mountain in the Lobasha region. And I was living in a nomadic tent, what we call a *ba*.

One morning very early I heard our dogs barking. At that moment I was dressing my son, putting on his *chuba*. My daughter was sleeping. When I looked outside, from the window of the ba, I saw many policemen together with a group of civil officials coming up toward our tent. The policemen were armed.

Among the civilian officers there was one Tibetan who used

to work as a servant in our house and who had been given a title and a position by the Chinese. But in his heart he was still very supportive of our Tibetan cause. He came in and he started comforting my son, patting his head. When I looked into his face I saw he was crying. Then I thought, "Oh yes. Now they have come to arrest me."

Then one officer told me, "You have to come with us." I asked where. She said, "Dri Tse Monastery." And then I knew I was being arrested. And there was a big lump of pain right here, and I said, "I don't want to go. Because this is my son. And I have another baby sleeping over there. And there is nobody to look after them. So I can't go."

Then one of the policemen slapped me here, on my right ear, so hard that still today I can't hear well in that ear. Then they started kicking me with their boots, hitting me with their rifle butts on both sides of my body. I fell down on the ground and immediately they tied up my hands behind me.

My son, who understood that I was being manhandled by these Chinese policemen, he was crying and screaming, "Oh my mother! They are taking you away! Mother! Mother!" And he kept clutching to me, trying to hold on to me and not let go. When he tried to hold me, to cling on to my chuba, a policeman kicked him, hard, so that he went up in the air and landed five feet away. But my son kept coming back to me, and each time he would be kicked or hit.

So, after a short while I was badly beaten. I had gotten up and was knocked down a number of times, but I still refused to go with them voluntarily. They had tied me with my hands behind my back, so they just dragged me by the rope out of the tent. And as they dragged me along my son kept running after me, crying and screaming for his mother, and each time he came to me he was kicked and beaten and thrown away.

All the other Tibetans camping in that field had gathered around, and they were pleading with the Chinese, "Please don't take her away. She has no one to take care of her babies." And while I was being dragged away, I turned around to look at my daughter, who had been sleeping, and I saw that my daughter, who was just a baby, had the idea that her mother was just playing with some grown-ups. She was laughing, thinking it was all a big game.

And the last glimpse of my son, the last time I saw him in my life, was when I was being dragged away. I saw him for the last time from a far distance, he was wearing a yellow chuba, running after me and crying for his mother.

5

Dri Tse Monastery had been converted into a prison and police station. It was about a quarter mile from the tent where I was arrested. All this distance they dragged me along the ground because I completely refused to walk on my own.

When we reached the monastery the Chinese policemen complained to the officers, saying, "She was very stubborn. She wouldn't listen to us. She refused to walk."

They said, "If she is so strong, let her try this." And they hoisted me up to the ceiling, hanging me from the rafters by the rope which tied my hands behind my back. As I was hanging there I began to choke on mucus, it was gurgling out of my mouth. I remember looking down on the ground and everything began spinning, and eventually I blacked out.

Afterward, when I woke up, I realized I had been taken down and I was in the middle of a group of Chinese policemen. They decided to take me to Kanze. Again I refused to go, insisting I could not leave my children. They tied me onto the saddle of a horse, tying my feet to the horse and my hands behind my back, and they took me to Kanze.

At Kanze I was put in a cell by a Chinese woman warder. She took the belt from my chuba, and also the laces from my boots and the tassels from my hair – anything that you could use to hang yourself. There were no windows in the cell. It was dark. On the door there was a great lock that rattled when it was opened. I was thrown into the cell with four other women. One woman stayed in each corner, and in the center was the slop bucket, our toilet.

I looked around to see if I recognized any of the four other women, but I didn't know any of them. None of them said anything to me because prisoners were not allowed to talk to each other. During the night they all tried to sleep. I pulled my chuba up over my head and tried to sleep also. But there was a corridor running along the wall on my side of the cell, and all night there was the noise of people going up and down.

As I lay there trying to sleep, suddenly, in my left ear, I would hear a child crying for its mother. This made me very upset, because I was thinking of my children. I was very unhappy. I could only sleep for a little bit, then again my children would come back to my mind. For the next three days, most of the time I just lay and wondered what would happen to my two children. What was happening to them, who was looking after them, how are they doing. I was constantly thinking about this.

On the third day they called me up to the prison office. There was a Chinese police chief and about four other policemen in the room. There was also a Tibetan translator. At that time I didn't understand a single word of Chinese.

They started by telling me, "You should tell us everything frankly and fully. Now there is no one to look after your two children. If you answer truthfully whatever we ask, then we will send you back to your two kids. If you do not talk, then in your whole life you will never go back to your home."

They said, "You are the leader of the women's resistance group, so you have to tell us the names of everyone who was involved. If you give us all the names, then tomorrow you can return to your children. If you tell us the truth, it will benefit you. And you should also think about your two children. If you don't talk to us, then you will be executed." They stressed the point when they mentioned execution, to frighten you.

This interrogation went on for a long time. I said, "I had no helpers. Whatever I did was because I do not like the Chinese and their methods. Especially because my husband died of poisoning, and I suspect it was you Chinese who killed him. And my father also died under mysterious circumstances. So it is my personal dislike of you Chinese, your policies, your atrocities against Tibetans. It is because of these things I oppose you people. Aside from that, my friends are not involved. They are not concerned with my opposition to your presence here. It is only my own personal grudge that makes me oppose you."

Then they said, "If you are not going to talk today, you go back down and think it over. As we said, you should tell us honestly, give us the names of others involved, and tomorrow you will be released and you can join your children. Otherwise you will be executed. Those are your two choices. Think it over."

I was sent down to my cell, and there I thought over what will happen. What if I give them the name of just one woman? I realized that that woman would experience the same brutality that I was suffering. I remembered that those other women also have children, they also have families. And I determined, I promised to myself, that I would not give even a single name to the Chinese. Whatever happens, I will not tell them anything. Whatever the charges, I will take it on myself.

6

About a week later, they opened the cell door and took me up to the same office. Straightaway they asked me, "Now we want to know what you have thought over, what is your decision?"

I said, "I have thought about it a lot. And from my side, whatever I know, I have already told you. To be truthful, I have no names to give you. Even if I lied, I could not give you any names. I have nothing else to say."

They responded by handcuffing me with my hands in front. Then they started kicking me with their heavy boots, on both of my thighs. When you are hit or kicked so hard like that, your flesh turns into a hard kind of lump. Now, still today, I have trouble with my legs because of those beatings. After this terrible beating they threw me back in the cell and said, "Think it over again."

They didn't take the handcuffs off. After that first beating I was left in handcuffs constantly, they were never taken off.

When I had to go to the toilet in the bucket in the cell it was very difficult to lift the hem of my chuba. It was also difficult to eat or drink tea, so I was not taking much food.

One of the women in the cell with me, her name was Lhaga, she would help to feed me. When we were given some *tsampa* she would knead the tsampa for me. Actually you were not allowed to help other prisoners, it was against the rules. But she would help me to eat, and when I had to use the toilet she would help me with my chuba. She is now here in Dharamsala, she has become a nun and she is in retreat. When we met here, when we recognized each other, when she told me who she was, then it all came back to me again.

In Kanze jail, these interrogations went on over and over, in general it was every week. When the beatings didn't make me talk, they used other methods. The worst thing was this: They would insert slivers of bamboo underneath my fingernail. The bamboo was about four inches long. They pushed the fine bamboo under the nail, they would push it all the way through, so that it came out again behind the back side of the fingernail. And, ooohshsh, it hurts very very much. The pain is so much – it just makes you moan.

And while they did it they would be questioning me about my companions, "If you don't tell us the name of your confederates, this is what you will get."

They did this to me many times. Many, many times. Always on the same finger. And after the first time, by the next week, that finger was already an open wound, swollen and scabby and sore. Then they would again insert the bamboo in the same finger. So they did this to me over and over and over again.

Here, look, you can see the second finger of my left hand, it is still swollen, permanently mutilated by that torture.

In the cell, after these sessions, we would quietly ask each other, "Did they torture you with the bamboo? What did they do to you?" And some would say, "Oh yes. They did it on this finger here." And some would say no. We would show each other and talk about what they were doing to us.

And then one night there was a noise at the door of the cell. They opened the lock and there were many policemen at the door. They unlocked my handcuffs and then cuffed me again behind my back, then they tied my arms to my body with ropes. They brought me together with about ten other prisoners, a vehicle came, a truck, and we were thrown into the back of the truck, just like loads of cargo.

That night the ten of us were taken to thamzing. I was the only woman. There were three *Rinpoches* – reincarnate lamas – and the rest were men prisoners. We were taken to Lobasha. There was a huge crowd that had been called together – thousands of people. All these people were assembled from the three districts in the region. Officials would announce the dates of these sessions and the people would have to come.

So the ten of us were lined up, each prisoner had a policeman standing on either side. You had to kneel with your head down, and you were not allowed to lift your head. My first thought was that there must be people here I know. Maybe they will have my children with them. I lifted my head to look but immediately a policeman hit me and pushed my head down.

It is the standard practice in thamzing that the people who are made to criticize and beat the prisoner are the victim's friends, relatives, loved ones. So for me, there was this Ugyen, our old servant who had come with the police to arrest me, and some other women I had known. Before the session the Chinese had already tried to brainwash these people, telling them all the bad things I had done, saying that Adhe is opposing the Chinese, opposing the Communist Party, opposing our policies, she is a bad woman. They were told all this beforehand.

But none of them came forward to beat me or criticize me. They said, "Oh no, we don't have anything against Ama Adhe. If it were her husband we might have something to say, but we have nothing bad to say about Ama Adhe." So they were sent back to the crowd.

Then one Chinese woman came forward. We Tibetans traditionally wear our hair in long braids. This woman grabbed my braids and jammed her knee into the back of my neck, pulling back on my hair. Then she started denouncing me, "You are someone who doesn't like the Communist Party of China. You are a counter-revolutionary. A leader among the reactionary elements."

And while she was hurting me this way she said, "Now you can see whether you have won or whether the Communist Party of China has won. You are nothing but a prisoner, but still you have the nerve to lift your head to look into the crowd."

Then she threatened, "Up till now you had two eyes to see. But today we are going to make you use only one eye. We are going to blind you." Then she tried to ruin my right eye. She began punching my right eye. I don't know whether this woman had a stone in her fist or not, but after the beating my right eye swelled up terribly. It was swollen completely shut. That whole side of my face became blue. There was a bad feeling in my eye and I was very afraid that it was permanently damaged.

During the thamzing this Chinese woman made the lamas drink her urine, forcing them to drink it. When they refused to drink it she splashed it in their face. She sat on the neck of the Rinpoches, just like sitting on a horse, and she screamed at them, "You have swindled the people with your religion."

While the others were being beaten and humiliated in this way, although I couldn't see with one eye, I quietly and carefully tried to look into the crowd. When I looked at the people, I could see that all of them were crying.

So one by one they gave thamzing to the ten of us. When

they were beating the lay prisoners the crowd was fairly calm. A few people from the crowd would shout at the Chinese. But when they began to torture the Rinpoches, then they would shout from the crowd, "Why are you treating our lamas this way! Why is a Chinese woman torturing our lamas!" But then immediately the soldiers would arrest these people and they themselves would be imprisoned.

The thamzing lasted from early morning until about midday. After the thamzing we were once again handcuffed and tied up and thrown into the truck like baggage, and we were hauled back to Kanze prison.

About two or three days later I was again called to the interrogation room. They told me, "You never told us anything. But now it doesn't matter, because your mother has now told us everything we want to know. She has given us all the names. And we are holding her here."

Of course I was very upset to hear this, but I just said, "Well, if my mother knows something it is her own personal knowledge. But I don't know anything." Of course they were telling me a great lie, but it upset me very much. As usual they denounced and cursed me and I was returned to my cell.

And again after two or three more days I was called back. And again I told them, "I don't have anything to tell you. Whatever I have told you is all that I know. If I had something to tell you of course I would tell, because I have my two children with no one to care for them. I have already suffered enough under you. Since you have told me that you plan to execute me, go ahead. Please go ahead and execute me. I do not want to suffer any further."

They replied, "You don't have to tell us to execute you. It is already decided. You will be executed. Within the next few days you will be dead." And once again I was sent back to my cell.

7

One day I and another inmate were called out of our cells. They took a wooden board, like a billboard with some Chinese writing on it, and hung it around my neck. We were taken into a yard where many prisoners were gathered, about thirty prisoners tied up with their hands behind their backs. Only I had the billboard hanging in front of my chest, so I thought, this must be the day. Last time they said they would execute me, so today must be the day.

Immediately I began thinking about my children. Other than that I felt I had nothing to worry about. By this time I had so many atrocities committed on my body, I thought, alright, they will shoot me in the back and that will be it. But the thought of my children just would not go away. It kept creeping into my mind, that they would be left behind, orphans, with no one to look after them.

Then suddenly there was a noise, I looked over and I saw my brother-in-law, Pema Gyaltsen, being brought into the yard. He also had a big board hanging around his neck. And when I looked at him, he was just smiling at me. Then I noticed that the letters on the board on Pema Gyaltsen's chest were written in red ink, while mine were written in black ink.

From the prison we were marched to the adjoining army base, maybe a half mile away. There were many soldiers waiting there, all armed and ready. Once we reached this army camp Pema Gyaltsen and I were singled out and made to kneel down.

They told us, "Now you better look at each other properly." Pema Gyaltsen was tied up with a rope, that special, terrible way they have of tying you up, it is very painful, it pulls the arms out of the sockets and you can't breathe.

Then they announced, "Today we are going to execute Pema Gyaltsen. But Adhe, we are going to let her suffer for the rest of her life. She will be imprisoned for sixteen years. And for her whole life she will suffer." The other prisoners were kneeling down on the other side, watching. We were told to stand up, to stand erect, with Pema Gyaltsen beside me on my left.

I told Pema Gyaltsen, "Now you must pray to the Triple Gem." He was just laughing and taking it easy. Suddenly he was shot twice in the back of the head, he fell in front of me. His brains and blood were splattered all over the left side of my chuba.

Immediately the Chinese said to me, "Now look. Look at him." Then from the loudspeakers they played music to celebrate. They told the other prisoners, "We have executed Pema Gyaltsen. We have taken our revenge on him. Ama Adhe will have to suffer for a lifetime. So all of you should look to see what has come of these two Tibetans. If you oppose the Communist Party of China, this is how you will fare."

Then they roughed me up and they said, "Now whatever support you have, you bring it here now. If you have the support of the Dalai Lama, go ahead and bring it here now. If you have the support of America or some foreign country, let us see it now."

8

I was arrested on the sixteenth day of the twelfth Tibetan month in 1958. I was in Kanze prison about five months. It was not like the first jail they took me to, Dri Tse, which was originally a monastery. Kanze was built to be a prison, built up against a mountain, very secret, very secure and controlled.

In the cell there were five women altogether. There were no beds. We slept on the floor. In the center was a big wooden bucket for a toilet. You just go and relieve yourself there. No matter how filthy it smells, you just have to sleep there on the floor.

We got two meals a day. For breakfast they gave tsampa at

ten in the morning. The evening meal was at five in the evening. Mostly it consisted of tsampa and a small bun that we call *momo*. It was just enough food. Not much, but enough to live on. They brought the food around, the door would open and the cook would serve the food in the cell.

As for washing – never. We couldn't even wash our hands.

No exercise. Never. We were always locked in the cell. Always. Except during interrogation sessions. Otherwise we were simply locked away in our cell.

We were not allowed to speak to each other. It was very difficult to break this rule, because inside the cell itself there was a spy among the prisoners. This woman Lhaga, who helped me, she once told me, "Don't speak. There are spies in this cell. They will report you." So after that I was afraid to say anything.

Sometimes, when we had to go out and empty the slop-buckets – at ten in the morning and five in the evening – if you were doing that job with someone you trusted, then you might whisper to each other and talk a little bit.

It was in the fourth Tibetan month of 1959 that a group of prisoners were transferred to Dartsedo near the Chinese border. We were taken in a truck under armed guard, one soldier with a machine gun in front, and three armed guards in the rear. There were about twenty-five of us. All except me were monks. And among the monks there were many lamas and tulkus. We were all tied together, so one of my hands was tied to the arm of a Rinpoche, and the other hand to another monk.

None of us knew beforehand that we would be transferred that day. At breakfast they gave us a lot of tea. Of course if there is extra, the prisoners will drink a lot of tea to make their stomachs full. After the morning meal we were called and taken away. It was a very long drive, we were full of tea, and during the trip they did not stop the truck for the prisoners to relieve themselves.

For myself I just thought it would be terribly disrespectful, an insult, to relieve myself in the truck in front of all these lamas. But the road was so rough that when the truck bumped up and down it would knock the breath out of you. I saw how some of the monks, and especially some of the elder ones, they just had to urinate sitting there in the truck.

It was sometime in the evening that we reached a place called Gadag. It was an area of many labor camps and prisons. So at Gadag Lung Trang – that means in Chinese, agricultural labor camp – we were let out of the truck. And then I could see that most of these elder monks and lamas, their *shamthab*, the skirt of their robes, was wet from having to urinate while we were bouncing over these rough roads.

At Gadag Lung Trang the monks were all kept in a separate room. I was kept alone in another small room which was locked up and guarded by sentries. Early the next morning, without giving us any food, we were again taken away in the truck with armed guards.

We reached Dartsedo that day around lunch time. We were given some food – one blackish momo and a glass of black tea. Then immediately we were told to go cut and carry stones for building. We were each given a contraption to carry the stones, a wooden plank with a ledge at the bottom, with ropes threaded through so that you wear it on your back like a rucksack, and you carry the stones on this. I had never seen anything like that before in my life, so I didn't know which was the head and which was the tail of the thing. Unwittingly I put it on upside down. Immediately one of the guards started beating me on my face. He yelled, "You better be careful! Don't show us your contempt! If you wear this rack upside down how will you carry stones!"

I said, "I've never seen a thing like this in my life, so how should I know how to use it?" He told me, "Shut up and go to work."

When we went out to collect these stones we had to march in double lines. You were not supposed to break the line, so you had to keep up with the march, whether you were carrying a heavy stone or an empty rack. At the far end, about a kilometer away, there was a stone quarry where other prisoners were blasting and cutting the stone. At the quarry, while you fetch the stones, the guards are always keeping an eye on you.

Then, returning with the stones on our backs, some of the elder monks who were not used to this kind of physical work, they would get weak and couldn't keep up. The guards would berate and beat these old lamas for being too slow.

Sometimes Tibetan civilians would gather to watch these scenes, and you could see the people crying and grabbing at each other with frustration at not being able to do anything to help. After a while, since the elder monks couldn't keep up, they were just locked up in their cells and only the younger ones had to go out to work.

At that time there were three hundred women at the prison. Some were old Ama-la's, with hair gone completely white. Some were nuns. Some were women of my age. And these three hundred women were from all different parts of Tibet – there were so many dialects being used some people couldn't even understand each other.

Some were brought from Lhasa, taken to Gormu, then to Zhiling, then by train to Chengdu. From Chengdu, Dartsedo is very near. There were women from Lhasa, Derge, Chamdo, Lithang, Chatring, Amdo, Kanze, Nyarong, there were nomads, women from all over.

Most of the Tibetans who were left alive after the battles with the Chinese were arrested and brought here. Sometimes we would talk to each other, "Did you leave any children behind?" Some would say yes, some would say no. And those who had left their children behind would say, "Oh you are very lucky. You don't have any children to worry about."

From among these women ten of us were assigned to clean vehicles, especially the buses. While we were cleaning the buses we could see all the other trucks that were parked there. We could see trucks full of golden statues, shining in the sun. Religious images of all different sizes were piled high in the back of these trucks.

Some of the others were afraid to look up, because there were always guards nearby. But sometimes I would look around to see what I could see. I would whisper to the others, "Just look. All of our religious treasures are being loaded in these trucks." And in the evening when we went back among the other women I would tell them, "Now our country, Tibet, it has lost its mothers – they are here in prison. It has lost its deities – our statues are being carried away to China, loaded into these trucks that I saw today."

This prison in Dartsedo was formerly a big monastery, Ngamchoe Monastery. The monastery was plundered of its statues and other religious objects. The shrine rooms and sleeping quarters were turned into prison cells. Many incarnate lamas and important monks were imprisoned there. All the monks were kept in the main assembly hall. The women prisoners were kept in rooms surrounding a courtyard with ten or twenty women together in each room.

One day I was summoned by a prison official. I was scolded by this officer who said, "Yesterday after you cleaned the buses you were telling the other prisoners about all your statues being taken away. You better be careful, otherwise there will be only one way to deal with you."

After a while I was assigned to work with the three women who took care of the pigsties. The pigs were kept for the Chinese staff to eat. By this time the food situation at the prison had become very bad. We were not given momos anymore, we just got thin corn gruel, or oat gruel. We were fed one mug of this three times a day.

There were two times a day for the monks to empty their toilet pots, times when they could go outside. Near the entrance there was a small stream with flowing water, and after emptying the buckets they would try to wash their hands or put some water on their heads. The monastery courtyard was paved with huge slabs of stone. What I would do is take bits from the pig food – which was made up of garbage and leftover scraps – and I would scatter bits of this pig food around the courtyard. And avoiding the guards who were posted on the roof, I would signal to these monks where to find the food, and they would immediately grab it and eat it. When you are hungry, if you can get something like that it is really good, you consider yourself very lucky to get something like that to eat.

One day while I was working in the pigsties, from a room that had a small window I heard someone calling out, "Aro! Aro!" which in Kham dialect means, "Hey there! Hey there!" When I looked through the window I saw two men inside. Both of them had been shot in their thighs. They were just sitting there with white cloth covering their legs.

Right away they asked me, "Are you the sister of Juguma?" That's the name of my elder brother who is now in Nepal. My first thought was that now the Chinese have killed my brother. I asked them, "Has my brother Juguma been killed?"

They said, "No, no." Then they told me some good news. They said that His Holiness the Dalai Lama had successfully escaped Tibet and reached India. My mind suddenly became very happy, to think that His Holiness the Dalai Lama had arrived safely in India.

They said that after His Holiness had left, when the Chinese started bombarding Lhasa and the Norbulinka area, they also attempted to escape. But the Chinese were shelling all the roads in and out of Lhasa, to stop people from escaping. Both of them were wounded in the shelling. All their friends and companions who were travelling with them were killed. These two survived only because they were wounded in the leg.

"Where is your native land?" I asked them. They said they were from Derge in Kham. They had met my brother in Lhasa around the Norbulinka and they had fought together. They told me that my brother was able to escape to India.

At that time these two were in very bad shape – they were almost dying. The food at that time was so poor, and they were wounded, so their condition was really deteriorating. So from the pig food I would pick out chunks of radish and other bits of food and I would squeeze it into a big lump, and I would aim to throw it through this little window so that it would land on their lap. If it fell on the floor they wouldn't be able to get it because they couldn't walk, so I would aim for their lap, and immediately they would grab it and eat it.

After I heard this great news, when I came upon some monks emptying their slop buckets I would immediately tell them that His Holiness had escaped to India, he was safe in India and the Chinese were not able to get their hands on him. This of course made everyone very happy. And I told everybody, "Now for us, even if we die, it doesn't matter. Because when His Holiness returns things will be better."

This gave me so much happiness, but most of the prisoners had not heard the news. So I started singing a native song, a folk-song from a proverb my father used to tell us. We would sing it when the whole country was covered under a layer of snow:

The snow has fallen, but don't be sad,
After the snowfall, comes the warmth of the sun.

When the other prisoners heard me singing this song they knew right away that I must have some happy news. So everyone would try to come to me to hear what good news I had to tell.

9

The four women who were tending the pigsties at Dartsedo were Ngangtso Wangmo from Lithang, Dolkar and Yangchen who were both from Chatring, and myself. All four of us were in our twenties.

The Chief Warden of the prison was a Chinese man named Trang Tsu Do Trang, he was the head of the whole prison. He repeatedly and regularly raped all four of us. One by one, he would call us to his quarters, supposedly to clean his house, and he would forcibly rape us. Then he would threaten us to make sure we didn't tell anyone. He was especially strict with me.

Afterward he would make us take some kind of pill, a medicine that smells of musk. It was dissolved in water, and he would make us drink this. Later I found out that if you take this you won't become pregnant.

The four of us would cry, and tell each other, "He is abusing us like this and we don't even have any control over our own bodies." But when we discussed it among ourselves we realized there isn't much we can do against this abuse. Out there in the prison the prisoners are dying of starvation, getting nothing to eat. Here there are four of us working in the pigsties, at least we get this leftover pig food. Our stomachs are full. At least we have that.

Then one day he was transferred and a new officer came. We were very happy to hear about this.

10

I continued to leave pig food in hidden places for the monks, but I began to see how wasted away they were looking. Their eyes were sunken in their sockets, their cheekbones sticking out, their heads looked big and their necks very thin. They looked just like hungry ghosts. It was frightening to even look upon their faces.

The food at Dartsedo was insufficient from the beginning. At Kanze we used to get momos. But at Dartsedo we were only given gruel of corn or oats. Everyone was slowly starving. The four of us who were tending the pigsties were the most healthy, because we could eat the pig food.

Dartsedo is a big area, and there are three main highways going out, one to the north, one to the east and one to the west. At the junction of these three roads there are military checkpoints. Minyatago is the highway going down to the Lobasha region. Yarlotago is the road where they piled the corpses of all the prisoners who died of starvation or were executed. They dug huge mass graves along that road, and that is where they dumped the bodies. In those days, if you had to go into that area you had to hold your nose because the stench was so horrible. Even now, if you go there you will see the bones. If we went there today I could show you where these mass graves are.

Every day they would deliver nine or ten truck loads of bodies out there. Some days less, some days more. Usually eight, nine, ten trucks.

Of course the labor was continuing, the main work was constructing new prison buildings. The entire construction job was done with the forced labor of prisoners – quarrying and carrying the stones, the carpentry, the masonry – every aspect of the job was done by prisoners.

We woke up at seven in the morning. At eight we got breakfast, and started work at nine. Lunch time would depend on when we finished our morning work. Then there was a one-hour break because the prison guards needed a rest after lunch. Then work again in the afternoon. So we worked four hours in the morning and four hours in the afternoon. After dinner there was the two-hour study session. These reeducation meetings were non-stop, they were never interrupted, and they went on every night at every prison.

At these meetings the Chinese scolded and punished those prisoners whose behavior they did not like. They would tell us that Mao Zedong is everyone's father. The communist nation of China is the best country in the world, China is number one. And they said, "You are hoping and waiting for the help of the Dalai Lama, but he is wandering all over the world, alone. He is kowtowing to imperialist America and many other countries, but he is not getting support from any of them. The Dalai Lama is in a world where he is not able to look after his health. So you are lost."

Prisoners who were beggars in earlier times, those who spoke Chinese, or who cooperated with the Chinese, they became special prisoners and were used as spies to check up on other prisoners. The Chinese would tell these characters, "You just check to see what the prisoners are discussing, who is speaking against the Chinese, and what they are saying. You report to us and we will give you money, we will release you." Sometimes they would really release a prisoner, saying, "This prisoner is really good. He has reported to us about the behavior of other prisoners, so we are going to release him." In front of all the other prisoners they would make a show of releasing him.

So eventually one of these spy-prisoners said in one of these meetings, "After Adhe sang that song all of these prisoners, their faces were glowing. Even the monks, everyone looked so happy. There must be some other meaning behind this song." He also accused me, saying, "I saw Adhe taking pig food for the monks."

Shortly after that I was called in to the office. In the pigsties there were troughs, hollowed out wooden logs where we used to put the pigs' food. They brought one of these troughs and made me kneel on that, and I had to raise my hands straight up in the air, and they started interrogating me. "Why were you singing that song? What was the meaning? Was it a message for the prisoners, that they shouldn't worry because there will be happier times? What happier times? What are you thinking?"

I answered, "It is just an old folk song from my native land, it reflected my mind and I was singing it. What happier times could there be? Everything is gone. So many people are dead. I was just recollecting an old native song."

Finally they charged me with three things: First, that after cleaning the buses I spread the word to the other prisoners that all the statues were being transported to China. Second, instead of giving the food to the pigs I was giving it to the monks. Third, I was singing this song.

They threatened me with execution and said, "If you don't begin to think straight we will execute you. On top of the crimes you committed here, you have been one of the main leaders of the resistance that opposes the Chinese liberation."

Then they pointed out that of all the women in that prison I was the worst criminal, with the most serious offenses and the heaviest sentence. None of the others had experienced what I had, with my brother-in-law's execution, and despite all this, they said, I was still acting against them.

For almost four hours they made me kneel on the trough. They had raised my chuba so that my knees were bare on the sharp edges of the rough wood, so my knees were raw and bleeding. Here, you can still see the scars on both of my knees. Afterward, when I was walking away, I was wearing my boots – traditional Tibetan boots – and I could feel they were wet inside from the blood that was pouring down my legs.

Finally they told me I would no longer be assigned to the pigsty. I was locked up in my cell and they said, "Now you think things over carefully."

While I was locked up in my cell I would watch others working outside. I would watch the monks coming out to carry their slop buckets, looking around for food in the old hiding places. But now there wasn't any food.

11

The third road that runs out of the junction in Dartsedo is the Gyanagtago, this is the road to China.

In the autumn of 1960, after I had been in Dartsedo Prison for about one and a half years, once again I was transferred. Many of the women had already died of starvation. Out of those who were left they selected one hundred, all of them around the age of twenty or so. We were put together with two hundred men, and this group was transferred to a lead mine at a place called Gothang Gyalpo, just over the border between China and Tibet.

We walked from Dartsedo to Gothang Gyalpo, three hundred prisoners in a double line, escorted by armed guards. It took us five days. We were given decent food because without it we could not have made the trip. We got some momos, and even the soup was thick and had something in it. When you licked the spoon there was really something there. In Dartsedo, there was nothing to lick, just water.

Each prisoner carried their own bag of personal belongings. I myself had hardly anything. Just my mug for soup. In fact, I was still in the same chuba I was wearing when I was arrested two years before. That chuba was everything to me. The sleeves of my chuba were my pillow, one side of the chuba was my mattress, and the other side was my blanket. At Dartsedo we had no other bedding or blankets.

During this march I decided to commit suicide by jumping off a bridge. I had made my prayers to the Triple Gem and I had decided to jump when we crossed the Chagsam Bridge that divided Tibet and China. But I couldn't do it. While we marched we were tied together, in groups of six or seven prisoners. I couldn't get away from the other prisoners.

When we finally arrived at Gothang Gyalpo it was an incredible scene: So many prisoners working all over this huge lead mine. They looked like bugs, like ants going in every direction. There were thousands and thousands of them swarming over the mine, and when I looked around, I saw they were all Tibetan. Their physical condition was the same as at Dartsedo – starvation. Many were leaning on walking sticks, otherwise they would not be able to hold up their heads.

The prison was placed in a location with rivers on two sides and a great mountain behind, so there was no chance of escape. They had dug a huge open pit mine in the middle of this mountain, and from there they were extracting lead.

The prisoners were grouped in work units of ten. Everyone had a small hammer. The lead ore would be brought down from the pit, and the prisoners would crush it piece by piece with their hammers. After each day's work a prison official would weigh how much each prisoner had broken that day. I don't remember what the quota was, but if a prisoner was not able to accomplish the correct number of kilos of broken rock every day, then he would be punished in some way – possibly he wouldn't be given a meal. Or he might be given only half a mug.

The food was the same food, corn and oat gruel. Sometimes I would pretend that I was sick, that I didn't have any strength to work. Then I would be assigned to the vegetable garden where they grew food for the Chinese guards. There you had a chance to eat some of the vegetables, whatever they were growing there.

Whether you worked in the lead mine or the vegetable garden, the military control was the same. In all directions there were armed guards keeping watch while the prisoners worked. When you wanted to relieve yourself you had to stand up and raise your hand and ask for permission. You had to say, "Boko Jesu," which means something like, "Excuse me Sir." You would look at the guard carefully and if he gave a little nod of his head, yes, you could go. If he didn't react at all, if he just ignored you, no, you couldn't go.

I didn't become ill, but any green thing I found, no matter what, I would pick up and eat. Some of the prisoners were Kuomintang (KMT) – Nationalist Chinese prisoners – these KMT prisoners, when they found worms in the fields they would eat them. There was a red worm and a white one, they would just pick them up and eat them. I myself could never do it. I couldn't eat those worms. But grass and weeds, any vegetable thing I could find, I would eat.

After some time there was no strength in my body to walk. I couldn't even go from here where I am sitting over to the door of this room. If I stood up I would just fall over. I didn't even have the strength to tie up the belt of my chuba, so it was always hanging loose, and when I walked I would step on the lining, so the lining was coming out, it was all coming apart.

In those days, when you got your soup, while you were served you leaned with all your weight on your walking stick. Then you would drink it down immediately, because if you tried to carry it away, you would just fall down and spill it – then you would have nothing to eat.

When the prison staff saw the cook carrying the soup to the prisoners they would gather together and follow along behind the cook in order to watch the scene for their amusement. When all the soup was served out the empty pot would be placed in the center of the group of prisoners. Then, on a signal, the prisoners would all go for the pot, desperately trying to get something out of it, sticking their hands in and licking their fingers. And because the prisoners were so weak they would fall over and stumble and roll around, and the pot would be pushed and pulled in every direction and the prisoners would be fighting each other for a chance to lick this empty pot. The Chinese officers would roar with laughter; it was a very funny show for them.

When I watched this scene I would always cry. I would wonder, why is this happening? We are the same human beings. Why are we suffering like this? Why are these Chinese making our people starve. And I would pray to His Holiness, and to the Triple Gem, to please bless us and protect us so that we won't have to suffer like this any longer.

Sometimes the prison officials would say, "Let's go down and watch the prisoners." They would take their old used tea leaves up to the top of a small hill, and they would throw out these old tea leaves. Immediately the prisoners would rush there, falling over themselves, and they would dive into the tea leaves, eating them like it was good food. Some prisoners who ate a lot of tea leaves, their lips and mouths would be stained black. And the Chinese officers would just laugh and have a good time watching this scene.

Right now I can see it all so clearly, I feel as if I were right there at this moment. Sometimes when I am eating my dinner, eating a good meal, suddenly the faces of my fellow prisoners come and appear before my eyes, and immediately there is a big lump stuck in my chest, and I don't have any appetite, I lose my interest in food.

When prisoners are dying of starvation, all they think about is food. They will be groaning and crying out, "Oh, may I have a big piece of bread to eat. May I have a great bowl of tsampa to eat." Like that they will be talking about all different foods, and crying out for them. They shout and cry out like this, and then it gets weaker, until they are just mumbling about food until they die.

In the cells the prisoners slept in rows, two rows down the length of the room. The space for each prisoner was about eighteen inches. Since all of the prisoners were nothing but skin and bones, we could fit in such a space.

During the night the prisoner next to you might be shouting and crying out for food. Then, while you are sleeping there beside her, you feel her body getting cold. And then you think, maybe she has died. In the morning, when everyone wakes up, they gather up all the bodies of those who have died and they put them in the hall. Many of my cell-mates died beside me like that, and I felt the cold of death in their bodies.

At night most of your dreams are about food. You see yourself eating a big meal of fresh bread, or tsampa, enjoying a delicious meal, and in your dream, no matter how much you eat there is always more, the food is never finished. And then the next morning, when you wake up you know it is a dream, and you feel so hungry, so starved for food.

There was one prisoner named Thubten Dhargye, he is alive today. One time when a prisoner died in his cell he tried to eat his flesh. But the guards found out about it and he was tied up in ropes and taken away for thamzing. After this incident they made a wooden enclosure outside the cells to dump the dead bodies, so the corpses were not left in the hallway anymore.

When I had a chance I asked Thubten Dhargye, "How much did you really eat? What was it like, eating human flesh?" He said, "There was nothing there to eat. It was only the skin and the bone, there was no meat there. And before I could even eat any of the skin the Chinese caught me."

There were two types of death among the prisoners. There was one group of prisoners who died while praying to His Holiness and to the Three Jewels of Buddhism. And then there was the other group who were always groaning and crying out for food.

I tore off a strip of cloth and I tied 108 knots in it to make a rosary. I started praying quietly on my own, doing Tara puja. I thought, before I die I should prepare myself with prayer.

My condition deteriorated, until finally I couldn't even walk. I just sat there, maybe saying mantras. And one night I felt that my nose was getting very cold. I thought, I don't know what is happening, this is very strange. Maybe now it is my turn to die of starvation.

The next morning I heard rushing water, like a waterfall or a stream. And when I looked up, I saw that I had been thrown into the wooden cage that they built to hold the dead bodies. I realized where I was, and I felt so sad, and I made a final prayer to His Holiness and the Triple Gem.

Then the workers came around to carry away the corpses, and when they saw me they yelled out, "Hey this one has her eyes open!" And I was carried back to my cell.

My own chuba had been taken off me, and I was in an old tattered rag of a chuba. Some other prisoner had switched my chuba for this rag I found myself in.

There were almost no women left, they had all died. From the hundred women who were brought with me from Dartsedo, only four were left. Since there was no other place to keep me I was put in with these three other women, who were tending the pigsties.

In 1962 the head of the prison administration was transferred and a new head was brought in. The old warden's name was Ma Ku Tra. The new man's name was Bhe Ku Tra. *Ku Tra* is the title – it means a very senior official, a top official.

While they were handing over the documents and records of the prison, this lead mine labor camp, the old warden told the new one that 12,019 Tibetans had died of starvation in that camp over the three years of 1960-1962. This conversation was overheard by Tenzin Norgay, a Tibetan who worked on the staff of the prison. When he heard this he was so shocked that he immediately came and told the doctor what he had heard, that so many Tibetans had died in that place. They discussed and argued about this because it was so shocking.

This information got around to other prisoners, and I came to hear of it at that time. I can never forget that figure – 12,019.

12

Back in my native land the people encouraged my brother Nyima – the second youngest of my mother's children – they encouraged him to take up a collection of food, and to try to bring it to me in prison. They told him to go around the community and beg for the food, and they did it this way because if he did not openly go around and beg for the food the Chinese might suspect him of stealing it. So he collected the food and he travelled to Gothang Gyalpo to find me.

Of course by that time not many were left at Gothang Gyalpo, not many had survived. One day my brother came to the prison carrying packets of tsampa, butter, dried meat, cheese, and tea. When he arrived at the prison the Chinese officials did not allow him to give the food to me. They said, "You are not allowed to take this food inside, because we are taking proper care of the prisoners here. They don't need your food. At Gothang Gyalpo no one has ever come before to give prisoners food, and you are not allowed to bring food here."

There was one KMT Chinese who was assigned to be the prison doctor. Actually it was just for show, so they could say there was a prison doctor, he couldn't really do much good. But his mind was not like the Communist Chinese, he didn't have a harmful motivation, and he was alright with the prisoners. This doctor argued with the prison officials about my brother and said, "Why don't you let him give her the food? He has come a long way to meet her and give her this food." My brother was crying when they wouldn't let him in. His feet were covered with blisters from all the walking he had to do to reach this remote place. And the doctor insisted it was better to let him in to give the food.

Finally the Chinese made my brother taste little bits from all the bags of food – to check if there was poison, I suppose. And then the food was given into the custody of the doctor.

Before they allowed me to meet my brother, the prison officials warned me, "You better show a happy face and never say anything about starvation. If you tell him that you are starving, or that you have suffered severely here, there will be serious consequences for you. But if you say I am not starving, I am well, everything is alright, we might give you some of the food."

So I came out smiling as they ordered me, and I just looked at my brother. When he saw me he lowered his head and started crying. Because the sight of me, the condition I was in, was inconceivable to him. But as for talking, we didn't have even a single exchange of words, because the moment he saw me he started to cry. And there was nothing he could say.

Later, when we met after my release, he recollected this moment: "When I looked at your face that day it was a face I could never imagine. Your eyes sunken into the sockets, your cheekbones sticking out, the sight of it was horrible. I couldn't stand it. There was nothing but the shape of your bones." He told me that for months after that visit he couldn't eat, because every time he sat down to a meal he saw my starving face.

The Chinese, before ending our meeting, told me to tell him that I was not starving. But I refused, how could I deny I was starving, it was obvious to see. Finally my brother left.

From the following morning, every day the doctor brought me a wooden cup partially full of tsampa. And he advised me, "If I leave the bag of food with you, you will eat it all in one go. That will not be good for you in your condition. You could die from that. But if you eat it a little bit at a time, and build up your diet each day, then you will recover. So each day I will bring you a little more food."

So the doctor took charge of the food and told the Chinese he would look after it. He was very helpful, this doctor was a good man. He didn't like the communist authorities. And he is alive today, working somewhere in China.

When I had that first cup of tsampa I was very happy. Then I immediately wanted another cup. But slowly over the next days the doctor increased my diet, and finally I was eating a full cup of tsampa each day, and of course I was very happy.

During those days my fellow inmates kept coming up close to me and saying, "Oh you smell of tsampa." I think it is true that if you eat tsampa you smell of tsampa. And they would ask me, "How much did your brother bring? How much did you get? How much do you eat every day?"

I began to think, alright, I am getting enough to eat. But these people are still starving. Maybe I should share it, distribute it to the others. But then there won't be enough, I thought. It would just be a little bit for each person. So I was thinking and thinking how I could solve this problem.

Eventually my health improved quite a bit. I was able to walk and to work. So finally I decided to tell the doctor what I wanted to do with the food, because I wanted to help the others. I asked him, "How about you helping me to arrange to make a good soup for everybody?"

The doctor was taken aback. He said, "Can you really give it up like that? Are you sure that is what you want to do with it?"

I said, "As far as I am concerned, I have decided. I want to share this with everybody else, because I can't bear to see them running after me, telling me that I smell of tsampa. So I have decided this is what I want to do."

So the doctor arranged for a big pot. A huge pot that had belonged to the monastery in Gothang Gyalpo. He got firewood and he called me to make the soup. We cooked it up and it was served to every prisoner. Every prisoner got a mug full. Some would just gulp it down immediately on the spot while it was still so hot they were sweating as they ate it. But some would take it back to their cell, where they could add more water and eat it slowly.

By that time there were very few prisoners left. I couldn't say exactly how many, fewer than one hundred. All my fellow inmates were very happy with my decision and they were all coming over to thank me for sharing my food, and saying, "This was brought by your brother, but you have really helped all of us." They said they would pray for my long life and pray that I could someday return to my native land.

The prison authorities did not make any trouble over this because it was all arranged by the doctor. Afterward, when the prisoners thanked the doctor he said, "Don't go around saying that I am a helpful person. Don't say that." He didn't want the authorities to hear that he was benefiting the prisoners.

By the time 1963 arrived there were only the four women prisoners left, perhaps fifty or sixty prisoners altogether. Then the whole area was emptied, cleared out. Everyone who was still alive was transferred back to Dartsedo, along with all the guards and prison staff. Gothang Gyalpo, where at least 12,000 Tibetans had died of hunger and slave labor, was abandoned. A deserted lead mine.

13

Near Dartsedo was a labor camp in an area known as Simacha. Simacha was a camp especially for women prisoners. We four women survivors of Gothang Gyalpo were transferred to Simacha. There were about fifty other women, from Dartsedo prison itself and other camps. The work we had to do was vegetable gardening. Growing the vegetables that were eaten by the Chinese staff.

We cultivated all kinds of vegetables, cabbage, chili peppers, radish, all of this was for the cadres and the guards to eat. But while we were working we would steal and eat what we could.

Sometimes we would try to smuggle vegetables for the other prisoners who were not working in the gardens. The prison guards ran a security check at the entrance, before we returned to our cells, and we were not allowed to take anything in with us. So we made secret pockets inside our chubas and although we were under the watchful eyes of the guards while we worked, we would try to stuff some vegetables into these secret pockets when they were not looking. And no matter how much they searched us, the guards never found the secret hiding places in our chubas.

Most of the women who were locked up in the cells were old ladies who were too old or too sick to work. The able-bodied prisoners all worked in the gardens, but these older women were given jobs like carding and spinning wool.

Once we were inside the cell we gave them the food and they would immediately eat it, covering their mouths so the guards would not see them eating. Since we were constantly stealing and eating from the vegetable garden, after some time we all became fairly healthy.

Occasionally the prison officials would scold us, saying, "You people don't think at all of work, you are always thinking about food. I know you are stealing vegetables because you are looking better."

As usual, in our cells we had no beds, no mattresses, but each prisoner was given a small woolen blanket. The toilet was still a bucket in the cell.

The prison guards and staff were women. Mainly Chinese women, though there were also some Tibetan women on staff. Most of these Tibetan women officials were married to Chinese men, but they were very helpful and supportive of us. When they were being watched by Chinese staff they would pretend to be very strict, always scolding us. But when we were working in the gardens, stealing vegetables, these Tibetan guards would just look the other way.

Since some of the women in Simacha had come from Dartsedo, I inquired about the Dartsedo prison – what had once been Ngamchoe Monastery – where I had been imprisoned together with hundreds of monks and lamas from all over Tibet. I asked them if they knew what happened to these monks. They told me that all of them had died.

There was one day there when seven high lamas all passed away. I knew three of those lamas myself: there was Lama Sogyal Choephel Gyatso from Nyarong, Dukor Shabtrul from Dukor, which is north of Kanze, and Bhabu Tulku from Derge. *Huofo* – living Buddha – is the Chinese word for Tibetan lama. When seven such high lamas all passed away on the same day, the Chinese were just amazed.

There was one old woman from my native region named Sonam Palzom. She didn't tell me what had happened to my son, but she told me about some of the events in our home country after I was arrested.

There was a lama called Lama Rinzin, who was popular all over the Kanze area. Everyone knew him. He was a very elderly lama; all of his hair was white.

Sonam Palzom told me, "After you were arrested Lama Rinzin was selected for thamzing. Before they took him his attendant told the lama, 'Tomorrow you are going to be put through thamzing.' And the attendant started crying. The lama said, 'No. No. There is no need for you to worry. In the end we are all bound to die. So there is no use in worrying about these things now.'

"So that night the attendant went to sleep as usual in the corner of his room, and the lama was in his bed. In the middle of the night the attendant heard a loud *pop!* He lay there wondering, what is that noise, what is happening? He couldn't sleep very well, and in the morning he got up and he found that Lama Rinzin had passed away during the night. So he would not be going to thamzing."

Normally when Tibetans die, during the funeral procession there is the breaking of the skull of the deceased. This is symbolic of the consciousness leaving the body to move on to its next life. But this lama, through a special practice called *powa*, had intentionally transferred his consciousness to another life. So they could not put him through thamzing. He was already gone.

Then I remembered something that happened at Go-thang Gyalpo lead mine. There were a few prisoners there who had the job of looking after other prisoners who were very sick, who were too weak to get up. One of these helpers told us about a lama who had been at Gothang Gyalpo. When people were dying of starvation this lama would console them and reassure them that in the future there would be a better life, peace, and liberation.

Then the lama began telling people, "Maybe my time has come now." The lama had brought something with him to the camp, something wrapped in cloth. He said, "Please bring it to me," and he told his helper to close the door. From the cloth he took out a yellow shirt and he put that on. He sat in meditation posture, and he began to perform some kind of ceremony. His hands were placed in some kind of special mudra, and when you looked at his posture, he was fixed, just like a statue. Sitting there, in that meditation posture, he passed away.

Afterward his body was thrown on the pile with the other dead Tibetans.

14

I was held at Simacha for a little over two years. At the beginning of 1966 I was transferred to another camp with a vegetable farm at Minyag Rangakha. The Chinese call this area Shingducha. It is about four hours' drive from Dartsedo, but it is still under the authority of Dartsedo District. The Chinese were operating twenty-one different labor camps in the area. At that time all the women prisoners were transferred from Simacha to Shingducha. We heard later that Simacha prison was converted into a school for children, but I don't know for sure.

In Shingducha the work was the same, tending the vegetable gardens. These gardens filled the needs of all the guards and staff of the twenty-one camps in the region. Here the food for the prisoners was a bit better. We got small momos and a little bit of cooked vegetables.

In general the women prisoners were in much better condition than the men because we got to work in the gardens. Some of the men worked in the fields, some of them were assigned to construction projects.

Before 1950 the Chinese never lived in our region. But after that time, whatever area they found to be a good location for a settlement, if there were some Tibetan houses there, they would demolish those Tibetan houses and move the Tibetans to another place. They gave the Tibetans very little compensation, and then they would quickly build Chinese houses. All over Kham they did it like that.

It was the prisoners who built these new settlements. Prisoners who carried the stones, who made the bricks, who did the carpentry work, who built the houses. But when you look to see who is living there, it is Chinese, not Tibetans.

I remember some of the old women telling us, "Before, in our day, we had big fields where we could camp and hold picnics. We would go up in the mountains for picnics and horse races, songs and dances. Now the Chinese have built many buildings in these parts, and in many areas they have completely changed the place. You don't even recognize the places we used to know. Now, even though it is our country, you can't even recognize your own native land."

Take for example the mountain forests. During the days of independent Tibet these mountains and forests were considered sacred. In many of them you were not supposed to cut the trees, and you weren't supposed to hunt. That was the law. In those days only people in groups could venture into those forests because they were so wild and thick, so full of every possible animal.

But when the Chinese came they devastated these forests. Using prison labor, as well as paid Chinese lumberjacks, they cut down trees over vast areas. All the wildlife disappeared. All the wood from these forests was transported to China. At the same time they started building settlements in these wild areas. So the whole region became unrecognizable.

I think that is the reason why the Chinese Government doesn't allow visitors into this part of Tibet. Because the people would see. There has been such an enormous influx of Chinese. If you go there today, you won't see many Tibetans. In our own native land you will see many more Chinese than you will see Tibetans.

15

One day in 1967, twenty of the healthiest women prisoners were called together. We all wondered what was going on, where were we going? We were taken to a hospital, perhaps a mile or so away, and we were told to wait there in a big hall. This was the biggest hospital in the area, for Chinese staff and officials, not for the public. There were different hospitals for the Chinese workers and for the Tibetans.

We were all sitting on chairs in this big hall. In the center there was a heater and we were being looked after very well. They were bringing us something to drink, the Chinese called it *futucha*. It was a clear liquid, very sweet, maybe molasses, maybe powdered glucose. We were told to drink a lot of this. The Chinese doctors were pushing it on us, urging us to drink it, constantly bringing us more. After a while our faces became all red because the room was very warm and we were drinking so much of this drink. And we were asking each other, what is going on? Why are they being so nice to us today?

Then a group of doctors entered the room in gowns. We were told to put out our arms. They took bottles about this size, about a pint, and they extracted blood from our arms. It hurt a little when they put the needle in, but while they were extracting the blood there wasn't any pain. So from each of the twenty of us they extracted this volume of blood.

Then we knew the reason they were being so nice to us, it was in order to extract blood. One of the prisoners said that if we drink this sweet drink maybe it will strengthen our blood, maybe we should drink more of it. So we all started drinking more.

After about an hour or so, the doctors came again. And again they extracted the same volume of blood! We all became very upset then, because they had already taken blood from our bodies, and we knew that we would not be getting good food to build up our strength afterward. When I looked at the faces of the other prisoners they had become very pale.

Of course after giving blood a person is not going to die right away, but afterwards, we found that among all these women their health began to deteriorate. They became sick and they got weaker and weaker.

There was one woman named Rinchen Dolma from Chatring who fell ill after this incident, and about one year later she died. There was another woman, Yondrung Palmo from Nyarong, she also got sick and eventually died. And Tsering Lhamo, from Kanze, we were from the same native land. She had a feeling like a lump in her abdomen. She would tell me, "I have this pain here. There is some kind of growth here, which started after they took our blood." She also eventually passed away.

Of course there was a doctor at the prison, but that was just for show, so there was no treatment for these women. If an outsider visited the prison they would say, "Oh yes, there is a doctor here." But it was a doctor in name only. In reality these doctors never seriously treated a prisoner or gave them useful medication. So these women fell ill, and due to lack of proper medical care, lack of proper food, they were never able to recover their strength, so they just became weaker and weaker and eventually they died.

My own health before they took blood from me was not as poor as these other women. But one problem that began after they took blood, and has continued until now, is that I get cramps in my calves and legs. I have had those cramps since that time. Sometimes at night, in bed, when I want to roll over, I can't do it right away, I have to move slowly and carefully, because if I move too suddenly the cramps start.

Many of the other women who survived also became ill and weak and developed various problems from this. There was a woman named Riho from Nagchu District, a place called Drakho. She would get giddy and dizzy when she walked. Sometimes she would faint. One time she fell and cut herself on the back of her head so they had to give her stitches. She is still alive today, and when people ask her what is wrong with her, she says, "Oh, I have had this problem since that time they took blood from us in prison."

16

In the region of Shingducha there is a prison called Chen Yu, in Chinese. It is very high security, with very high walls and many armed guards all around. This is a prison where they hold those who are sentenced to over twenty-five years or life imprisonment. Around the beginning of 1968 a group of us were transferred to Chen Yu Prison, mainly prisoners who were considered problems by the Chinese, who were not co-operative and didn't listen to their ideas.

At this new prison they told us, "You people were made to work in order to reeducate you, but it didn't help to change your minds. Now you have to use your minds and get a proper education in order to change your stubborn brains." And so, for a year we were not assigned to any work, but we had to constantly attend indoctrination classes. Of course at every prison you had these reeducation sessions for two hours every night. But now, at Chen Yu, that was all we did.

During these classes they would tell us that His Holiness is wandering around begging for help from America and other foreign countries but he is not finding help from anyone.

Then they would say, "America is just a paper tiger. When you look at the paper tiger it looks very fierce and powerful, but if it falls into the water, it just dissolves. America is the enemy of the world. No other country likes America. But the Dalai Lama is begging for help from such a place. So what reason do you people have for hope? If you have faith in such a person, it is like a dream, a fantasy. You hold on to the dream of many happy things happening, but then when you wake up in the morning these things are not there. It is just a dream. Instead of these fantasies it is better for you to realize that the Communist Party of China is good. And see that China under the Communist Party is the biggest and the greatest country in the world. And Mao Zedong is the father of all the citizens of the world.

"So you should consider this, and realize it. And then think, 'In my early days I opposed the Communist Party of China. But I made a mistake.' You must think like that. And thinking like that you should generate love for the Communist Party of China. And work along the guidelines set forth by the CPC. If you think in these terms, your sentence may be reduced. You may have the opportunity to return to your family, you will be able to return to your native land. Otherwise, if you fantasize that the Dalai Lama is coming back, or you dream that some foreign country will help you, then you will suffer for your whole lifetime in this prison."

Every afternoon after lunch the prison staff would take a one-hour rest break. One day, after one of these indoctrination sessions, while the officers were resting it started to rain. Some of the prisoners started joking, "Now it is raining. America is just a paper tiger. With a rain like this America has probably disappeared."

But unfortunately this was reported to the authorities, and some prisoners, including me, were punished. That night we had to kneel down for two hours and raise our arms above our heads. When we couldn't hold our arms up any longer and they started to droop, the guards would immediately kick us on the elbows with their heavy boots. And they would say,

"You are all very bad. Even now while you are being reeducated you are showing your dislike. We will investigate this and find out who instigated this talk."

Then one day all the women prisoners were called in and we were taken to the meeting hall. It was full of Chinese guards and officials. They sat us down and they cut off our hair. They cut our hair short like the Chinese women. Then the soldiers gave us round hats that covered the ears and buttoned under the chin. We were told to take off our Tibetan clothes and we were given Chinese clothes, Mao suits made of cotton, and shirts. We had to pile all of our chubas in one corner, and after dressing us in Mao suits and Chinese hairstyles all our Tibetan clothes were burned.

Then they formally started the meeting and they announced, "From today onward all of you have to speak Chinese. From today onward if anyone is found speaking Tibetan she will be prosecuted. From today, everything is Chinese. There is no Tibet. You are not to wear Tibetan clothes, you are not to speak Tibetan language. Now there is no more Tibet. Only China. You are not allowed to murmur prayers or recite mantras. Every prisoner is expected to report it if they hear any others speaking Tibetan or reciting mantras. Those who cooperate and report these rule-breakers will be rewarded with release from prison."

Among the prisoners who were listening, the old women, white-haired and toothless – they didn't understand any Chinese, and now they were not allowed to speak Tibetan, so from then on they had to sit as if they were dumb, they couldn't say anything.

But when the Chinese told us this, of course they had to use a Tibetan translator, because these elder prisoners didn't understand what the officials were saying in Chinese. I myself knew some Chinese by this time, as it had already been ten years since I was arrested.

This was the time of the Cultural Revolution. Sometimes at the meetings they would bring thankas and use them as cushions on the chairs and sit on them. They would say, "Now you

can see whether your deities and sacred beings exist or not."
These were Chinese women officers, they would sit on our
sacred thankas, and we were forced to look up and watch this.
And as soon as you saw something like this you would feel
such a pain inside. Because you know these deities, these are
your own objects of worship, and it made you feel so bad.

So for one year we underwent this reeducation regime. But
for myself, I had always believed that whatever the Chinese
say, it is a lie. I didn't have even a fraction of belief in what the
Chinese told us. I had made a personal decision to trust my
own understanding of what I saw and what I experienced.
Whatever they told the prisoners, I would simply disregard it.
Although openly I never opposed the Chinese authorities –
because if I spoke out the results would have been terrible –
inside I was always opposed, even when I kept quiet.

Some prisoners would pretend that they liked and agreed
with what the Chinese were saying, but inside not many prisoners trusted the Chinese words. Sometimes they would
make a great show of releasing certain prisoners, but these
were mainly informers and spies.

For myself, I always thought, even if they repeat their ideas
one hundred or one thousand times, I will always believe the
words of the lamas who said even if you are suffering right
now, in the end there will be happiness. And I also thought
about His Holiness, who had escaped, and was outside trying
to help us. I always believed that he would come back to his
people.

I was determined that I would remember all these years of
suffering under the Chinese. All the brutality I was subjected
to. So I always tried to review and remember these events.
That is why I remember things very clearly today, because I
was determined and I made every effort to remember them. I
decided that when all the Tibetans who had escaped into exile returned, I would tell them everything that happened in
our country. That determination kept all these memories fresh
in my heart.

17

A year later, in 1969, we were transferred back to Shingducha and we resumed our routine of working in the vegetable fields. At that time there was a Tibetan woman on the prison staff named Drangkho. She had married a Chinese man when she was young and ended up with a job as a prison officer. She was very helpful to the prisoners. She would always say, "We are Tibetans. They are Chinese." So to that extent she was one of us.

Drangkho liked me, and she would tell me, "You are a very strong Tibetan, and you should stay that way. You should remain unmoved, no matter what the Chinese tell you. Because ultimately, they cannot enter your heart. You should not be like some others who waver back and forth, trying to be clever. Because if you do that, in the future it will only bring more problems for you. But if you remain firm, if you never bend to what the Chinese tell you, you keep a strong mind, that will be the best way."

She somehow arranged for me to work in the kitchen as a cook's helper. There was a Chinese woman working there and Drangkho told her, "You know Adhe? When we send her to wash clothes she does a very good job, she is very reliable. Maybe we should get her to work in the kitchen." So with her help I got the job working in the kitchen.

Drangkho told me, "When you go to fetch water never attempt to escape. You won't be able to escape and you will land me in big trouble. But if you work carefully in the kitchen you will have enough to eat. And since they took that blood from you, you need the extra nourishment."

Sometimes I was assigned to carry the food out to the prisoners working in the fields. Of course there would always be an escort with me. When I looked around I saw all the new roads and highways built in the region. And on these new roads half of the trucks you saw were transporting timber from Tibet to China. Many of the other trucks were carrying religious statues. But this time it wasn't the smaller images that they took away after 1959. This time they took the great statues, the large images from the monasteries, and they cut them in half, chopped them into pieces, and hauled them away in trucks. Many were broken up with axes or hammers. They would just smash them to pieces.

To see these sights was very depressing for me. And not only this, but during those days the Chinese would bring huge loads of scriptures into the prison and pile them up in one room, and they would get a group of prisoners working to tear up these scriptures into little pieces. They would dump the shredded scriptures into a big drum full of water, then they would add mud and the mixture would be used to plaster houses.

In 1968 many new prisoners arrived in our camp who brought us news from the rest of the country. They told us, "Now everything is finished. Everything is destroyed. The religion has been destroyed. There is nothing left." Most of these women were nuns who refused to get married, or who were openly telling the Chinese what they thought: "You are destroying everything that belongs to the Tibetans."

One of these newcomers said, "His Holiness has been able to flee along with many other capable Tibetans. These people are alive, which is good. But if you look at the remaining Tibetan society inside Tibet as a hand with five fingers, then the thumb and the first two fingers have been chopped off. These categories of Tibetan society have all been killed. Killed to such an extent that if you go up into the forests where they fought you will find countless skeletons of dead Tibetans. So what is left in Tibet are just the last two fingers, the weakest fingers, these are the Tibetans who are left. The only ones left are the small children. There is hardly anyone left that we would know. Our generation is gone."

Then I said, "Among the prisoners, all the elite of Tibetan society, the educated, the officials, the lamas and scholars, all have perished – at Gothang Gyalpo lead mine, and at the other camps. Now our land has no mothers, it has no religion, His Holiness has fled the country." Now and then we would pray for his early return. Then we would just sit there and cry.

In each of the twenty-one *lung trang* – agricultural labor camps – in the Shingducha region there was one section where the cattle confiscated from the nomads were raised by prisoners. The livestock was for the use of the Chinese who would eat the dairy products and the meat.

On Tibetan New Year – what we call *Losar* – of 1970, when they slaughtered yaks for the Chinese staff's celebration, the women's section and the camp opposite us were very fortunate to be given the heads and limbs of the slaughtered yaks. All the prisoners were very happy, really overjoyed to hear that we would be getting some yak meat for New Year.

The women's section got five yak heads. The chief cook in the kitchen of the women's section was a former Kuomintang Chinese woman, very unpleasant, a nasty person. Her name was Li Hu Yeh. Now, the Chinese woman who was head warden of our prison, and this head cook, they got together and made a secret plan. When the yak heads were brought to the kitchen to be prepared for cooking I found these two cutting out the tongues of the yak heads. Cutting out all of the tongues. When I saw this I asked, "What are you doing? Why are you taking the tongues away?"

The head cook replied, "You keep your trap shut. It's none of your business. You don't have the right to say anything here."

The women's prison warden was named Nukashi. She was a very fat lady. As soon as I spoke up the head cook whispered something to Nukashi. She just smiled at the head cook and then she left. By now I had become very angry, because I knew that all the other prisoners were so happy about this special food for Losar. Especially the older women, they were so excited at the idea of having some meat on this special occasion. And I thought, if the tongue is cut out what is there left to eat? The tongue is the main piece of meat in a yak head. And it is considered a kind of delicacy. So I thought, what will the prisoners have to eat? It will just be bones.

Then I decided that I would not take my eyes off those

tongues. I would just sit in that kitchen without moving and watch those tongues. And if the head cook told me to go fetch water or firewood, I would just say, "Oh today I have a splitting headache. I just can't move." So I just sat there and waited.

Soon I found the head cook quietly put the tongues into a bag. And then she left with the bag. I chased after her. I was much stronger than she was, I grabbed her and pulled her down. I yelled at her, "What do you think you are doing? Why are you taking these tongues away?"

She said, "Nukashi ordered me to bring them to her."

So we were fighting over this bag of yak tongues, and finally I was able to get hold of two of the tongues. And as soon as I had those two I ran to the kitchen, cut them up and threw them into the pot of soup.

Then the head cook started crying out, shouting, "Adhe is beating me! Adhe is attacking me!" Soon the prison guards came to see what was going on and then Nukashi arrived, yelling, "What's going on here?"

Immediately the cook took her aside and whispered to her. Of course I was yelled at and scolded. But this time I was not afraid because this warden, who was a very senior officer, was trying to use these yak tongues for her own benefit. She was taking the meat for her own personal use, so I knew I was in the right.

Then the guards started roughing me up, pulling my hair, beating and hitting me. In the melee I hit the cook. And to the warden I just stood up and raised my head and said, "Go ahead and kill me!" And then I pushed the fat woman and she fell over.

Then the Tibetan woman officer, Drangkho, arrived and asked, "What is going on?" I told her what was happening: That these two were stealing the tongues from the prisoners' New Year's food. The five yak heads were given to the prisoners by the prison office. And for the last few days the prisoners had been talking and getting excited about this happy occasion, getting the chance to eat yak meat for Losar. And now these two women are trying to steal the tongues from the prisoners.

When she heard this Drangkho said, "Why are you taking

these tongues away? These were given by the office to the prisoners. This was not meant for you to take away."

Then Nukashi replied, "Are you taking the side of Adhe?" There followed an exchange of strong words between those two. Then the two of them started to fight and wrestle with each other. I joined in and I pulled Nukashi's hair and I grabbed her leg and she fell onto the ground. By the time the prison guards could break it up Drangkho had a hold on Nukashi's hair and she was pulling it. Finally the two of them were separated.

Then Nukashi said to the other prison staff, "Adhe was not only assaulting me, but she also beat up the head cook." Straightaway I was locked up in a small room. After a while Drangkho came to my cell. She said, "Don't worry. I will report that Nukashi stole those three tongues from the prisoners and intended to use them for her personal benefit."

I was handcuffed and left in solitary confinement for three days. Then a Chinese official came. He asked me what happened, and I told him the whole story. He said, "The incident over the tongues is one thing. But, first of all you beat up the head cook, and secondly, you touched Nukashi, the warden. Now, you have been in prison for twelve years, but in that time you haven't behaved properly even for one single day. You better be careful, because you have a brain like a stone in the water. You are stone-headed. You just don't change. If you are not careful, if in the future you touch other staff officers, there will be only one way to deal with you, and that will be execution."

They kept me in solitary confinement for a week. After that of course I was no longer working in the kitchen, but returned to work in the vegetable gardens with the other prisoners.

But the two tongues that I grabbed got into the pot of soup for our New Year meal. My fellow prisoners thanked me for all the trouble I went through trying to see that the tongues were not stolen from us. They said they were sorry that I had to undergo all these problems with the Chinese for their sake. But they were happy to have yak meat for Losar.

18

There is a place called Nagchuka which lies on the border between Lithang and Minyag Rangakha. During 1972-1973 I was working in the forests of this region along with many other prisoners who were forced to cut timber. We were driven to this area in the morning and in the evening we went back to Shingducha prison camp. The women's job was mainly to pick up the branches that were too small to be cut for lumber. This wood was hauled back to the prison for fuel.

Actually there were all different sizes of logs which were not of the quality to be taken to the Chinese market. Some were huge logs, and they had to be loaded onto the trucks. There were wooden planks slanting down off the back of the truck and we had to roll these logs up the planks and onto the truck.

In these forests you could see many, many civilian Chinese also cutting trees. When you looked up into the forest you saw great piles of felled trees stacked up in different sections. They would work from one side to the other until they had cut down the entire forest and there were no trees left.

They were also doing some replanting in the forests, but they were transplanting a small tree that only grows well if it rains; if the weather gets dry it dies immediately.

The Tibetan prisoners working there were kept separate from the Chinese lumberjacks. Some of the wood was turned into charcoal, which means burning it slowly in a closed pile. The Tibetans were used mainly for this dirty work. And the women picked up the leftover timber.

In this region the traffic on the roads was very heavy, because there were so many trucks hauling away this timber and charcoal. Most of the trucks were military trucks. They would come up to Tibet loaded with supplies and ammunition for the army, and when they returned to China they would transport timber from Tibet. When we returned to the camp they would make us cut the firewood that we had loaded onto the trucks. This was very difficult. There were very large chunks of wood and you needed a lot of strength to do that work. We used axes, or wedges and mauls. At that time I developed blisters and then great calluses on my hands. It was not possible to take breaks when we were cutting this wood, because a guard would always be sitting on a chair next to you watching.

In 1974 I completed sixteen years of imprisonment – which was the sentence I was given in 1958. One day Nukashi, the warden of the women's section called me in. She said, "Today you have served sixteen years in prison. And during all these years of imprisonment at Kanze, Dartsedo, Gothang Gyalpo, and here at Shingducha, you have never behaved properly. You hold onto the idea that you would like to have a knife in your hand and then you could eliminate all the Chinese. For these reasons, you will not get an unconditional release. For your whole life you will be under the black hat."

In those days when a prisoner was released they would be labeled as having a "black hat." Under a black hat your movement is completely restricted. Your speech is restricted. And sometimes you have to report weekly about your behavior. And they pay you a nominal wage for your work.

Nukashi told me, "Your bad behavior in prison hasn't hurt us. It is only harming you." She told me about one prisoner in the fourth unit, named Lhamo Tso: "This woman was imprisoned for the same reason as you. But since she listened to us, she has returned to society. But in your case you won't be able to do that."

I replied, "Maybe because you stole our yak tongues you are treating me differently. But as a prisoner I have worked in many places, so if you don't treat me properly I know many other staff members who will help me. Your superiors might like to know how you stole food for your own use."

"We will see what you say to the others about how I mistreat you. I will tell the other officers that you are acting insubordinate," she warned. Again we started quarreling, she made threats, and our interview ended.

19

I was transferred to Mafutra, a labor brigade where we had to work in a flour mill. It was a huge complex. Technically it is not a prison, but is called a *lemi rukha* – labor brigade. The main difference is that they do not lock the doors. And you don't have to relieve yourself inside the cell. And when you are working there are no armed guards, just civilian staff overseeing the work.

During the day the prisoners – that's still what we were, we really had no freedom – were laborers in this flour mill. One of the main jobs was to pack the flour into sacks. You would carry the empty sacks to the machine and as the ground flour came out you filled up the sacks. Then you had to weigh it. There were maybe fifty or sixty prisoners working there. All of them were Tibetans like me who had completed their prison sentences.

The working conditions were definitely different because we were not watched by armed guards. We got time to relax, but that was only by avoiding the Chinese staff who were supposed to be supervising us. We nicknamed the staff, calling them the "jackals." Someone would say, "Uh-oh, a jackal is coming." Then everyone would pretend that they were working very hard. Or, "The jackal has left." Then we would relax.

During my sixteen years in prison every prisoner was given 2.05 *yuan* a month. This was the wage while I was in prison. Of course it was really nothing, but to the outside world the Chinese could say that they were giving a wage to their prisoners.

At Mafutra they paid us twenty-nine yuan a month. This was your income, your livelihood. And from this amount you had to meet all your expenses. From the twenty-nine yuan they would deduct rent, electricity, and food.

In the morning there was rice soup. In the afternoon there were momos, sometimes with vegetables, sometimes rice with vegetables. At night there was something like thukpa – noodle soup. We were given a coupon to account for the food that we ate, and this coupon had to be used very carefully.

Because if you ate too much your ration would run out and you would end up having nothing to eat for the rest of the month. So you could not just eat as much as you wanted, but had to maintain a strict diet according to the amount of food that was rationed.

Of course at the mill, when we were grinding tsampa we would have a chance to steal some, and then we would enjoy eating a lot of tsampa.

We slept with five in a room. And still they gave us no beds and no blankets.

After working there for one year I was transferred to Watra. Watra is a labor brigade where they make bricks – a brick factory. Our work was to dig the mud for the bricks.

Whenever I was sent to a new prison the Chinese would transfer my file. They always made a point of informing the authorities at the new prison about my background. So when I was transferred from Mafutra to Watra they sent along a letter. The new warden looked it over and said, "Oh, this prisoner is a serious offender." So at each prison they would keep a special vigilant eye on prisoners like me.

Of course the officials at these labor brigades were actually plain-clothes policemen. They wore civilian clothes but they were not civilians. They all carried pistols.

One day I was assigned with some men to go and cut wood in the forest. Each prisoner was supposed to bring in six hundred *gyama* of wood – about three hundred kilograms. All this wood was used for baking bricks. We would go to the forest, spend the day, and come back. They would also take a cook. In two different pots they would make two different kinds of tea, one for the staff and one for the prisoners.

The trees in this forest were thin, smaller-size trees. We were each given a sickle to cut them down. The men prisoners, who did this work all the time, had sharpened their sickles beforehand and they could bring down a tree with two strokes. But for me it was very difficult to cut down a tree in two swings. I would have to hack away at it. The wood was then tied in bundles and transported in wheelbarrows.

It was a very steep mountain, difficult to work on. The men would always try to cut the forest in a zigzag pattern, working along the contour. But I didn't know the system so I would try to work my way straight up, and I would be slipping and falling. It was very difficult for me to fulfill my quota of six hundred gyama per day. I had to keep an eye on the staff and, when they were not looking, I would try to borrow some wood from someone else's pile. My friends would help me, but sometimes I still couldn't fill my quota.

When we returned in the evening they would weigh what each prisoner had cut that day. When I didn't meet my quota, that evening at the reeducation meeting I would be called up to stand in front and I would be criticized, "Why didn't you accomplish your work quota today?"

I would reply, "I am the only woman prisoner among these men. I cannot cut as quickly as they do. That is why I can't meet this quota."

They would say, "You are trying to lie. You are just shirking work. When you opposed the Communist Party of China you had all the strength and means you could muster. But now you say you don't even have the strength to cut wood."

This was a difficult time for me, very stressful. During the day I was constantly worried about fulfilling my quota, and then in the evenings I had to face these meetings where I would be criticized and humiliated in front of all the other prisoners.

There were occasions when I was loading wood onto the truck and I was not able to control the wheelbarrow. I would slip and it would fall over. All the staff would point and laugh at me.

It was at this time that I met Rinchen Samdruk. When I was facing a problem he would help me. When he came to my aid the staff would try to stop him from helping me. Rinchen Samdruk would argue with them and tell them, "You know a woman can't do as much of this work as a man. Why are you sending her to cut trees? Why don't you send her with the other women to do other work?"

Eventually I was moved to other work, carrying stones on my back for construction projects.

20

For the workers in the labor brigades the Chinese had a rule that every three years well-behaved prisoners were allowed to visit their relatives for one month. Those who did not behave well were allowed a shorter visit.

I was given a letter of permission to go to visit my family in my native land. It said that I had to return in fifteen days. At that time my brother-in-law, Phuba, the husband of my eldest sister, was also held at Watra. The staff warned me, "Just remember that we have Rinchen Samdruk and your brother-in-law as a guarantee. If you don't return they will be punished." I was supposed to show this letter to the local authorities immediately upon my arrival in Lobasha.

So when I arrived I handed over the letter to the local administrator. He read the document and he found that I had been in prison for all these years, and of course the letter described my behavior. He said to me, "During your fifteen days here you are not allowed to speak about different things among the public. If there is any trouble, any political unrest or talk, if something happens while you are here, you will be held responsible."

And when I finally saw Kanze, although it was my native land, it was completely unrecognizable. I saw that all the monasteries were sacked and completely destroyed; only ruins were left. And there was almost no one left from the people I knew in 1958, only those who had been small children then, who of course I didn't recognize now.

Of the women I had worked with in our secret women's committee, about five of them had survived. One night they came to see me, and after telling each other our stories we all just broke down in tears.

While I was travelling to Lobasha, I had it in my mind, thinking, now my son has grown. He will be alive. Maybe he has been taken away by the Chinese. So I asked these old friends, Where is my son? They couldn't answer anything. They just kept crying.

So then I asked my brother Nyima, the one who came to Gothang Gyalpo to give me food. He was the one who finally told me, "There is no use for you to worry about this. Don't be upset. But your son, after your arrest we tried to comfort him, but he just wouldn't listen to anyone. He was uncontrollable, he ran away, and he fell into the river and died."

A few years later, when I was finally released, I asked my friends again, "What really happened to my son?" But they couldn't tell me the exact truth. They wouldn't give me the details because they thought I had suffered enough, and it would just trouble me more.

Honestly, I still don't know exactly how it happened. But it seems he became so distraught, seeing his mother being beaten and bound and dragged away, I believe now that it was too much for his young mind. Apparently he just continued wailing and crying for his mother. When my neighbors and friends tried to comfort him or feed him he wouldn't listen. They tried to hold him but he would bite their hands. He ran away, and until the time he died, when he fell into a river, people were not sure where he was. It all happened very soon after my arrest.

I was very close to my mother. I loved her very much. I asked about her, but she was gone also. After my arrest, all the property of my family was confiscated by the Chinese. Many of my brothers and sisters were imprisoned. My mother was left with nothing. No food or utensils in the house. The neighbors would try to help her by leaving tsampa for her, but ultimately she died of starvation.

My brother Ucho – the one who was held with the local leaders under house arrest – he also died of starvation. He was kept in that same fortress where they were originally held, and eventually the conditions in that prison became like Gothang

Gyalpo, and there he died of starvation. Of course it was not just my family, but many, many other Tibetans died of starvation during those years.

The eldest son of my step-mother, whose name was Chokley, was subjected to thamzing in Kanze. During the thamzing he was beaten with rifle butts. It seems that one rifle hit his liver, so he died from that.

And Pema Gyaltsen, who was executed before my eyes, his wife Bhumo was my middle sister. She went mad and eventually died.

So in such a harmonious and beautiful land like ours, this is what it had come to. My mother, my stepmother, three brothers and sisters, and three other family members, they were all buried close to each other. Still today you can go there and see their graves. But at that time it was very difficult for me to visit this place – I was not supposed to go there; and if I was seen by the Chinese I would get in trouble.

But one night I and my brother went up to the graveyard. There we made a small fire, and I started talking. I made a vow in front of their graves, "You have all suffered and died, and I also have been oppressed and brutalized for all these years in Chinese prisons. But when the Dharma returns to our land, when His Holiness returns to our land, then I will dig up your graves, and take out your bones, and I will perform proper ceremonies for you."

Other than that there was nothing else I could do. My brother was worried that this would emotionally upset me too much. He was afraid that it would hurt me too much and I would get sick. So he wanted to take me away from that place. So we left.

While I was in Lobasha I stayed with my brother Nyima. He constantly advised me, "Never think about these things. It will only make you depressed and ill. It won't do you any good."

My daughter, who was four months old when I was arrested, had grown up. One of my friends, Drolma, took her in after my arrest. She nursed her and brought her up together with her own daughter. Her name is Tashi Khando. I was taken to see her by my brother. He told her, "This is your mother." Of course we didn't know each other, we just stared at one another. Slowly, slowly we approached each other, and I took her hand, I held her, and then she was crying on my lap.

She told me that when she was younger, there was another woman named Adhe in our area. At first she thought this other Adhe was her mother, and she went to see her. But this woman said, "No, no, no. I am sorry but I am not your mother. Your mother is in prison, but she will be coming back soon." And she gave Tashi Khando some good Tibetan food to eat. This is how she found out that I was in prison.

When we were left alone she would take my hand and hold it and she would say, "Now I really have my mother." I tried to calm my daughter and reassure her. I didn't speak of all the things that I had been through. Because if I told her too much about my prison life she would become very angry and opposed to the Chinese, and from that she would just suffer. So I tried to reassure her, telling her that I would be released very soon and I will come back. There was no need to worry.

Before I left, my brother told me that they were trying to arrange the marriage of Tashi Khando to a boy from a local family, and the mother of that family was an old friend of mine. So I said that was fine with me. After I left, the mother of her new husband was very helpful to my daughter, caring for her as if she were her own child. They became a happy family.

When I talked with my friends from the Women's Committee they told me, "To protect us you took on all the responsibility, you bore all the charges, and because of that you have suffered for all these years. When you are finally released we want you to come back and live here, so that we can look after you. You won't have to work. We want to look after you for the rest of your life." They even brought their sons to me, and told them, "If something happens to us, when we are gone, you should always take care of this lady." And in our tradition in Kham, when you promise something you hold the hand of the person and you make your promise. So in that manner all these young men, the sons of my old friends, took my hand and promised to me that they would look after me when I was finally released and returned to my home.

And during that visit I also met Ugyen, the old servant who led the police to my tent when they came to arrest me. I always knew that he had no bad intentions toward me, that he was just being used by the Chinese. I knew him so well from before, and when we were operating the women's underground he had given me many useful bits of information concerning the Chinese, about what they were saying about me.

By this time he was a very old man, just reciting mantras and prayers. He cried when we met. He said that after my arrest he was so dazed he didn't know where he was or what he was doing. And even now, in the night, when he recalled my son clutching at me and being beaten, he couldn't bear it.

The condition of Buddhism in my native land was that there was no place left to practice our religion. Nothing had survived destruction. And the entire sangha – the large sector of monks and nuns in our population – they had all perished. The monks, lamas, and the whole educated class were gone.

For the survivors there was only one hope – relying on His Holiness and the Tibetan community in exile. Everyone would constantly pray for happier days in Tibet, and they would pray for the success of the Tibetans in exile.

So after exchanging all kinds of information with the surviving Tibetans my fifteen days ended and I had to go back. They had warned me of the consequences if I did not.

It is a one-and-a-half-day bus ride from Lobasha to Watra. While I was travelling I passed the scenes of some of my earlier experiences: the place where I was arrested, where I was dragged away by the policemen, and where I saw my son for the last time. When I saw this place from a distance as I was riding away in the bus, I was suddenly filled with emotion and pain. I was overcome by the memories.

I remember another sight I saw on that trip. There is a river called Shingchu which runs through this area. As we drove along the river it was filled with logs, timber floating down to China. And on both sides of the river there were huge stacks of logs, thousands and thousands of logs stacked along the riverbanks. This river goes to China, to the region of Hanyang, where iron bars block the logs, and there they pull them out of the river.

21

When I returned to Watra my brother-in-law asked me all about the conditions back home. Since he was quite old I didn't tell him too much. I didn't want to upset him. But then, when I myself started to think about all that had happened, I became very depressed. I just thought, now there is nothing left. And after that I couldn't work. I just sat on my bed.

My friends told me, "Don't do this." And the Chinese supervisor came and said, "Who incited you not to work?"

I replied, "There is no one to incite me. But now I have seen with my own eyes the condition of my country. Before, when I worked for you, making bricks, carrying stones, cutting wood, I thought I was doing this work because someday I would have the chance to see my mother, to see my children and my brothers and sisters. But now I have seen the truth – all of them have been killed, or they have died of starvation. Now, no. If this is the way things are, I will never work."

Then the Chinese boss ordered other prisoners to drag me out to work. But they just stood there. They didn't listen to him. I said, "Now there is nothing left for me. I don't care if you shoot me right now. You decide. I don't care."

My brother-in-law and Rinchen Samdruk told him, "You better execute her. Because she has seen everything with her own eyes."

Actually, by this time I was mentally very distressed, very disturbed, because I was dwelling on how my family had perished and how the land had been completely transformed. After visiting my native land, and then coming back to the labor camp – it had a great impact on me. Everyday I would laugh for long periods, kind of hysterical fits. I couldn't control myself, I would just laugh and laugh. And then some days I would cry uncontrollably all day. And sometimes I would just be singing. And I never wanted to sit down. I always wanted to be moving, moving. I couldn't relax, couldn't sit still. When the other Tibetans saw my condition they would cry and say, "Now Ama Adhe has gone mad."

One of the disciples of Jamyang Khentse Rinpoche was a prisoner in our area. He was quite old, and he was assigned as a watchman in the fields to make sure that cattle didn't eat the crops. One day, on our day off, Rinchen Samdruk and my brother-in-law took me to see this old lama. He was a kind of scarecrow, sitting out in the middle of the field. I was hysterical, singing and laughing and crying.

The old lama said, "It is so sad. Adhe has suffered so much, and now she ends up like this." He did moxibustion on me. All over the body. On the head, all around the spine, on the shoulders. It is done with a special herb that is rolled into a stick and then burned at the tip and held over different parts of the body. The heat was scorching. It was very painful, but when it was over I found it very relieving.

After about one month, slowly, I found myself regaining control of my mind. From the moxibustion I had sores all over my body, and they took a long time to heal. But mentally I felt much better. I stopped crying and laughing and singing, and I was able to just sit down and relax. My mind was settling down.

One day they announced that today there will be no work, just a meeting. Lo Kasu was the leader at Watra – *Kasu* is the title. In the meeting he said, "Adhe is a very bad woman. For all these years we have tried to reeducate her. But nothing changes in her head. She pretended to be mad, she was singing and crying and laughing, and even telling us to execute her. She is a very bad woman. So from today onward no prisoner is allowed to speak to her or associate with her. She is a bad element."

But my friends didn't listen to that. Instead they were very helpful and friendly to me. When we were divided into groups of ten or fifteen for specific work, all the others in my squad would say, "Oh Ama-la, you just relax here and take it easy. We will do the work. You are sick and you need the rest." And some of the older prisoners told me, "These Chinese are always trying to condemn you. But for us you are doing the right thing, we are with you."

And when people back in my community heard about my state they were all trying to send me food, butter, meat, and cheese to such an extent that I couldn't eat it all.

My daughter came to visit me around this time – it was around 1976 – after my nervous breakdown. She heard that her mother was not well so she came to see me. At that time I was recovering from the breakdown and the moxibustion and I had returned to work. My daughter told the camp supervisors, "My mother is very ill, so I will work in her place." They didn't object. So for twenty days my daughter took my place at work and this gave me time to rest.

They only allowed her to stay for a few weeks, and when she left to return to Lobasha, Tashi Khando cried continuously. I told her, "Nukashi, the fat woman warden, once told me not to corrupt my daughter's mind with my 'incorrect way of thinking.' Nukashi told me, 'Explain to your daughter that the Chinese are good. And never tell her the things that have happened to you. Don't spoil her brain with your ideas.'"

We laughed together at this, and she said, "Mother, you don't have to tell me what atrocities the Chinese committed on you. I know. And I know these are things we must never forget. I will tell them to my children, and they will tell them to their children. During the past twenty days while I worked in your place, I have listened to the stories of the Tibetan people who are forced to work here. And no matter what methods the Chinese use to try to control my mind, I will never forget that my own mother is one of the few survivors from among thousands of Tibetans who starved to death and were executed and were tortured to death. No matter what method they use, these things can never be erased from my mind."

She told me that when she was growing up one of the worst things for her was not having someone she could call her mother. All the other children would call for their mother or talk about their mother, and she would think, all these other kids have their mother, but what about me, where is my mother? And every time she thought about her mother there was a lump of pain inside her heart.

In Minyag Rangakha there is a great snowcapped mountain named Sha Jara, very high, and very sacred in that land. It is the sacred mountain of that region. At the base there is a very large lake. One day in 1975, suddenly a black nomad's tent appeared sitting on the lake. The Chinese were terrified, they were amazed. This was not natural. They were looking at it through binoculars, trying to figure out what it really was. And then suddenly the tent disappeared, and it revealed a huge green lotus, floating on the lake.

This made all the Tibetans very happy. Everyone in the region went to the lake to pray and offer scarves and other special offerings. They prayed that the Buddha's teachings would remain and spread in Tibet. And they believed it was a sign that His Holiness the Dalai Lama would return to a free country. This was one year before Mao died.

The Chinese were so terrified that they bombed this lotus. All the Tibetans were coming out to offer prayers and scarves. The Chinese didn't know what to do to stop it, so they tried to blow it up. After they bombed it, when you picked up a piece it felt just like grass. The people all came down to pick up bits of the lotus that were floating on the lake. They took their pieces of the magic lotus home and put it on their altars.

22

In 1979 the Chinese began to institute their so-called liberalization. Exiled Tibetans and foreign visitors began coming into Tibet. And then the first delegation from His Holiness was arranged to come and investigate the conditions in Tibet. Just before the first delegation arrived in our area there was a meeting at our labor brigade. They said, "From today onward there will be no more black hat. From today onward no one will be kept for life imprisonment. All the prisoners will be released."

"But," they said, "all the reactionary leaders, the ringleaders, these people will be kept behind, because these are the people who incited the masses. They will be detained and the rest will be released." So at that time more than half the prisoners were released from Watra.

Just before the delegation came to our area the Chinese told the public that when they arrived the local citizens should dress up in clean Tibetan clothes, should carry prayer wheels in their hands, and go out as if they were on a picnic, having a good time, singing and dancing.

At Watra itself we were summoned to the big meeting hall and they told us the same thing, "When the delegation comes don't wear Chinese clothes, put on Tibetan clothes." And on that day there would be no work; everybody must come for this important meeting.

On the day they arrived I told Rinchen Samdruk and my brother-in-law, "You two go to the meeting. I will just pretend that I am sick and I will stay here. Today, if I am not able to tell these visitors what has happened in my life, I will not be satisfied."

They said, "Today, we don't think you will have a chance to speak. But there will be many other visitors to come, so you can tell your story, slowly, slowly. If you try to do something today, the Chinese will just punish you further."

So they went to the meeting and reported that I was sick and unable to eat. The Chinese said, "If she is sick just lock her door and don't let her go out."

But I slipped out of the camp. The main road is very close to the camp, and I went there and I saw a long line of cars coming. I tried to reach someone in one of the cars, someone from the delegation. I saw someone, I think it was Lobsang Samten, the leader of the delegation and the elder brother of His Holiness. I tried to flag them down but the driver just drove around me. They didn't stop, and Lobsang Samten just waved to me. That was it.

They drove on to the town and had the meeting. Afterward people told me, "Today we saw the brother of His Holiness. The Chinese told us to wear Tibetan clothes and to carry mani wheels and malas, but they already took everything. There aren't any chubas left. But we are happy. We were able to see him, the brother of His Holiness."

Before the delegation arrived the Chinese paid Tibetans to quickly restore the monasteries that were visible from the highways. But all the ruined monasteries in the remote areas, which are not easily seen from the highway, these they ignored. They gave nothing to fix these up.

Some Tibetans, to needle the Chinese, would say, "Oh you are now giving out money for restoring monasteries. We also have a monastery in our village that we want to renovate. Please give us money." But the officials would answer, "No, no, no. This is not meant for your monastery." And they wouldn't give them anything.

Of course they didn't really restore them to their former condition. They would just demolish the old ruins and then rebuild a small chapel. But some of the elder Tibetans were very moved by this, once again having a place to worship. They didn't have any of the materials, any Buddha images or religious objects to make a proper chapel, nothing to put on the altar, so they began to make clay statues, and on the walls they tried to put up paintings or photographs of different deities.

As all the monks and lamas and tulkus had perished, there wasn't anyone left to stay at the monasteries. If you looked from the road you might think, "Oh there is a nice monastery up there." But it was just for show. Just a facade.

When the Tibetans would go into these temples, immediately they would begin to cry, because they are nothing like the real temples from the days of independent Tibet. They are just walls, just a building. There is no main image of Buddha, nothing on the altar, no murals, so any Tibetan going in there would feel empty.

By this time my daughter was married. She told me, "Now you should find some way of getting out of this labor brigade. I and my husband will look after you when you come back home. There is no need for you or Rinchen Samdruk or your brother-in-law to work – we are going to look after all of you once you are released."

We decided on a plan, to have my brother in Nepal write a letter saying that he wanted to come visit me. Eventually a letter arrived from him in which he asked, "Since all the prisoners are supposed to be released, why are you still held in prison? I am going to come to visit you, if I can meet you in Lobasha."

He also wrote a letter to Kanze District authorities saying he wanted to come visit me in Lobasha. The Chinese were quite worried by this letter and the Kanze District cabled Dartsedo District and told them, "You have to release Adhe. If you don't release her her brother won't come."

At that time the Chinese had told the world that all the prisoners in Tibet were released. They wanted as many exiles as possible to return to Tibet, to make it look like Tibet was open and normal. But if my brother came to visit and found me still in prison it would be a big embarrassment to the Chinese.

Using these letters for leverage, certain Tibetans who held official positions in the local administration used their connections and influence, and ultimately I was released from Watra in 1985.

The supervisor of all the twenty-one prisons in the Minyag

Rangakha prison complex was a man named Tsu So Gye – *So Gye* is his title. When I was released they called me to his office. He said, "Now we are going to send you back to your home. You have never bowed to the Chinese during your imprisonment and we have never been able to instill in you Chinese ideas. During the entire twenty-seven years of your imprisonment we have not been able to reeducate you. During all these years you have been stone-headed. But no matter how much you oppose us and our policies, it is just like you are picking up a stone and dropping it on your own feet. It doesn't harm us in any way.

"Your brother is now coming from abroad to visit you. You are not allowed to speak to him or to the public about those who died of starvation in prison, those who died of execution, and so forth. All these things you are not allowed to speak about. And if you tell stories to the people, we have our helpers among the public and they will inform us. In that event you will not have time to spend with your brother, or your daughter, or with your friends – you will be back in prison."

I was given a document of release and told to take this letter to the regional office in Lobasha. I was released along with Rinchen Samdruk – the two of us together. My brother-in-law had already been released.

When I got word of my release I quietly organized a small party for the other prisoners that I was close to. At that time there were about forty left in the labor brigade. There was a common room and we could quietly arrange such meetings when someone was released. We would comfort each other, and pray to meet after we were all released, and offer to help in whatever way we could once we were outside. And we would have something to eat, and if possible, exchange scarves.

At my release party I told them, "Now it seems the time is good for us. I don't know whether His Holiness himself is coming soon or not, but already his brother has visited our area, and on the roadside monasteries are being renovated.

"But we must never forget what happened to the thousands of our fellow prisoners. I, for one, can never forget what I went through during all these years in prison. Perhaps in the future there will be people from the outside coming to our area, and we will find an atmosphere and opportunities to tell our stories. If such a chance comes, I myself will spend day and night telling each and every detail to such visitors."

We all promised that we would not forget what we had seen with our own eyes. Someone said, "Unlike you, Adhe, many of us have forgotten so many of the things that happened. But still the important events are fresh in our minds, and we will keep them in our hearts."

Initially, when I first realized that I was free, of course I was very, very happy. But when I looked at my situation again, it was like staring at a blank wall, because I realized that my mother had died, my brothers and sisters had perished, my son had died, and even the earth and stones of my native land had been altered since the coming of the Chinese. There wasn't anything that I recognized from the time of my arrest. Of the people who survived, most were children when I was taken away. So for me it was like moving to a completely new region, it was not the country that I had known. When I thought about this, in my mind it was like a great void. Coming home was a moment when I felt so happy and so sad at the same time.

23

When I arrived in Lobasha, straightaway I took my letter of release to the regional office, and the District Commissioner read it carefully. Once again he warned me of the consequences of telling people about my life. He said he did not want to hear that Adhe is saying this and that. He warned me not to tell my daughter or my relatives or my brother – when he came to visit – about the persecutions I had experienced in prison. He said, "Normally when people are released they have understood the Communist way of thinking, and they become good citizens. But in your case you have resisted re-education."

My friends later told me that before I arrived the Chinese called a big meeting in Lobasha where they announced, "Soon Adhe is going to be released. When you look at her she is just a woman. But in reality she is someone who tries to undermine the Communist Party of China and she incites people in the society against the government. So you people have to be careful of her. We will give incentives to anyone who reports to us if Ama Adhe tries to defame the Chinese Government, or if she starts to sing subversive songs. If she does this you should report to us immediately."

So when I arrived my friends told me, "Please be careful. They said this about you before you came." And even my daughter said, "Please mother, don't go outside the house. Just stay here and relax."

And the children of the town, after hearing so much Chinese talk, they became curious about me and they would sneak around all excited to see what this so-called Ama Adhe looked like. But then they would see that it is just an old woman, just like their own mothers. So they would go away saying, "Oh this Ama Adhe is just an old Ama-la."

Of course among close friends who came to visit me, bringing gifts of tea or butter, to these people I would tell the whole story. Among the public, I would keep a watch out and if I found someone who was trustworthy, I would tell them the truth too. I would tell them everything.

Even Tibetan officials who were working for the Chinese, they realized the hardship I had been subjected to and they would come quietly in the night to meet me and talk to me. And they told me, "Although the Chinese Government says all kinds of things against you, we consider you a very good person, a patriot and a freedom fighter." These were people who kept little shrines in their homes with water bowls and offerings of incense. On the altar would be photographs of Chinese leaders, but inside the frame, behind the picture of Mao, they hid a portrait of His Holiness the Dalai Lama.

They would tell me how delighted they were to find that even after twenty-seven years of imprisonment, during which the Chinese had drained my entire energy and strength, "Still you have your determination as a Tibetan, and they have not been able to brainwash you."

They said, "Although we work for the Chinese, it is only because we are paid by them. We need this work for our livelihood. We have no alternative." For them to openly support the Tibetan cause would be like sending themselves to prison. They couldn't openly speak about Tibetan independence, but in private they would say, "We are not Chinese. We are Tibetan. His Holiness is our light. In the future there will be happiness for us, for the Tibetan people."

All these Tibetan officials helped me a lot. Especially in getting me the passport to come out of Tibet. It was all arranged by these officials. I went to the Kanze District Office with the letter from my brother. I said, "Now I want to go to Nepal to bring my brother back."

But the Chinese said, "Oh no. You don't need to go. Maybe you could send one of your nephews."

I kept trying and trying. I stressed to them that for my brother it was important to meet me. He wanted to take me on a pilgrimage, and then we would come back together. But the Chinese didn't trust me, and they said, "No, no, no. There is no need for you to go."

It was the Tibetan officials who did a lot of the planning and maneuvering in order to get me my passport. Finally we came to the administrator who actually issues the passports. To this person we stressed that we were actually doing something good for the Chinese Communist Party – that my brother would be coming back from exile, and this would be favorable to the CPC and unfavorable to the Dalai Lama. But without sending Ama Adhe it will not be possible.

I was called in to the Kanze District Office where they asked me, "If you are sent to bring back your brother, what are you going to say?"

I replied, "I will tell him, 'Now you should come and return to your native land and be with your family, whom you haven't seen for so many years. The situation is good. There is no use in leaving your old bones outside your own country.' I will tell him that, and tell him that I have come to pick him up and bring him home."

Before I went to that office, the Tibetan officials who were helping me told me what they would ask me and what I should reply. So I was well prepared with all the answers.

The officer responded, "Well, if that is the case, then it is okay. You can go." And he went on to lecture me, "You have been in prison for twenty-seven years, but you have not been reeducated. So you should think this over very carefully. If you bring your brother back we will not bother you any more in the future. We will give both of you pensions, and we will never trouble you again. For your brother, there is no use in his staying around the Dalai Lama, he should return to his native land because that is where he belongs. If you come back with him you don't have to worry about your house or your salary – we will provide you with everything you need."

I just nodded my agreement to the man who was going to give me my passport.

But even after Kanze issues the passport, it still has to be stamped by Dartsedo District. I thought it would be quite difficult to get the stamp I needed from Dartsedo. But with more planning, and by using various means, we were able to change the minds of the officials there.

One point we made to them was to say, "Oh no. Ama Adhe would never stay away. She has her daughter here, and her relatives. She will definitely come back. And if she brings her brother back with her that is even better for the Communist Party of China." So by stressing these points, finally I got the stamp I needed.

Now there was one last obstacle: I didn't have any money. After so many years in prison, I really had nothing. But the surviving old Tibetans, and some of my old fellow-prisoners, and even the Tibetan officials, they all arranged for my travelling expenses.

These people told me, "You must not waste your trip. We

in Tibet who have suffered under the Chinese, according to our tradition we will tell our children the story, and the truth will be passed down from generation to generation, what the Chinese did in our land. But apart from that, we have only fists against the military might of the communists. But in your case, you now have the opportunity to go to the free world where there won't be any restrictions on you. So you should inform the world in detail of what has been going on. And of course you must have an audience with His Holiness the Dalai Lama and tell him your story."

I remember very clearly my friends telling me this, and encouraging me to speak out on their behalf, in order to, as they said, "bring light to the hopes of the Tibetans in Tibet."

I told them, "Every one of you can rest assured that I will tell everything, whenever there is an opportunity. I am someone who has suffered for many years, but still I have these events engraved in my heart. So you do not need to worry, I will tell the world."

All of these meetings were in the night. And since there wasn't a single Tibetan who had not suffered at the hands of the Chinese, everyone had information to give to me, for me to carry out of Tibet. We would discuss these things through the night, and in every case we would end our talk in tears. And we would take each other's hands, and touch our heads, and they would kiss me good-bye with their blessings.

On the day I left all my friends and relatives came to say good-bye. My daughter was crying, and to calm her and comfort her I said, "Today I am not being arrested by the Chinese. I am going to India to see His Holiness, and then I will come back with my brother." I couldn't tell her that I was going to stay in exile, because then she would not have let me go.

Then I travelled, together with Rinchen Samdruk, to Lhasa, which took about a week. Some of the officials had managed to arrange an official Chinese car at a special discount – it was much better than the hard bus ride. It is about 1700 kilometers to Lhasa.

Most of the traffic we saw on the roads was trucks transporting timber or medicinal herbs which are picked in the mountains. In the nomadic regions, you also saw loads of wool.

Once I was in Lhasa I went on a pilgrimage around the surviving temples and monasteries. I went especially to pray for all my relatives who had perished. I also went for the blessing of visiting the audience chamber of His Holiness the Dalai Lama in the Potala. There I saw his empty throne, with only a white scarf laid across it. That sight was very moving for me. It is to this room that the elders of Lhasa and other pilgrims come to pray that His Holiness will return soon to sit on this throne. While I was there they came to this room to offer their special prayers, and it was a very powerful scene. In the end I spent about four months in Lhasa.

In order to visit Nepal I needed a visa, and this had to be issued in Lhasa. But the Nepalese would not issue the visa until you bribed them. They were asking too much money and I didn't have it. So I went to a lama in Lhasa to ask for a *mo* – a divination – to advise me what to do.

I told him, "I have this passport, and there are many people travelling back and forth now. If I go without a Nepalese visa, will I be able to reach Kathmandu?"

The lama threw his mo and said it looked very favorable: "There is no doubt that you will have safe passage."

Rinchen Samdruk and I travelled by bus to Dram, the town on the border between Tibet and Nepal. There the Chinese border guards said, "You don't have a Nepalese visa stamp. They won't let you into Nepal."

I said, "I am just going to pick up my brother who is returning to Tibet. I am not going to stay long, I will be coming straight back. Maybe you have some means to help me cross the border."

And the Chinese guards said, "Why don't you try giving the Nepalese some money, then they may allow you to cross."

So I went down to the bridge, it's called Friendship Bridge, and in the middle there is a red line which marks the border of Tibet and Nepal. Right there on the border line I began to pray to His Holiness and Tara and all the deities to help me, and as I crossed the line there was a Tibetan standing there who grabbed my hand and said, "Are you Adhe?" I didn't recognize him at all, but he said, "I have been sent by your brother to pick you up and bring you to Kathmandu."

I was overjoyed to find someone there to help me. I said, "But I don't have a Nepalese visa, so I don't know if they will allow me across."

He said, "Oh, don't worry. If you pay them something they will let you in."

So at Potari, on the Nepalese side, we bribed the border guards and they were happy to give the visa. It was around midnight when we finally arrived in Kathmandu, in Swayambunath, where my brother was living.

My brother, who was seventy-nine at that time, was just lying on his bed, and the man who had met me went in and said, "Juguma, your sister is here." Then he got up and came out to greet me, and we embraced and held each other, and we wept.

Of course he inquired about the situation in Tibet. But since he was quite old I did not tell him everything, because I thought it might be too much for him. I told him, "There is no need to worry now. The whole of the six million people have suffered. It is not only the two of us. But now we are in the land where His Holiness lives. So you must do your religious practice, and things will be better in the future."

But as much as I tried to calm him down it was difficult. He would keep asking about different people from our native land. He would say their names and ask, "How is this fellow? And what about that family? And how is this uncle?" And I just had to lie. I would tell him they are fine, they are doing this or that. I just couldn't tell him, "Oh, he was executed. He was tortured to death. They died of starvation."

Since there wasn't anyone to look after my elderly brother, and he was always practicing his devotions, doing puja or circumambulating the stupa, he was very dirty and his clothes were covered with lice. So Rinchen Samdruk and I cleaned him and brought him new clothes and looked after him, and slowly his health improved.

Then Rinchen Samdruk and I went to the teaching by His Holiness the Dalai Lama in Varanasi, India. There was a special group audience for all the recent arrivals from Tibet. All of us in the audience were completely satisfied to have a blessing from His Holiness, and we were leaving the compound with our hearts full of this wonderful opportunity. But Rinchen Samdruk and I felt we had to see His Holiness personally to inform him about what had been going on in our region and in our own lives. So we left Varanasi to go to Dharamsala, where His Holiness lives.

At that time "Dharamsala" and "Dalai Lama" were the only two words we knew in Hindi. We had no one to help us on the way, but these two words were very useful to us. When we had to get on a bus or a train we would just say, "Dharamsala? Dalai Lama? Dharamsala? Dalai Lama?" And the driver would nod and we would get on board.

Finally one evening we reached Dharamsala. That night we stayed in the bus station because we weren't sure where we were. But the next morning we saw a Tibetan lady in the bus station, and we asked her, "Where are we?" And she said, "This is Dharamsala."

All the Tibetans who arrive here from Tibet are immediately registered and then looked after by an office of the Tibetan Government. They are given accommodation and food and so forth. We were given rooms at the Tibetan Government Hostel for recent arrivals. And soon we had an appointment for a private audience with His Holiness. This was in October 1988.

When we entered the room with His Holiness, we came in and we immediately just sat right next to the door. This was the way we were trained. Humble people like us could never get so close to such a great person. Three times His Holiness had to urge us, "Come up. Come up. Come up." Telling us to come sit close to him. When I saw His Holiness for the first time, immediately I was about to cry. But then I said to myself, "This is no time to cry. You have so much responsibility to inform His Holiness of the situation." So I buried my emotions and I told him everything. There were times when the story just overwhelmed me, I couldn't control my tears and I had to stop. And then Rinchen Samdruk would carry on.

The interview lasted about one and a half hours. Every time I mentioned the destruction of one of the monasteries or about the deaths of various lamas, His Holiness was immediately whispering prayers for them. And then I requested His Holiness, and through him all the other lamas, to pray for those who died of starvation, for all those who died without any traditional prayers or ceremonies, so that their spirits may be calmed. Immediately His Holiness made prayers for them also.

PART 3

THE MOMO GUN

Tenpa Soepa's Story

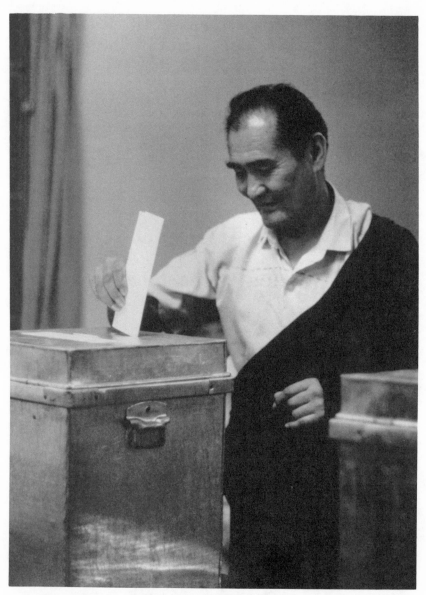

Tenpa Soepa casting his ballot for the first democratic election of the
Tibetan National Assembly, Dharamsala, India.

Photo by Lois Raimondo.

The Momo Gun:
Tenpa Soepa's Story

1

My name is Tenpa Soepa and I was born in 1934 in Lhasa. My father's name was Lungta Tsering and my mother's name was Dekyi Yangzom. Gomang Khangsar was our family title. We were a family of middle-class farmers. Our family home was in the village of Pagmo Shue, under Taktze District. But my father worked in his younger years as the steward of the estates of Lhading, and because of his work I came to be born in Lhasa.

When he got older my father resigned his position as steward and moved back to our village to farm for himself. The farm he cultivated and the house we lived in actually belonged to Lhading, but my father worked this land on a lease basis – basically he rented it from the Lhading family. So our income came from farming – that was our main source of livelihood.

There were eight of us in the family, six children and my mother and father. We children were four girls and two boys. I was the third child, and it seemed that my parents had a spe-

cial fondness for me, probably because, between my brother
and myself, I was more clever. And since I was a bit brighter
they thought I could do a better job with the chores around the
house.

Until I was eight or nine years old my father taught me reading and writing at home. Then, when I was ten, I went off to
school in Lhasa. It was a day school, called Nyarong Shar, and
I attended this school until I was fifteen.

At that time I returned to the village. But after I was home
for a while my parents said, "You can't just hang around here
and do nothing forever. You'll have to do some work." They
sent me to fertilize the fields. In the spring they used to fertilize the fields with manure, and they would carry the manure
on donkeys. A lot of donkeys would bring this manure, and
you would have to spread it here on this field, and another load
over there on that field, and so on. This was very hard work,
and while I was working, if I sat down, the ground was freezing. But when I stood up, it was too windy. So this was my first
job at home, and I was having a hard time of it.

I said to my mother, "Mom, I don't think I'll stay here any
longer. I think I'd rather go back to Lhasa." Both my parents
had the wish, and always advised me that, "When you grow
up, you should serve the Tibetan Government." That was
their main ambition for me.

So when I was sixteen they took me to Lhasa and there I
entered the Tze School. This was a government school where
young monks came from the three great monastic seats of
Lhasa – Ganden, Drepung, and Sera – as well as other monasteries, and were trained to go into the government service.
Each monastery would select a few young monks and these
boys would enter this school to become government officers. I
entered Gomang College of Drepung Monastery, and through
Gomang I obtained a seat at the Tze School. The curriculum
included Tibetan history, literature and culture, arithmetic,
and accounting. Besides these there were no other major subjects, and we didn't learn any foreign language.

For three years I studied at the Tze School. When I graduated at nineteen I went to work for the Tibetan Government as a *Tzedrung*, a monk official with the duties of a clerk or accountant. At first I worked in the Department of Revenue Sources, which oversaw the collection of taxes from the villages and farms, which were paid in the form of grain. But later there was a reorganization and I was transferred into the Grain Collection Office. I worked there until 1953.

Of course by then the Chinese had already entered Tibet. In the early part of 1954 the Chinese were building a road between Dithoe and Lhasa. The workers were Tibetan and the Tibetan Government was paying half the wages, so some of us were assigned to work on this project as paymasters. We paid the wages in grain and in silver coins. The Tibetan Government paid most of the cost, the Chinese paid the rest.

At that time they were planning His Holiness's trip to China. As soon as I returned from the road project I was appointed to a post in the delegation. I was an advance-man, my job was to travel a day ahead of the entourage and make arrangements for the delegation in each place that they stopped along the way.

It was in the fifth Tibetan month of 1954 that His Holiness left for Beijing. There was a large group of officials in the delegation who had work to do while travelling to China and on the way back. But while we were in Beijing and His Holiness was attending meetings we really didn't have that much to do. So we were sent on a tour and we went off to see "the four directions of China."

In our travels around China what became clear to me was that the general public had no real freedom. I had heard that before the Communists came to power there was private property, but when we were there, there wasn't one single private house left – everything was owned by the government, and everyone had to work for the government. And whatever the government told people to do, that was the work they had to do. There was no freedom to say, "I want to do this. I can handle that." You just did what you were told.

Of course the Chinese did whatever they could to please us,

because their primary aim was to win our hearts. I remember one night in Jilin Province they held a big dinner party in our honor. There I met a Mongolian, who was sitting by me and helping to serve me and explaining the different kinds of vegetable dishes. Then he asked me, "Do you have these kinds of vegetables in Tibet?"

I replied, "Yes. Of course we have these, and many others, because the land is very fertile in Tibet."

So the Mongolian leaned over and quietly said, "Of course I know that. I know there are all kinds of vegetables grown in Tibet. But the Chinese have spread the belief that nothing can grow in Tibet. They claim that Tibet is a barren land with no resources. They say this because they don't want any outside powers coming in and taking what is there. They want it all for themselves."

Years later I discovered just how widespread this propaganda was. When I was in Jiuzhen Prison in China the Chinese prisoners and staff would ask us, "Do you have houses in Tibet? Can you grow grain?"

We said, "Of course we have houses. Even the great Potala, one of the greatest buildings in the world, is in Tibet."

Then they told us, "But we always heard that Tibet was a barren place, with no civilization. And the people just live in tents and survive by hunting."

Even later, when we were in prison back in Lhasa, officials would come from China and say, "You Tibetans, before 1950 did you have rice to eat? Did you have cotton clothes to wear?"

We told them that we made woolen clothes ourselves, and we imported other cloth, including silk and cotton. In some areas of Tibet they grew rice, and some rice was imported. But they would deny it and say, "No. You didn't have these things."

The Chinese spread this image very forcefully to the world – that Tibet had nothing at all before the Chinese came. Now, when I look back, I can see that the main reason for this propaganda was to make it easier for them to swallow up Tibet. If there was nothing there, no one else would be interested in Tibet and it would be easier for the Chinese to take over.

While His Holiness was in Beijing, Jawarhalal Nehru came to China, together with his daughter Indira Gandhi. We went to the airport to receive them, and one day they attended a banquet together. I was nearby, and I was able to overhear a conversation between His Holiness and Nehru. Nehru said, "Tibet is the highest land in the world. Therefore Your Holiness must be careful that the waters in Tibet do not come flooding down on those below."

His Holiness replied, "This is true. Yes, Tibet is the roof of the world. But preventing the water from leaking down from the roof is the responsibility of those living underneath the roof. If they do not find a way to stop the water, then naturally the water will come rushing down."

We arrived back in Lhasa in 1955 and once back I was assigned to a new department called the Reform Office. When His Holiness was enthroned he decided that Tibet must begin to make major changes in the political and economic structure of the country, and in order to institute these reforms he established this new Reform Office. Representatives were chosen from all walks of life to work in this department: government officials, monks from the major monasteries, and representatives of the public from the different parts of Tibet. I was on the staff as a member of the standing committee which ran the office.

By 1956 the Chinese had already established their Preparatory Committee for the Tibetan Autonomous Region (PCART), and the Chinese wanted the Tibetan Government officials to participate in the work of that Committee. But our own Reform Office had a great deal of work to do on its own, and our government did not want its people to participate in the Chinese Committee. An agreement was made that officials on the staff of the Reform Office would not have to work in the

Chinese departments, and at first this was upheld. But eventually we were told we had to help with their workload, so we began to divide our time between the two offices. This was in 1956, and this arrangement lasted about three months.

Toward the end of 1956 His Holiness visited India for the Buddha Jayanti – the 2500th anniversary of the birth of the Buddha – and he began developing many new ideas for moving Tibet toward a more modern society. The Chinese were not too happy that His Holiness had his own active Reform Office. It made the PCART office unnecessary, and so, once again, the staff was reshuffled and I was moved back into the Tibetan Reform Office on a full-time basis, where I continued to work until 1959.

His Holiness had the idea from the very beginning, when he established the Reform Office, to bring a democratic system to Tibet. The Chinese point of view was that Tibet was a feudal system. It was in certain ways, but it was not totally feudalistic. For example, take my own case: I had no noble lineage, my father was the steward for a landlord, and later he was a farmer. Now, a farmer's son would not get a chance to serve in the Tibetan Government if it were a totally feudalistic society.

There were two avenues to enter the service of the Tibetan Government: one was from the monks' side, and the other was the laymen's side. Government servants from the laymen's side were mostly nobles, there it was by blood-line. But on the monks' side, whoever entered the monasteries and had the capability and the interest, they had the opportunity to enter the government. And the power of these monk officials, who came from all strata of society, was equal to the noble lay officials.

The work of the Reform Office was to reform the old system and to correct the injustices that were prevailing in our society. And during the time I served in this Office we did succeed in implementing some reforms. Previously, when government officials travelled around the country they could requisition horses and servants and all sorts of facilities from people in the villages. This practice was abolished. We also saw to it that many prisoners were released unconditionally. Debts were forgiven for those people who had become indebted to the state.

Under the old system of taxation the government would appoint a District Commissioner, but he was not given a salary. The amount of tax to be paid by his district would be fixed by the government. Whatever surplus that Commissioner collected above the tax due, that surplus became his profit – in lieu of salary. But under the reforms of our Office all the tax they collected was paid directly to the government, and the government paid them a fixed salary. Part of my job was to administer these salaries.

So the Reform Office had begun to make significant progress. But the Chinese did not appreciate these changes at all. The Chinese wanted to say that when they came to Tibet they did things to benefit the people. But here the reforms were being made by the Tibetans themselves. The Chinese were not at all happy with the work of our Office, and sometimes they put a stop to changes that they didn't like.

The first I heard about the Chinese? At that time I was only about seventeen or eighteen years old. People were saying "the Chinese Communists are coming." I didn't have any idea what that meant, what their customs or ideas were, but I did have the sense that someone from outside was coming, that some foreigners were coming. I didn't understand all the implications, but I thought it was not a good thing. I wondered what was going to happen, and there was a feeling of anxiety that people are coming from outside and who knows what will happen.

The public was full of rumors and everyone seemed to be very upset and fearful. They said, "The Chinese are Communists; they will do a lot of harm. They don't have Dharma. They don't have compassion. They will do a lot of bad things." This was the general attitude in Central Tibet.

One of my own first contacts was with a Chinese official I had worked with on the trip to China. After we were back in Tibet, in 1956, the Chinese set up a Tibetan Youth Organization, and this fellow told me I should join. Over and over he pushed me to join the Youth Organization. But I really had no interest in joining. He said, "I will nominate you as your backer to get you in. There will be a lot of advantages to you if you enroll in this organization."

It would have been rude to just flatly say no, so I told him I would ask my parents. The next day he asked me if I had talked to my parents yet. He kept after me, asking if I had discussed it with my parents. So then I started avoiding him. He would come to our house and ask if I was there, and my parents would say "No. Tenpa Soepa is not home."

When the Chinese first arrived they presented themselves very humbly. But then as more and more arrived it became clear that they were intending to take over the country. That's when the public became afraid. At first people trusted them, but as they became more aggressive the public started to get worried.

Not everybody thought that the Chinese were a completely harmful force. Perhaps ten percent of the people had high hopes that the Chinese might bring some good changes to their lives. One thing people were interested in was new schools. Previously in Tibet, although there were lower schools, there was hardly any opportunity for higher education. People wanted to go to school, but all the new schools were Chinese medium – the classes were in Chinese language. Although eager for education, they didn't like the idea that the schools were run in Chinese. For a lot of people it was a real dilemma.

Life was changing in Lhasa. Between 1952 and 1959 the biggest problem was the shortage of food, and because it was scarce the price went way up, grain went up, butter went up. For the poorer people it became very difficult. Before the Chinese occupation of Tibet, one *khel* of grain – about twelve kilos – cost about fifteen *gormo*. After the Chinese arrived, in

1956-1958, it shot up to over one hundred.

When the Chinese arrived they said they were going to give assistance in the production of grain, but what they really did was they began to buy up large quantities of grain to feed their army. In some places they bought the grain, in other regions they said the local government had to feed the army and they just took the grain without payment. By 1959 people were really feeling the squeeze of the grain shortage and the consequent inflation.

But the social and religious problems began earlier, at least from 1956, when the Chinese began criticizing respected people in Tibetan society. They began calling the monks "Red Thieves" and the lamas "Yellow Bandits," and saying that they were stealing from the people. They began attacking our religion.

And in the east, in Kanze, in Kham, the Chinese began their "reforms." They took over the fields and began to reorganize the agriculture. They said they were doing these things for the "liberation of Tibet," but actually all these changes began to make it difficult for the Tibetans to survive.

So in Eastern Tibet by 1956 there were economic problems caused by the land reforms, there were food shortages, and there were ideological problems because of the attack on religion. And for these reasons in Eastern Tibet there were demonstrations and a guerrilla resistance movement began to grow.

I already knew that the Chinese were against religion because I saw it myself when we were coming back from China. We were in Kham, where the Chinese were building a road, and there were Chinese guardposts set at regular distances along the way. One day I was travelling in advance of the main party and I went up to have lunch at one of these guardposts. But as I approached I found that they had built the steps and the paths out of Mani stones – stones engraved with the sacred prayer of Tibet. They were using these sacred stones for their footpaths. No Tibetan would ever walk on these. When I realized this I just turned around and I never went up to those places again.

Another problem was that if a Tibetan committed any small offense, even the slightest violation, he or she would be arrested and imprisoned. So people became very afraid. This strict police vigilance began right from 1952. If you protested even a little bit they would arrest you right away.

An opposition movement developed among the public in Lhasa and they sent letters to both the Tibetan and Chinese Governments saying that Tibetans could take care of their own affairs, they didn't need any help from outsiders, and the Chinese should go back to China.

As far as the Tibetan Government workers were concerned, they certainly were not happy to see the Chinese come in, though there didn't seem to be anything we could do to stop them. Many of us felt that as long as we stayed in Tibet we were in a hopeless situation, that the Chinese will just control us and there is nothing we can do. Many thought we should pack our bags and take refuge in a neighboring country, and then from outside the borders we could organize our resistance. But in reality we couldn't leave because His Holiness was staying in Tibet, and as long as he was there, the rest of the government was going to stay with him.

In fact, this was the reason so many government officials were stuck in Tibet and captured. Because when His Holiness finally did leave it was very sudden, and for many there was no chance to escape. But right from the time that the Seventeen-Point Agreement was put in force, most government people realized that Tibet was no longer a safe place for us.

In 1955, during the trip to China, I arrived in Dartsedo, near the Chinese border. When I got there we heard that people from all over the region were going to come for a blessing from His Holiness. In one area there had apparently been an outbreak of smallpox. We were worried that if a lot of infected people came the disease could spread.

I went out to do some checking, to see whether people with smallpox were arriving. In order to do this I put on a chuba and went out to circulate among the crowds in the market. I would pick something up and ask, "How much is this?" But before I could even ask the price the merchants would get mad at me and yell and almost beat me up because they mistook me for a Chinese! My chuba was a style worn in Central Tibet – much better quality than what the locals wore – I spoke Lhasa dialect instead of Khampa Tibetan, and we were also much cleaner than the local people. They assumed we were foreigners, and figured that we were Chinese wearing Tibetan clothes. So instead of telling me the price and trying to sell me things, they wanted to attack me. So already at that time the people in the east were hostile to the Chinese.

On the other hand, when we walked around wearing the distinctive chuba of a government official, everyone recognized that we were from His Holiness's delegation. Then all the people would come rushing up to us asking for blessings. We said, "We are not lamas. We can't give you blessings."

They replied, "It is the same as if you were lamas, because you are so close to His Holiness." And when we went to the market, if we asked the price of something, they wouldn't answer a price but just give it to us. It was obvious that they liked us very much because we were working for the Dalai Lama.

2

On the night of March 10, 1959, I was staying in a house nearby Norbulinka, the Summer Palace where His Holiness was in residence. Very early in the morning my servant, Gyalpo, came and told me, "The people are saying that His Holiness has been invited to the Chinese army camp tomorrow. The public is in an uproar and there is a lot of talk that they want to ask His Holiness not to go."

I wasn't too concerned but in the morning I set out for the Norbulinka at eight o'clock, an hour earlier than my normal routine. On the way I found crowds of people streaming down from Lhasa, and when I arrived at Norbulinka I found that the gates were closed. They had locked the gates to prevent the crowds from getting in. There were some government officials posted at the gates and I had to ask them to open up for me.

I asked them what was going on. They said, "His Holiness has been invited to a program at the army base. There is going to be some big National Assembly in Beijing and the Chinese want His Holiness to go. So in order to get him to the meeting they invited him to this show at the army base. Then they are planning to capture him and take him to China and keep him there. The people think this is a Chinese scheme and they are trying to stop him from going."

I found Kungo Tara who was with some representatives of the big monasteries and asked him what to do. Tara told us to go out and lock all the gates leading into Norbulinka and tell the guards that no one is to be allowed in. He gave us the keys and we went out to lock the gates and talk to the army guards.

When I brought the keys back Tara told me to go down to meet Kalon Sampho. When I arrived at the gate I found Kalon Sampho lying on the ground unconscious. We carried him over and lay him in the shade. I saw that Kalon Sampho had arrived at Norbulinka in a car with his Chinese bodyguard. They got out of their car and when the crowd saw the Chinese guard they began throwing stones. One of the stones hit the *Kalon* on the head. He was knocked down and his head was bleeding. I could see that some in the crowd had thrown knives which stuck into the car. We tried to calm the people down and once they realized that it was a Kalon in the car they cooled down and left us alone. We rushed him off to a hospital in Lhasa, and from there the Chinese took him to a hospital inside their military compound.

We went back inside where they were organizing a security plan. In Norbulinka there are two security rings. The outer fence surrounds the whole park, which is quite extensive. And then the inner fence encloses His Holiness's personal compound and residence. Two junior staff were sent to each of the gates of this inner fence, to join the army personnel who were already stationed to guard each gate.

I was sent to guard the gate at the back of His Holiness's compound. On the way there I heard gunshots. Someone came and told us that Phakpalha Khenchung – the elder brother of Chamdo Phakpalha, a high lama from Chamdo – had been killed by the protestors. He was a government official, and it was rumored that he had a very close relationship with the Chinese. As we heard the story, this fellow came down to Norbulinka in the morning in his monks' robes, but when he saw all the trouble he went back home and changed into a chuba. He came back riding a bicycle with a scarf wrapped around his face. But the crowd recognized him and suspecting him of collaboration, stoned him to death.

We remained on duty at the gate. Then someone told us that an important meeting was being organized, and we should all try to appear at this meeting. There were two government officials and some army guards at the gate, so we went to the meeting in turns. It was held at a large building in the Norbulinka park. It was attended by Tibetan Government staff – monks and laymen – and representatives of the public. They were declaring, "Tibet is independent. We must throw the Chinese out!" They had written a resolution to this effect and everyone was asked to sign the statement. So I signed this declaration and returned to my post.

On the 10th and 11th there were demonstrations around the Barkhor in Lhasa. The people were chanting slogans like, "Chinese out of Tibet!" "The invitation to His Holiness is no good!" "Chinese don't interfere in Tibet's affairs!" The protestors went to the Indian, Nepalese, and Bhutanese embassies and submitted letters asking the ambassadors to support the Tibetan cause.

At the Norbulinka Kalon Surkhang announced to the crowds, "The main fear of the Tibetan people is that His Holiness will go to the Chinese army base to see the performance. But His Holiness is not going to go. You should all go back to your homes." He repeated his announcement many times, but hardly anyone listened. Most of the crowd just stayed there encircling the Norbulinka day and night.

To the north of Norbulinka is a motor road. On the night of March 15th a convoy of Chinese military vehicles came rumbling down that road, perhaps five or six hundred trucks. Behind each truck was an artillery piece, and after every ten trucks there was a tank. At every major intersection they stationed a tank to guard the convoy as it rolled through. The arrival of such powerful reinforcements created a great deal of fear in everyone's mind. At that point many people went home and brought their guns down to Norbulinka. They were ready to defend it with a fight if they had to.

Now the government really became concerned for His Holiness's safety. The general feeling was that it was too dangerous for him to remain in his palace at Norbulinka, and after some discussion it was agreed that he had to move. Preparations for his departure were begun. No one knew of these plans except for people at the highest levels, the Kalons and so forth, and those like me, who were assigned specific duties. I was told not to say anything to anyone; the situation was to be kept completely secret.

Late in the afternoon of March 17th a volley was fired from Chinese artillery. The shells landed barely one kilometer from the Norbulinka Palace, where His Holiness lived. I myself saw where these shells hit – it was a muddy area near the river, and they made big holes in the ground.

Kalon Kundeling summoned me. He said, "You are not to tell this to anyone. His Holiness is definitely ready to leave. So, are you ready with your arrangements?"

"Yes," I said, "I am ready."

"Then go to Norbulinka, find Phala Dronyer Chenmo, he will give you some horses, and you bring them here." This they had already arranged. He also told me that on the way back I should stop at the house of His Holiness's personal attendant and bring his saddle.

I went to Phala Dronyer Chenmo's residence in the Norbulinka but he was not in. They told me he had gone to the *Kashag* so I proceeded up there. He was in a meeting and according to our protocol I could not request him to come

down to see me. Normally, I would have to leave a message
with his assistant or go to see him in his office. But this message was too urgent and too secret to give to anyone else. So I
asked one of the staff to go up and ask Phala to peek outside,
where he would see me.

But Phala did not come down himself. Instead the
Chikhyab Khenpo Gadrang, the ranking monk official in the
government, appeared and asked me, "What do you want?"

I didn't tell him anything. I just said, "Please tell Phala to
come down. I need to see him."

He said, "Just tell me what you need."

They worked in the same office, and I knew they had already discussed it before he came down, so I said, "I need a
horse." He immediately understood what I meant and went
back inside for some discussion. When he came back he told
me to bring the stablemaster.

I found the stablemaster and as we were coming back we
met the Chikhyab Khenpo on the way. He ordered the
stablemaster to give me five very good and very swift horses.
These were horses that were normally reserved for His Holiness and his entourage.

We went to the stable and he gave me five or six of the best
horses. Then, as instructed, I went to get the saddle from His
Holiness's attendant's house. But there they were very suspicious. When I asked for His Holiness's saddle they said there
was no one there who could give it to me, so I gave up on that
and just brought the horses.

Kundeling told me to get the horses ready and prepare their
saddles. He chose a good horse for His Holiness and told me to
saddle it well. Then he gave me my instructions. At about ten-
thirty that night, if everything was ready on the far side of the
river, they would fire a shot in the air. That was the signal to pro-
ceed. At eleven o'clock a vehicle would arrive in the lane behind my house. There is a small bridge there and the car
would stop by the bridge. He told me to take the passengers from
the car, put them on horses and lead them down to the riverbank.
They assigned a detachment of thirty soldiers to assist me.

Just before sunset Kundeling and the General of the Drabchi Regiment, Drabchi Debon, left the house. They told the servants in the house that if anyone asked for them, tell them they have gone out for an inspection of Jakya Karpo Hill. My servant and I left, leading the horses and my thirty troops back to my residence to wait.

At ten-thirty we heard the gunshot. There were still crowds of people around the Norbulinka and the shot caused an uproar, with people thinking that fighting had started. When I went behind my house I found people milling about the lane where we were to meet the car. I brought my soldiers and told the public they shouldn't be in that area and they should move farther away. I posted the army around the lane and instructed them not to let anyone through.

We waited, and exactly at eleven o'clock a truck appeared. In the back of the truck were the two Tutors of the Dalai Lama, and three Kalons – Liushar, Surkhang, and Shasur. They were covered with a canvas tarpaulin. I took them to my house and mounted them on the horses. I sent half our troops in advance, and with the other half guarding our rear, we proceeded down to the river.

At the river all the boats were being held on the far bank. We had arranged that I would signal the other side by making three circles with a red torch, and they would respond with the same signal and send a boat. I gave the signal and the boat came across. We all got in, the two Tutors, the three Kalons, myself, and our army detachment, and we crossed the Kyichu River.

I knew that His Holiness had already left because the escape was planned in three stages. First His Holiness's mother and other members of his family left. Then His Holiness, who must have gone at about ten o'clock. The gunshot was our signal that he had crossed safely. The third stage was my group which crossed at eleven.

On the far bank we disembarked and mounted our horses. There was no fuss over protocol; we just grabbed whatever horse was nearby, mounted up and rode off. After we had trav-

elled eight or ten kilometers we were close on catching up to
His Holiness's party. There is a pass called Che-la. Just before
we arrived at the pass Kundeling, who was riding in advance,
came back to see me.

He said, "His Holiness has an important letter and you have
to take it back to Lhasa." He gave me the letter. He told me to
spend the night in Niu District, on this side of the river, and in
the morning I should cross over and deliver the letter to Kungo
Tara, who was still at Norbulinka.

So I turned around, and with the letter tucked away, rode
back down toward Lhasa. At Niu District I met Ngawang
Senge – one of the leaders of the National Volunteer Defense
Army (NVDA) – and together we camped near the river, wait-
ing for dawn when we would cross. The guerrilla leader said,
"Since you are going back to Lhasa, I have a favor to ask."

I said, "That's okay. I will do whatever I can."

"When you get back, grab whatever arms and ammunition
you can find at Norbulinka and take them to your house. I will
come tonight with some men to pick it up. Then we can travel
back together."

I agreed to his plan. Before dawn I awoke and rode down to
the riverbank. But at the river all the boats were being held by
our forces. They were stopping everyone and no one was allowed to cross in either direction. I told the soldiers I had to
cross to the other side. They said, "Show us your pass."

I didn't have any identification with me, but my servant had
his. They knew that I was a government official, so when my
servant showed his identification they were convinced and
they went to get us a boat.

They were gone about half an hour. There was a large round
boulder by the riverbank, and I sat there and waited and
watched the river. A great feeling of sadness and depression
came over me. In my whole life I have never been sadder than
at that moment. His Holiness had fled. I could imagine the
scene in Lhasa. The Chinese are there, ready to start the killing. I thought, if I go back there....

Then I had an idea. Maybe I should send Gyalpo, my servant. He could go across and deliver the letter while I waited here. When he came back we could go on and catch up with His Holiness. I thought about this. Then I took out the letter to take a look at it. It wasn't sealed. I opened it and began reading.

The letter was from His Holiness to the government ministers remaining in Lhasa. It said that he had left secretly and suddenly and his plan was to stay at Lhuntze District, near the border, to await developments. Since he was accompanied by the Kalons and the Commander-in-Chief, in the letter he appointed two Acting Prime Ministers, Lobsang Tashi and Mindrug Bug, and another Commander-in-Chief of the army. He advised these newly appointed ministers to negotiate terms with the Chinese in a peaceful and non-violent manner. And he instructed them to keep him informed of their progress. At the bottom, it bore the signature of His Holiness the Dalai Lama.

I read the letter, and it was plain how very important it was. My country was in a desperate situation. I thought to myself, I am a government servant. It is my moral duty to go to Norbulinka and hand this letter over with my own hands. I can not give the job to someone else. Even if I die, then I have to die, but there will be no regrets. So I made up my mind that I would go.

Once across the river there is some distance you have to walk up to the Norbulinka. As I was walking along the path I heard a gunshot. When I heard the first shot I didn't pay much attention. But as I walked on I heard another and then a bullet passed right by me. I immediately lay on the ground and waited until the shooting stopped. Then I got up and hurried to the Norbulinka.

I found Kungo Tara and I handed him the letter. He asked me how things were going with His Holiness and his party. I said everything was fine. He seemed very happy to hear that. He offered me tea and we drank tea together.

As Ngawang Senge, the NVDA leader, had asked me, I told Kungo Tara I wanted to take some guns and ammunition to my house. Tara said yes, take as much as you can from Norbulinka. I got some men to help me and we carried about twenty boxes of rifles and ammunition to my house. With the stock of weapons I already had, my house was half-filled with guns.

Later, about thirty NVDA men came to pick up the arms. Ngawang Senge sent a letter saying that he couldn't come, but asking me to send the weapons with these soldiers. I gave them the guns. I thought, perhaps I should go with them now. But I was exhausted. I had not had a decent sleep for several nights. I decided I would sleep in my house that night. I went to bed and told Gyalpo not to wake me, that I would sleep until I woke up myself.

When I finally awoke it was three o'clock in the afternoon. I got up and ate. All the time I was wondering and worrying about what was going on at Norbulinka, so I went to see what was happening.

When I got there I met a lot of government workers. They were asking me, "Is His Holiness still here? Is it true that he has already left?" But I was sworn to secrecy, I couldn't tell anyone. I had to lie to my colleagues, so I said, "His Holiness? He must still be here. We have all been here together. Where else could he be?"

I went for a walk around. I arrived at the main gate as it was getting dark. A Chinese tank was approaching. On top was a machine gun and the soldier pointed the gun at us. Everyone ducked down behind the barricades. I didn't duck, I stood up. I had a gun in my pocket. I put my hand in my chuba and held the gun. The tank veered away. It didn't fire, and I just stood there and watched it drive off.

As it was growing dark I decided I would go home. But then I met some friends and they said, "You shouldn't go out at this hour. It's already dark and it is very dangerous." I still had my bedding in the guard's room behind His Holiness's residence, so I went there to spend the night.

It was about one o'clock in the morning, the morning of March 20th, that the shelling began. The first shells hit the

roof of His Holiness's residence and ripped open a hole expos-
ing his private rooms. Those of us sleeping nearby were jolted
awake by the pounding of the shells and the sound of glass
shattering all around. The lights went out, but we could see
chunks of the roof fallen on the ground behind His Holiness's
Palace. I found a rifle and went out.

I wasn't sure what to do, but I ran to the nearest barricade,
which had been built across from a Chinese truck depot on the
north side of the Norbulinka. I arrived to find a pitched battle
raging. There were many Tibetans and they were firing
through holes in the barricade. I joined them and began firing
my rifle.

We Tibetans have a saying, "You will know who has won
and who has lost a battle by the sound of their guns." And I
found out this is really true. When I tried to fire this rifle it
didn't make a sound, it froze up. I thought maybe the rifle was
too cold, it being so early in the morning. Then someone said
it had too much oil on it, because it was new. He took it to
clean it. I started firing my pistol. But we were shooting
through these holes in the mud barricade and there was so
much dirt and dust flying everywhere, it fouled up my pistol
and it got jammed.

When you first hear the sound of so many guns firing it is
terrifying, but after five minutes you forget your fear. The Chinese were well dug in so we could not see our targets clearly.
The shooting would come in waves. After a volley the air was
so filled with smoke that no one could see what they were
shooting at. Then all at once the firing would cease until the air
cleared, and then it would start again.

From behind our barricade we couldn't see how much damage we were doing. But their bullets were finding their marks
and many were killed on our side. When I saw my first few
deaths, there was so much blood, I felt some fear. But after
seeing a few die, I didn't get frightened any more. I saw others
picking up the guns of those who had fallen, and this gave me
courage. So the battle continued like this until sunrise.

Finally we realized that we could not hold this position if the battle continued like this. We needed artillery support and our nearest artillery positions were on Tze and Chokpori Hills. I went back to the Norbulinka to send a message up to these hills that this Chinese position across from the truck depot had to be destroyed by artillery.

When I got to the army command post they said they already knew about the situation at the truck depot. But the cables up to the mountains were cut. They had no wireless radios, so there was no way to make contact except by messenger. They told me, "We sent a few people up there with the message to bombard that position; whether they got there or not, we don't know. But we will send another group of messengers up to both hills."

On my way back I met Kungo Gedar. He said to me, "There is nothing we can do now but escape. We have to get away."

My mouth said, "Yes, you are right, we should run." But in my mind, I really didn't want to flee at that moment. His Holiness has sent me back, I thought. If I run away now, I will go to meet His Holiness, and he will ask me, "What is the situation in Lhasa, at Norbulinka?" If I had to say, "Well, they were shooting, and when I heard the sound of the guns I ran away," that would be shameful. I felt that I should stay longer to see what developed, so that I could give a full picture of the scale of destruction and the number of casualties to His Holiness.

By this time the Chinese artillery shells were falling like rain. A shell would fall nearby, there would be a lot of smoke and dirt, and everyone would scatter. So like that I lost Gedar-la.

Soon I ran into Taring. He said, "It's good we met. We can go together. But first come with me. I want to get the camera and film from the Palace. We will take as many pictures as we can, to show the world what is going on, then we will run away together. But if the Chinese get us, if we are about to be captured, we will shoot ourselves." So we talked about this as we went up to the Palace. We found the camera and film, but as we were coming back to take some pictures, another shell came in and I was separated from Taring.

Then my servant, Gyalpo, found me. He had brought food. He said, "You may not get anything else to eat, so you better eat this."

Shells were falling all around us so you couldn't properly have a meal. But he said, "If you don't eat, you're going to get hungry." So I began to eat, and then I noticed one of my staff nearby. I called him over and told him to have some food. We were standing up and eating this food. And just then a shell came in and the young staff member standing near me fell; he was killed. I thought, "Alright, if they kill me that's it. There is nothing I can do." And I just stood there and ate my food.

When I finished eating I told Gyalpo, "Now we all have to look out for ourselves. You can't be looking after me anymore. We are on our own now." And he left.

I heard that the Tibetans who were defending a fortified position we had near Chensel Phodrang, on the west side of Norbulinka, were starting to break ranks and flee. This was an important defensive position so I thought I better go up there and try to stop them from running away. But by the time I got there most were already gone. I told the others that we had to hold this position, but they weren't listening to me and just took off. Since I was alone there was nothing I could do.

A relative of mine, Gyaltsen Choeden, lived nearby. I met him and he said, "Very good. This has worked out well. Now we can escape together." We went up to his house to rest for a little while.

But once again my servant appeared. He scolded me and said, "You shouldn't be waiting around like this. Everyone is running away. We have to go." So I went with him and we went back through the Norbulinka.

As we neared the north gate we passed a group of eight or nine people and I saw my friend Reva Thubten. He was glad to see me and said that he would escape with us. He said he was carrying a lot of money so we could buy whatever we needed on the way.

But in the group where we were standing was a Tibetan militiaman who raised his gun, stuck it in my chest and said, "I am going to shoot you! You people in the government – we have been pleading for guns, but until now you wouldn't give us anything. You stopped us from getting the guns we needed. It's because of you that we have ended up in this state. Now I am going to shoot you."

I knew that weapons were not distributed to the general public because until the last minute the government was trying to find a peaceful solution, but at that moment there was no reasoning with this fellow. I reached for my pistol, thinking I would shoot him before he shoots me. But as soon as I grabbed my pistol a shell exploded right there. Those of us who weren't killed on the spot scattered.

A piece of shrapnel hit me here on my left shoulder. It was very painful. I immediately headed home, took off my chuba and shirt and checked the wound. My clothes were ripped, it had penetrated right up to the skin, but there was no wound, no blood. This gave me real confidence in the protection amulet I was carrying. These amulets contain an image or some texts which are provided by high lamas to protect you from harm while you are travelling or in danger. They also contain relics, cloth or hair or ashes of high lamas. They are called *Tsonsung*, which means "weapon protector," and they are specifically blessed for that purpose. So this restored my courage, and once again I went out.

When I got back to Norbulinka I heard that there was a meeting. I headed over to the meeting hall but by the time I arrived it was over and most people had left. But I saw Kungo Tara coming out with a few others. Tara said to me, "Good to see you. Listen. The Chinese have captured Chokpori Hill. We have to go up there to retake it."

So a small group of us went with Tara to the ammunition dump. We went inside and started carrying out boxes of ammunition. But while we were there messengers started coming one after another from the Tzechak Office to tell Tara that the results of the oracle had come and he was needed right away. They must have been consulting the oracle to find out whether we should continue to fight or flee.

Tara told us, "You wait here. Get the weapons together and I will come back immediately."

We waited some time for Tara but he didn't come back. But then Ngawang Senge, the NVDA leader, appeared. He must have heard the results of the oracle because he said, "Now there is no point in our staying here and fighting any longer. Our only chance is to escape."

I said, "If we go, how are we going to do it?"

He said, "You go back to your stables and get some horses. You've got all these weapons. I'll stay here and organize the guns and ammunition. We'll take as much as we can carry and we will go together." So I went down to get the horses.

When I got to the stables I found every horse was being held by a Tibetan fighter. There wasn't one free horse. I yelled at the stablemaster, "Look at this! You're not taking care of the horses. Now we have to leave and I need some horses."

He was terrified. He said, "Please Kungo-la, I can't do anything. You talk to these people yourself. If I say anything they will kill me."

What could I do? I took out my pistol and I grabbed a horse away from one man. I thought to myself, if this guy resists I will shoot him. Fortunately he didn't argue. I took the horse and left.

I sent my servant, Gyalpo, on the horse up to the ammunition dump where Ngawang Senge was waiting for me, with the message, "All the horses are gone. What should I do, come up to you, or will you come down here?"

While I waited I met Sandutsang Chondze Wangdo with some friends. He said that Chokpori and Jakya Karpo Hills had been captured. These positions commanded the only escape route so now it was difficult to get out. What should we do?

We gathered a meeting together of about forty or fifty people in the stables, where we discussed our predicament: The Chinese have reached right up to the outer perimeter of Norbulinka. They are about to overrun our fortifications, and behind those we have no more defenses. They have taken the two mountains and the escape route between them is controlled by the Chinese. Finally we agreed on a plan: We would stay here and fight until nightfall. After dark we would all escape together. We might have a chance of getting through in the dark.

We agreed to reassemble that night and the meeting broke up. There was one man who was wounded and bleeding badly. I brushed passed him and as I did I got blood on my clothes. The old superstition popped into my mind, that if you are touched by blood from an open wound your protection amulet will lose its power.

Just as this thought ran through my mind a shell landed and blasted the building. I was knocked to the ground. When the smoke faded I tried to get up but I couldn't. I had a machine gun slung on my back; using that as a walking stick I pulled myself up. I went into an adjoining room, where some other people were gathered, but then another shell hit and the roof came down on top of me. I was pinned down and it was only with great effort that I dug myself out. My left leg was badly injured. I tried to stand up but it was impossible; I couldn't walk.

I crawled out of the house. I felt very thirsty. I found a stone water trough for horses and drank my fill of water. Then I crawled over to the stables, but no one was there. The horses were panicked and going wild and I nearly got trampled.

I couldn't find anyone to help me, and there was no way I could handle a horse, so I crawled back to Norbulinka, which was about 150 yards away. In Norbulinka there is a small palace surrounded by a lake, and the lake is fed by a small stream. When I got to the edge of the lake I couldn't go any farther, so I just lay there, exhausted. Shells were landing constantly all around and the sky was dark with smoke.

I considered my situation. I can no longer fight, and now I have no chance of escape. If I am captured they will surely torture me. It would be better just to die right here. There were shells and bullets landing all around me and I lay there for an hour or so, waiting to be killed. But nothing hit me except flying bits of dirt.

Finally I decided that a Chinese bullet was not going to kill me, so I took out my pistol and prepared to shoot myself in the head. But when I was about ready to fire a thought came into my mind – they say that a person who dies in water, in their next life they have a very clear and lucid mind. So I thought it would be better to die in this water. I put my pistol away, crawled down to the edge of the water and jumped into the lake.

I sank down until I hit the muddy bottom. But then I just floated back to the surface. I went down again. And then floated back up again. I just wouldn't die. I decided this meant that I had too much air in me, so I opened my mouth and my eyes and let all the air out. I sank down to the bottom and this time I tried to hold on to the lake bottom, but there was nothing to hold on to, just mud. I bobbed up and down like that probably for half an hour.

Since I didn't die, I paddled over to a set of stairs and tried to climb out of the lake. But I couldn't get out. I was loaded down with hand-grenades and bandoliers of bullets, so I took off my chuba and threw it all in the water. Then I was able to pull myself out.

I crawled along, leaving a trail of water and blood streaming behind me. I crawled toward the Audience Hall where His Holiness used to meet dignitaries. Inside was a throne where His Holiness used to sit. I thought, if I am going to die, that is the place to die. As I lay there beside the throne I felt very peaceful and happy.

Then I heard Tibetans outside running around and shouting to each other, "The Chinese are at the gates! They are going to occupy the Norbulinka! We should fire the place. Let's burn it down." I thought, it's so hard to die. I didn't die in the water, and I probably won't die in the fire, either.

I crawled out of the building and made my way to a gate leading out of Norbulinka. As I was about to enter the gate a bullet hit me right here, in the forehead. Maybe it was fired from far away so it had no force by the time it hit me, but it just bounced off my forehead and fell into my shirt. It was very hot and burned all the way down my chest – I scrambled to get that searing bullet out of my shirt.

Inside the gatehouse I met my brother-in-law, my younger sister's husband. He said he was glad to see me. He took off his chuba and covered me with it. He asked, "Now what should I do?"

I said, "You can't stay here like this. You have to get out of here. Get across the river. Our people are across the river. If you can get there you can continue fighting. But you can't stay here, you will just get killed." Then I said, "Look, I can't go. Please shoot me." I asked him, I urged him to do it. But he couldn't. And then he went.

Then a young boy about seventeen years old appeared. He was standing against the wall. He said to me, "There is no more hope in fighting. The Chinese are inside the compound and there is no way to escape; all the routes are blocked."

"That doesn't matter," I said. "You just have to try to escape through the enemy lines. You may be killed or you may not. But the place you want to get to is the other side of the river. Our people are there and you can join them and fight back. If you go, you may be saved or you may be killed, those are your choices. But there is no point in staying here, because then you will definitely be killed."

The boy was about to leave. Although I wasn't a smoker I suddenly had an urge for a cigarette. I asked him, "Do you have a smoke?"

"Yes," he said. He gave me a cigarette and lit it. I took a few drags. I don't remember how many, but after a few drags on the cigarette I fell unconscious.

After that I don't remember much. I slept. About nine o'clock that night I suddenly woke up to a tremendous noise of gunfire. It was a machine gun firing nearby. I peeked out the door. It was dark but I could dimly see a lot of Chinese soldiers moving back and forth inside the Norbulinka gardens. There was a big storage room for firewood. Underneath that a Tibetan machine gun emplacement was firing fiercely and killing many Chinese soldiers. From that position the Tibetan gunner managed to clear the whole area. After some time the firing stopped, maybe he was killed, or captured, or maybe he ran away, I'm not sure, but the gun became quiet. Then the Chinese soldiers started moving in again; a lot of soldiers started pouring in. They were afraid to charge right into the buildings. They would fire into the buildings for a while and then call for the people inside to come out. Many people came out to surrender.

I took off my amulet box, opened it, took out the blessings inside and ate them. I looked around the gatehouse for a weapon. I thought if I fired at these soldiers they would shoot back and kill me. But it was dark and I couldn't find any guns around me.

So I crawled out to surrender. A group of soldiers saw me and yelled, "Stand up! Stand up!" But I couldn't stand up. They looked me over with a torch, and when they saw that my clothes were covered in blood, they said, "You go there by that electric pole."

I could see some Chinese soldiers guarding Tibetan prisoners. I thought, if they kill me they kill me, but I am not going over there. I crawled away. Nearby was a guardhouse, but it had two steps up to the door and I couldn't get up. But there was a small courtyard so I crawled in there. I saw about five people lying there. Because of the loss of blood I felt very, very thirsty. I called out, "Please give me some water. Please give me some water." But no one responded. I looked around at the others and realized they were all dead.

I lay there a while and then a squad of three Chinese soldiers came in. They called out, got no reply, then made the rounds of the dead bodies, kicking each body and shining a torch into the faces. They came to me – I was covered in blood – kicked me, and decided I was dead. They had another look around and then they left. After half an hour another squad came to look around. One of them kicked me in the gut very hard. I almost let out a cry, but I had just enough strength to hold it in.

There was a kitchen. I crawled in there and tried to get up

on a bed, but I couldn't. I lay on the floor and around one A.M. someone came out of hiding to drink some water from a water tank that was up on a table. I cried out for some water. He gave me some, I drank, and then I fell asleep.

After sunrise the Chinese came around again calling for everyone to come out. Many more people surrendered. From wherever they were hiding they came out and gave themselves up. I figured there was nothing else to do so I also came out.

The soldiers told us to "go over there," to a place where the prisoners were being rounded up. There were soldiers guarding, and some Chinese officials sorting out the Tibetan Government staff from the civilian prisoners. There were about five of us government officers. They separated us from the group and told us to go sit under a tree. The civilians were tied up with their hands behind their backs and led away by soldiers. I remember thinking, they are taking them away to be shot. It doesn't matter, after them they will kill us. I wonder when our turn will come. That was my thought. I found out later that these civilians were not executed, but were taken to prison.

Blood was still oozing continuously from my leg, although I had taken off my shirt and wrapped it around the wound. We were left sitting there all morning and into the afternoon. As the sun rose we naturally wanted to move to stay out of the heat, but if we tried to move even a little bit a soldier would kick us. The sun made my wound dry out a bit, which was good, but as it dried the shirt stuck to the scab and it was difficult peeling the shirt off, which really hurt. Finally, sometime after midday, a jeep arrived. They started to put us in the jeep, but then one Chinese official pointed at me and told me to stay there. They took the others away. I found out later they were taken to prison. I was left behind because of my serious injury.

It grew later and later and no one was attending to me and finally I was getting quite cold. I noticed a nobleman, Shokhang Jedrung, whom I knew. He was working for the Chinese. I called out to him, "Jedrung-la, Jedrung-la." He didn't really respond, but I yelled at him, "Whatever you are going to do with me please do it quickly, because I am going to die here." He sent a man who carried me on his back into a huge prayer hall called the Offering Temple.

In this hall they were holding all the wounded prisoners. It was completely full of people and there was hardly a place to sit. Blood was flowing on the floor like water. Many of them were about to die from their wounds. I sat there and watched people dying. It was getting quite cold and when someone died the people lying nearby would take their clothes. Near me was an old white-haired Khampa, he was badly wounded and about to die. I watched him. He was wearing a heavy cloak. I watched him, and when his breathing became shallow I grabbed his cloak and was about to put it on when I saw that it was completely soaked with blood. It was wet and dripping with blood. But I put it on anyway, and it helped to keep me a little bit warmer.

The next morning, at dawn, they gave us each a cup of tsampa and a cup of tea. My hands were completely covered with blood, the blood of many different people. There was no place to wash, but we hadn't eaten for several days. There was nothing to do, I just had to mix the tsampa and tea with my bloody hands. I poured the tea into the tsampa and made *pak*. And as I kneaded the mixture the pak became red, just as if it was a red torma. There was nothing to do but eat that.

Then they dealt with injuries. The lightly injured were treated with first aid right there. As they bandaged the wounds they would shake and scold and abuse the prisoners. Since my bone was broken they said I had to go to the hospital. They took me and several others with bad injuries and they just threw us into a truck as if we were a load of stones. That was terribly painful. The road was very rough and the truck was bouncing us around in the back, so it was a painful ride to the hospital.

I had quite a few wounds on my body, but most of them were minor. I discovered that these amulets really do protect us, because my chuba was full of bullet holes, but none of these bullets seriously harmed me. The only serious injury I had was the bone in my foot, which was shattered.

When we reached the hospital my two companions were admitted and put into a room which had about forty or fifty wounded Tibetans stuffed into it. I was separated and put into a small room alone. There was nothing in this room, no bed, nothing at all. They took my clothes, which were drenched in blood, and gave me white hospital clothes, and they gave me a blanket. A soldier was stationed guarding the door. I lay down on the floor with half the blanket underneath me and pulled the other half over me, and like that I spent the night.

That night there was no medical attention and no food. The next morning a nurse came in, she was a Tibetan, but she wasn't allowed to talk to us. In one hand she had a big bowl with tsampa, in the other hand she had a thermos with hot water, and she carried a small mug. There was only one mug, and she was in a hurry. I figured out that if I took the hot water first she couldn't wait while it cooled off enough for me to drink it; she would just leave and I wouldn't get any tsampa. So first I took a mug full of tsampa and immediately poured it on my blanket, then I held out the mug for the hot water. Actually, what we normally call tsampa is the roasted barley flour that people eat. This stuff was what we normally feed to horses and mules – barley ground together with raw beans. It is very bitter and barely edible.

When I finished eating I got medical treatment. The bone in my foot was shattered into little pieces. They made me stand up on it and it was excruciating. While they were treating me they were yelling and scolding me. I understood a little bit of Chinese and I heard them yelling at the other prisoners too. "We are giving you medical treatment. You people don't deserve this. It is because of your fighting that all the buildings around here have broken windows and the roofs are destroyed. Look at all the destruction you have caused. And now here we are caring for you." And while they were scolding me like this they were poking their instruments and their fingers around in my wound. It was more like torture than medical treatment.

The first day I kept quiet and tolerated this. And the second day again the doctor was poking around in the wound. It was agonizing, but again I tolerated it. I could see that he was just hurting me, that what he was doing had no benefit for my wound. So on the third day, when this doctor came around to give me his so-called treatment, I protested: "You are not treating me for me to get better. You are just torturing me! Now I am not taking any more of your treatment!"

As I was using forceful language another doctor heard me and came in. He said, "What is going on here?"

I told him what was happening. "He is not treating my wound. He is making me stand on the leg, and poking around, just to cause me pain!" So then this new doctor said he would attend to me.

I noticed that there were a lot of Tibetans in that hospital who were having their arms and legs amputated. As I watched through my open door I saw doctors coming down the hall playing with these amputated limbs. But I could see quite a few Tibetans whose wounds did not seem very serious also having their limbs amputated. I realized that they were performing a lot of amputations for no reason. Just out of cruelty.

After a week the doctor came to me and said, "We have to amputate your leg."

"I won't have my leg amputated," I told him.

"If we don't take it off it will become badly infected and you will die."

"If I die I want to die in one piece, not with my legs cut off." That's what I told him.

I was finally convinced they were doing unnecessary amputations when I met Lobsang Gyaltsen, an acquaintance of mine, who was a policeman – actually he played trumpet in the police band. I met him in the hospital one day and he had a small wound on his arm, nothing serious. Then the next thing I knew they took his arm off. I asked him "You just had a scratch. Why did they cut off your arm?"

He told me his story: "They said, 'We are going to amputate.' I told them again and again, 'No, I won't have it amputated.' So one day they came and said, 'We have to take you for some special medication.' They took me out to another room and they put a blindfold on me. I saw so many strange things, like a play dancing before my eyes. I didn't know what was happening. Later, when I got back to my ward, and I was lying in my bed, I discovered that my arm was gone. Until then I had no idea they were going to amputate." So like that, they drugged people and tricked them into having their limbs amputated.

The name of the hospital was "The People's Hospital." It was in Lhasa, just near the Potala. I stayed there a little more than two months. Every three days I was taken into an interrogation room and asked many questions: "How did you organize the revolt? Who were the key figures in your revolt? Who was working with you?" When I didn't answer they would point guns at me and say, "Now we are treating your wounds. But if you don't answer our questions we will kill you."

My attitude was, whatever happens I don't care anymore. I told them, "It is up to you whether you kill me or keep me. I am in your hands. But I have nothing to say."

Sometimes a Chinese official whom I knew would come round and advise me, "Tell them the truth, talk straight, tell them whatever you know. Many others are talking anyway. You are still young. Don't waste your life." Sometimes he would come with his "friendly" advice, and sometimes others would come and give me the hard line.

Two of the nurses were Tibetans. One was called Aminya; she was a Muslim. The other was from Kham, named Ani. They were not allowed to talk to me. The guard usually kept an eye on things and the nurses were very afraid of the guard. The food was meager, every morning and evening one cup of tsampa and tea. The nurses were not supposed to bring us anything else.

I felt sorry for them. They showed a lot of sympathy for me. They really cared about their fellow Tibetans and knew the food was inadequate, but they felt helpless to do anything. Later things got a little less strict, with less attention, and the guards would wander off. When the guards were away these two nurses would take chances and bring something extra to eat. They ate in the canteen and weren't allowed to take anything away. So they would sit at the table, eat part of a momo and then hide the rest. They secretly carried this off and when no one was watching they would pass my room, throw the momos on my lap and quickly leave. They couldn't do this very often but to me it showed their sympathy for a fellow Tibetan.

Before I left the hospital things got still more lenient. One day the nurses told me, "The Chinese officials showed a film in the hospital in which the captured Tibetans and their weapons were put on display. You all had so much equipment, guns and ammunition, there were so many of you. How could it be that we lost the fight?" They asked me that with tears in their eyes.

It was funny in a way. There wasn't much I could say. I told them we were just outgunned. They had better weapons and more men. There was no way we could win.

Time went on; the wound would not heal quickly. We thought there was some sort of chemical substance on the bullets which prevents the wound from healing. Finally after two months they put a plaster cast on my leg and sent me to prison.

3

I don't remember the exact date, but it was in the fourth Tibetan month, in 1959, that they took me to prison. Two officials came in and told me I was leaving, but said nothing about where I was to go. They brought me down to a jeep waiting in front of the hospital and drove me to the General Military Headquarters of the Chinese forces. There they were holding Tibetan Government civil servants, high lamas, and abbots of the monasteries – the leaders of Tibetan society.

At the prison they left me for some time while they discussed where to put me. In that prison there were four different levels of incarceration. One was high security, very strict; two were intermediate; and the last was fairly lenient. They decided to put me into one of the middle level cells.

There were about seventy prisoners in that wing, some prominent people among them: Tomo Geshe Rinpoche, who is now in America; Lhau Tara, who was the Chief Secretary at that time – he died in Tibet; and Ribur Rinpoche, who is currently working at Tibet House in New Delhi.

It was one very long room. We slept on wooden planks laid across bricks on the floor, and there was a thin mattress on top of the wooden surface. The prisoners had to go out to work all day. I couldn't go to work because of my leg, but my colleagues came back each day and told me what they were doing. The work was all within the army base, which was quite extensive. Mainly they were put to work demolishing fortifications that the Chinese had built to defend against an attack.

At night they would give us "political reeducation classes." We would have to study and discuss Chinese newspapers. Sometimes Chinese generals would come and ask us questions and we would have to give answers. At this stage I don't think they had any planned program of reeducation. Their questions had no particular point. Each officer would come and just ask whatever questions he liked. "Do you realize why you are here?" "What is the reason why you had to be put in this prison?" Like that. There was no emphasis on Communist indoctrination, not yet. They were just trying to distract our minds. They wanted us to have no leisure time, so they would either put us to work, or call a meeting. This way people never had time to think.

The food was decent food, it was the same food the Chinese soldiers were eating. There was a toilet, not very nice but outside the cell. And in the morning we were able to wash with water from a well. After washing up in the morning we got food, and then went out to work.

It was all pretty much improvised at this point. They hadn't really planned for this. From our side, we prisoners didn't think we were in so much trouble. We didn't think we had done anything terribly wrong. All we did was to say that Tibet is an independent country. And since it *is* an independent country, where was the crime? We thought they would hold us for five or six months and then release us. One friend of mine, an old government official, told me, "It will be hard for me. I know too much, too much history, too many stories about the Chinese. But you all are young, junior officials. After six months they will let you go."

Every two or three days authorities from outside would come to interrogate us. In the hospital I hadn't told them anything, and I continued to keep quiet after I arrived in prison. But every day the prisoners would return from work and we would be gathered in these study sessions, where each prisoner had to tell what it was he had done – we organized like this, I fought with the Chinese like that. As these reeducation sessions went on, there were many whom I worked with and fought with who were telling what we had done. So I began to think I was just being stupid by not talking. First of all, I thought, the Chinese have completely taken over and they already know everything, so keeping quiet wasn't benefitting anyone. And secondly, those who didn't talk were treated as hard cases and it was causing me unnecessary trouble.

The main reason I had not talked was that I knew that His Holiness was going to Lhoka, that he was planning to stay in Lhuntze District, and they were planning eventually to return. I believed that they would return and I was constantly expecting to see the NVDA pouring over Jakya Karpo Hill. I would often look over in that direction with real hope.

But since everyone else was talking about what they did, I decided that if I kept quiet it wouldn't make any difference. So I told them a little about my post at Norbulinka and what my work involved. I told them what I did during the fighting and how I was wounded. But I didn't tell them anything about helping with the escape, how we left, how I came back with the letter, or about the future plans of His Holiness.

But once I had begun to talk the interrogators started pressing me, "Now you have begun to talk. But you are not telling us everything. You are not telling us the most important things that you know. If you tell us everything it will be better for you. So think it over."

The interrogations went on and on. They went on pressing me to tell more, but I insisted, "That is all that I know." Eventually they started getting very angry and abusing me. They accused me of hiding the truth from them, and finally they moved me to a cell in the maximum security wing.

Actually, they had a pretty good idea of what my involvement was. But I remembered the pledge that I took at Norbulinka, that I would keep as an absolute secret the planning and departure of His Holiness. The Chinese might learn about these things from other sources, but I resolved that I would not be the one to tell them.

So they put me in a cell. It was a tiny room. It was just big enough to lie down in either direction. I was put in with three others, Donpo Kasur, Lha Gyari, and Jangchi Mentoepa – the Governor of the Jang region. In the windows there were iron bars, then an iron screen, and then glass windows. We couldn't see outside, and from outside no one could see in. The door was also covered in iron. The light was a bulb hanging from the ceiling which was half inside and half outside the cell. There was one small slop bucket for a toilet. And there was a mattress.

Outside there was a corridor for the guards to keep watch. There was a small hole in the door and a guard would peek inside once in a while. We were not allowed to talk to each other, we were not allowed to lean against the walls, not allowed to stretch out our legs, and not allowed to close our eyes. We had to sit up like this all the time. If the guard saw you doing any of these he would come in and beat you with a club.

It was a military kind of regime. In the morning they blew a whistle, and you had to get up and straighten up your bedding. Then they would take us out – there was a courtyard outside – and we would take three rounds of the circle. That was our exercise. Then we washed and were taken back. When we made the rounds in the courtyard we could not talk because the guards were always watching. But even if we were allowed to talk you couldn't hear a thing, because the prisoners were in shackles, and the clatter of the chains on the ground as they walked was deafening.

Then they put us back in the cell. We were taken to the toilet once in the morning and once in the evening. We were taken in groups, cell by cell. The cells were in rows, but staggered, so that you could not see another cell when you looked through the hole in your door. They would take each cell to the toilet and then bring them back, you would hear the door clang as they moved up the row, one by one.

All the prisoners were Tibetans, except for two Chinese. One had frostbite on his foot. We heard that he was spying for a foreign country and while he was trying to get away he got frostbite in the mountains. The other was given the nickname of "Momo Gyakpa," which means "Fat Dumpling." He had been a Chinese army officer in Lhoka, but he joined the Tibetan resistance and fought against the Chinese. Eventually he was executed.

At night the guards blew a whistle and we had to be in bed within fifteen minutes. We had to pretend to sleep whether we were sleeping or not, otherwise the guards would yell at us.

There was one senior guard who had a hairlip. I don't remember his name but we used to call him "Hairlip." He had a pet monkey. He would bring this monkey down among the prisoners and set it loose. It would get excited and jump all over us and bite. Hairlip would laugh and enjoy it when the monkey bit us. Some of the prisoners developed nasty wounds. He would come around frequently to play this game. And if we misbehaved ourselves he would beat us with an iron rod.

In October the thamzing began. They took a prisoner out for thamzing, and then brought him back. Some had to be carried back, as they were so badly beaten they couldn't walk. I remember one who was barely alive. If a prisoner did not tell them what they wanted to hear during interrogations and re-education sessions they would take him for thamzing, where the public would punish him. They would gather all the people and the Chinese would announce that this prisoner is not cooperating, he has done such and such things wrong, and then the people were supposed to beat him up and abuse him.

Some were also crucified, like Jesus, but they didn't use nails. They tied your arms outstretched to a wooden cross. You couldn't bend over. Then they beat you. Some people were beaten almost to death. Doctor Tenzin Choedak was beaten so badly that when he came back he couldn't take off his shirt. It had to be ripped off, his back was so swollen and bruised.

There were a lot of young boys in the prison and a lot of the beatings were carried out by these kids. The Chinese would tell them that if they performed this thamzing they would get good jobs, or they would be released soon. And of course young boys don't know any better, so they would go ahead and beat the other prisoners.

The prisoners were also given punitive labor. For example, they would make three people pull a cart that was normally pulled by horses. They would have to haul loads of firewood or fertilizer or stone. Sometimes they would have to pull these carts for a distance of one hundred kilometers.

Or prisoners were taken to a swamp near Lhasa where they would have to dig mud and work half-submerged in the slime. Or prisoners would be sent out to clean toilets in public places. The intention of having us do this kind of degrading work was to frighten the public. People would see the former nobles and government officials doing these horrible things; naturally they would feel too frightened to actively oppose the Chinese.

But the public still found ways to show their sympathy. The old beggars – those who had previously been beggars – would have great pity for these prisoners who had previously been nobles. The prisoners would be working hard with nothing to drink. The beggars had nothing themselves except their old tin cans, but they would fill these with water and set them down some distance from the sweating prisoners. Then they would sing, "Here is water if you want." Such messages they would sing in their songs. So the prisoners would come over and drink from these tins.

It was also common for people on the streets to buy presents, candy or cigarettes, and throw them into the back of the carts that the prisoners had to pull. People couldn't approach the prisoners directly, but this way the prisoners who went out to work could bring back special treats to the prison.

In this way the Tibetan public showed their sympathy for us. The Chinese would proclaim that we were reactionaries, traitors, feudal landlords, and thieves of the people, but it was clear that the sympathy of the people was with us.

During this time my leg still had not healed, so I wasn't sent out to do these jobs. But my friends went out every morning and came back in the evening and told me these stories, and whatever goodies they brought back we would eat together. My problem was the opposite of hard labor. I just had to sit in my cell with absolutely nothing to do all day long. I had to sit like that for two months. At least if you were taken out to work you were free to move around. You were getting some exercise and you were with other people.

They let me send a letter to my parents though we weren't allowed to meet. After I wrote they began to send me packages of clothes and food from time to time. They weren't allowed to bring these to me directly, but the packages got to me through the prison authorities.

One of my cellmates was Donpo Kasur, who had suffered from some minor mental problems even before the uprising. In fact he had resigned as Kalon because of his illness, though I don't think it was anything serious. Although in the cell we were not allowed to talk to each other, when we went to the toilet we would whisper back and forth. He used to ask me, "Do you think I could escape if I ran away?"

I told him it would be impossible to escape from this place, there are guards everywhere. But he said, "If I could just get as far as the river I could jump in and commit suicide."

I told him, "You shouldn't try anything like that. You are already old and there is no reason for you to do that." I remember it was on October 23, 1959. He found under the bed some kind of ointment bottle, a heavy glass bottle. He started bashing himself on the head with it, trying to kill himself. After a few blows the guards came rushing in. He attacked the guards, trying to smash them. Finally he was overpowered and restrained, and a high prison official came down.

He already had shackles on his feet, now they manacled his hands behind his back. Then they beat him up. He was over seventy years old but they beat him terribly. Immediately I was pulled out and put into another cell.

The next morning they took me for questioning, "What happened? Why did he do this? What did he say?"

I told them straight, "His mind was disturbed. He had some mental problems before which caused him to resign his post as Kalon. He didn't say anything special to me. We didn't have any conversation about it." When asked if this was the truth, I said yes and signed the statement. Then they took him up for questioning, but what happened there I don't know.

For two days I was kept outside my usual cell, and then on October 25th they came and told me I was being moved. They took me out along with ten or fifteen other prisoners. Some were out working that morning but they brought them back and immediately put them in the prison van. They put our bedding in first, then we had to pile in and they drove us to Norbulinka. Part of Norbulinka had been turned into a prison.

Two days later, on October 27th, they gathered all the prisoners for a meeting. There were many prisoners. They read out the names of all the prisoners and they selected about three hundred. They pulled us aside and sent the rest back to their cells.

I remember that the name of the official from the Security Office was Ching Du Ren, and Kesang Kotrang was acting as his interpreter. They told us, "You prisoners have to go to China in order to be reformed. There you will undergo reform through labor. According to your situation and your crimes you will be assigned different types of work. Your fate will be de-

cided according to how well you work. We are sending you to
China because it will be easier to feed you there; we won't
have to transport the food all the way up here. Remember that
on the road during your transportation, and after you arrive,
you have to obey all the rules and maintain strict discipline."

They told us we were not allowed to see our families before
we left. They said, "If you need clothes or anything else you
can send a message through us, and we will contact your family. But you cannot meet them."

But the day before we left the family members of the prisoners who were being deported assembled outside the prison,
crying and calling out for the Chinese to let them see their
loved ones. They made such an uproar that the prison authorities finally gave in and allowed us to meet. The families had to
stay outside the wall. We remained inside, and one at a time
we were called to a doorway to meet our family members. Chinese guards and officials surrounded us.

I went to the doorway and found my mother and father and
brothers and sisters. My mother had been crying so much her
face was all swollen. When she saw me she just took my hand,
she couldn't utter a word. She took out something from her
pocket, it was a small bag of money. She insisted that I take it.
I said, "I don't need this." But she insisted I take the money.
Other than that, she couldn't say a word. That was the last
time I saw my mother's face.

We were warned not to say anything about where we were
going. I told my parents that wherever we were, I would write
to them immediately. This was the most important thing to
them. There wasn't much else to say.

With all the friends and family of the prisoners there must
have been two hundred or three hundred people, and all of
them were crying. They were terribly worried. I saw them behind my parents, they were calling out, "You people help each
other. Look after each other."

There wasn't much I could say but in order to comfort them
I said to the crowd, "You who are staying here, please treat
each other as if you were one family. If anyone is having a

problem help each other with the spirit of one big family. We who are going away will also consider ourselves as a family and look after each other. So you do not need to worry about us. Please don't lose your courage."

At two A.M. on the morning of October 29th we were woken up. Another group of Tibetan prisoners was bringing us food. They were full of sympathy and kind words for us, some were even crying. They said, "You are about to go. We will be taken later. But don't worry, it will be alright." They pressed the food on us, saying, "Please eat. We made really good food for you. It's very good. Please, just eat a little. It's very tasty." But there in the middle of the night, about to be deported – we had no idea where or what would happen to us – we could barely swallow a bite.

At dawn we left. There was a line of trucks and they loaded about thirty prisoners into each truck. They were trucks without roofs. In the front there were two guards, and in the back there were two guards with guns. As we travelled out of the city we met up with many other vehicles loaded with deportees coming from all directions, I have no idea where they all came from. Eventually I think there must have been 3000 prisoners in the column. After every few trucks full of prisoners there was a truck mounted with a machine gun and cannon and full of Chinese soldiers.

From the moment they first told us they were taking us away to China my thoughts had been black, and I had a kind of numb feeling. I just remembered the story from earlier in the century of Liushar, a noble who was captured and chained and carried away by the Chinese after a battle between the Tibetans and the Kuomintang. After he was taken to China no one ever heard of him again. That is why I felt numb, I felt that our fate would be the same. I thought, I will never live to see Tibet again.

The convoy went by way of Drepung Monastery, and once you are over the pass at Drepung you can't see Lhasa anymore. At that moment my mind suddenly lightened and I felt a kind of peace. Maybe because I had this sense of renunciation, maybe because I felt sure we were heading for a firing squad. But as Lhasa slipped from our sight I felt I could see things more clearly, and as we travelled I wasn't troubled by any further fears.

That night at dusk we arrived at a place called Jang Damshung. We stayed there one night. The army put up tents with fifty or sixty prisoners jammed tightly into each tent. It was too uncomfortable to sleep, so we just sat there, with soldiers patrolling outside.

Each day as we travelled we were allowed out of the trucks twice – once in the morning and once in the evening. The trucks would stop, the soldiers would jump down and station themselves all around in a circle, and we would go into the circle to relieve ourselves. As soon as you had your turn you jumped back into the truck right away.

At the next stop, when we reached Ngachu, they fed us. They gave us each one mug of rice porridge and one momo. I can't remember if it was morning or evening. The next stop was a place called Karmug. There also we were given the same treatment. We were put in an army tent, and we couldn't sleep or go outside. We just had to sit like this. Everyday they fed us only one meal. And so we travelled on to Amdo.

In a place called Amdo Toema we spent one night. There they put us all in a big building. They filled that hall with prisoners, and still there were more. Where the overflow stayed I don't know. We were crammed in with no place to sleep. A couple of people died there. I remember one woman who passed away while holding her little child in her lap. The next morning snow was falling, the ground was covered with fresh snow. They tied a rope to her legs, dragged her outside, and dumped her body in the snow.

There was no roof on the trucks. It was freezing cold and the wind was very strong. When it snowed the snow would stick to us. If we tried to brush it off the guards screamed at us. If we moved at all they would lower their rifles and point them at us. The situation was almost unbearable. We were just this side of dying from the cold.

Along the road we could see why our guards were so jumpy. We saw many burnt-out guardposts and even some tanks that were destroyed by Tibetan guerrillas. This was Amdo, where the guerrilla war had gone on for years. But now there were only soldiers travelling on the roads. We saw no civilians.

So they hauled us in trucks to the northeast corner of Amdo, to a place called Luyang where there was a railway depot. At Luyang they organized us into groups of two hundred to three hundred. Then they read out lists of names and lined us up and put us into steel railroad boxcars. In our boxcar there were seventy-six people. They put us in and locked the door from outside. There was no window so it was pitch black inside. You couldn't see a thing.

Because we were so tired from the road journey, and it was dark, and slightly warm from the heat of our bodies, we all slept. I don't even know how many days or nights we travelled because it was completely dark. When we finally arrived and they let us out it was afternoon. At the station we saw that our boxcar was standing there alone; all the others had been taken somewhere else.

They unlocked the door and ordered us out of the boxcar. There were seventy-six of us, mostly government officials, village leaders, lamas, abbots and monastery managers. We were held at the station for an hour and then trucks came and carried us another twenty-five kilometers or so. We arrived at a large fortress-type structure, with guard towers at all four corners and a wall all around. We were taken inside.

We could see immediately it was a very shabby place, in poor repair. There were a few Chinese people about, but they were all curled up and hunched over in corners. I assumed we would be staying the night there and then moving on. We thought it was some kind of hospital or sanatorium. It never occurred to us that this was our final destination.

When we arrived we still had the soap and towels that our families had given us in Lhasa, so we started washing our hands and faces. When the Chinese prisoners who were hanging about saw this they started laughing at us. We thought they were just laughing at us because we were Tibetans. But it wasn't long before we realized what they were laughing at: a bunch of naive newcomers enjoying a civilized refinement, when, unwittingly, they stood at the gates of a barbarous existence.

That night they gave us thukpa, some kind of soup. I don't know what it was made from but it was very thin and completely black. They brought it in a big brass pot. They said, "This is your food." It was too disgusting to look at. None of us ate a bite of it.

In the morning we were given little bite-size momos. They were also black, made with the same black ingredient. We waited around most of the day until they came to induct us into the prison, to take our names and give us work assignments.

It is interesting to note that from the time we were captured in Lhasa we were classified as "prisoners of war," and this is what we were called here at Jiuzhen Prison. The Chinese word is *Phuluk* – prisoners of war. The Tibetan equivalent term is *zung mag*, literally "captured soldiers." The prison office was called "Prisoner of War Camp Office." Of course this indicated Chinese acknowledgement that we were prisoners captured in a war between two governments. Later our designation changed. We became "reactionaries" or "counter-revolutionaries." When we finally returned to Tibet, if we called ourselves *zung mag* the Chinese would scold us and say, "You are not prisoners of war! You are counter-revolutionaries!"

We were divided into three categories – those who could perform the hardest work, those who could do the middle level work, and those who could only perform light labor. Since I was young they put me in the group for the hardest labor. I told them my situation, "My leg is injured. I can't walk. Please assign me to light work."

"That is not possible," they said. "If that is your situation you need to give us a pass from a doctor."

So I went to see the camp doctor. He asked me what happened. I explained that I was wounded by a cannon shell in the fighting at Lhasa. When he heard that, instead of giving me a medical certificate he gave me a great harangue, screaming that I was a bad element in society.

Our first work assignment was to dig a canal for water. But it was winter and the ground was frozen solid. It was almost impossible to dig. The ground was so hard that when you struck it with a pickaxe sometimes the handle would break. If you broke a handle you had to compensate the prison by paying three *motse*. In actual fact there was no purpose to this canal, it was just make-work. Once they realized it would be impossible to dig a canal in the winter they changed our work assignment to agricultural work.

The prison was called Trang Jao Agricultural Labor Camp. It was located in Jiuzhen in the province of Gansu. It contained over one thousand prisoners. There were seventy-six Tibetans, the rest were Chinese. The prisoners were the people that the Chinese Communists considered the worst type of criminals. People they thought could not be released because they would stir up trouble in their communities. There were former Kuomintang soldiers and officials from all over – Beijing, Shanghai. If they couldn't kill them they sent them here.

The place had a climate of extremes. For three months in the summer it was unbearably hot. When you were working in the fields and you stopped for lunch, if you wanted to sit down to eat you couldn't sit because the ground was too hot. If you stayed standing you might at least get a bit of a breeze. In the winter the weather was incredibly cold. The snow would pile up on the grass roofs of our huts, and when the sun came out it would melt and drip down. But before the water reached the ground it would freeze again, forming long icicles hanging down from the roof.

The soil was very alkaline. There was a white mineral that would leach out of the ground when it rained, and in the winter it would blow around in the air. They say it is very unhealthy. The only crop that grew there was wheat.

Previously this region was a wasteland. People just couldn't live there. Since they couldn't find anyone to live in this wilderness in 1956 they decided to build prisons there. Prisoners don't have any choice. They can't say, "I don't think I want to live there." So they brought prisoners and made them build their own prisons and begin to cultivate the land. And of course to guard the prisoners they settled army regiments. When we got there the total area under cultivation was more than one thousand *mu* – over one thousand acres.

So our work was to cultivate the land and to break new ground for cultivation. We had absolutely no machinery to help us. It was all done by human labor, using picks and shovels. While we were there we turned many acres into useable agricultural land. Each prisoner had to turn over one mu per day. If you didn't finish your allotment you were not allowed to eat lunch, and in the evening when you returned to the prison you would face thamzing.

Of course some prisoners were healthy and strong and some were weaker. If a healthy prisoner finished his work he was not permitted to help a weaker prisoner. Everyone had to do his quota by himself. In the fields, every work unit had a work site which was marked off by red flags in the four corners. You had to stay inside those borders; if you crossed the line the guards shot you.

After ten or fifteen days of doing this kind of work our feet were covered with blisters and sores. It became very hard to walk, and when you tried to push the spade in with your foot you would fall over. If you fell over like that, immediately a guard would start kicking you.

At harvest time the quota was the same – one person had to harvest one mu per day. The workday started in the morning before the sun rose. In the evening at sunset they would take us back to the prison.

In the morning when we got up they gave us one small mug full of thukpa. Although we called this thukpa, in reality it was no thicker than dishwater. As soon as we finished the thukpa they would blow a whistle. At the whistle we had to line up according to work units and they took roll call. First they counted the number of prisoners. If everyone was present we went straight out to work. If it didn't add up they called the roll by name. If someone was missing, everything would stop until they located the missing prisoner. If he was sleeping they would wake him up. Some would try to hide but there was no possibility of hiding; they found them and brought them back.

When a prisoner became ill or exhausted he would just lie under his blanket in the morning. Then the guards would drag him out by his feet. It didn't matter if he couldn't walk, they would drag him out to the fields, right out to his work place. But these prisoners couldn't do any work, they couldn't even stand up. They would just lie there in the field, and there they would die. Many died just like that, lying helpless in the fields.

In the afternoon, for lunch we got one small momo, bite-size, which you could just pop whole into your mouth. They were also made from that weird black flour. And with that we got one mug of hot water. Nothing else. In the evening, when we came back, we got another mug of thukpa.

Sometimes they would give us vegetables. We call it vegetables. Actually it was weeds that grew at the edge of the fields. These weeds were cut and dried on the rooftops in 1956 for pig food. It was left piled up on the roof and had become rotten. But this rotten fodder, cut in 1956, is what they fed us in 1959. And they only gave us each half a cup of that.

In our diet there was never one drop of oil or fat. And not even a pinch of salt. Every day we got one tiny momo and two small mugs of thin gruel. Officially the food quota for a prisoner was four kilos of flour per month. That was the stated ration. So how much food were we getting? If you divide the four kilos by ninety meals in a month you will understand our diet. It comes to forty-four grams – one and a half ounces – per meal. That was our food ration.

Chinese holidays were special occasions. During these celebrations we would get special food, and sometimes we would even get meat. Some livestock were kept in the prison – cows to give milk for the staff and oxen and horses for work. If one of

these died they would cut up the meat into four portions –
three quarters would go to the staff, and one portion was to be
shared between one thousand prisoners.

So if an animal died naturally we would get meat, but they
never slaughtered any animals intentionally for these occasions. Prisoners were assigned to look after this livestock and
when a festival was coming up we would ask the prisoners in
charge of the animals, "Which one of these animals is weak?
Which one is about to die?" And I don't know how it happened, but it always turned out that under the supervision of
the prisoners one animal was always sick enough to die just
before a festival.

But gradually we were starving, so we began to look for
sources of nourishment wherever we could find it. When we
dug the ground, worms might come out. If we saw a worm all
the prisoners would run for it and if you got it you immediately
popped it in your mouth, otherwise it would be taken away. It
would wiggle around on your tongue, so you had to bite down
on it quickly.

The livestock was also fed on grain, and in their excrement
undigested grains of wheat would come out. We would pick
these grains out of the manure pile and eat that. We ate a lot of
this grain, but actually, if you looked closely at the kernels, it
usually was just a husk. The nutritious part was already di-
gested by the animal.

Sometimes, digging away in the fields, we would find bones.
Human bones or animal bones. We would eat this too. It had
no taste. It was like dry Tibetan cheese; you would just chew
on it. Even if we knew it was human bone, still we would eat it.

If we were working in an area and we came across a tree everyone would immediately run to the tree and eat all the
leaves. The younger ones would climb the tree and the others
would stand underneath and eat the leaves that fell down.
Some leaves were so tough they were hard to swallow. And the
bitterness was unmentionable. But you couldn't be fussy
about the bitterness. You just ate it.

And there were various types of grasses and wild vegetation

growing along the paths and the edges of the fields. The Tibetan doctor Tenzin Choedak was in our group, and of course he was an expert on herbs and wild plants. He could recognize which plants were poisonous and which were edible. We would ask him, is it okay to eat this or that grass, and we would eat whatever he said was safe. But we weren't actually allowed to do this. You had to be very fast and sneaky, because if a guard caught you eating grass you would get a beating.

At this time, if you looked in the toilet it didn't look like a human being's toilet. All the stools were green from the grass and undigested leaves. What came out of us was of a worse quality than horse manure. It was nothing but grass and green fibre, it didn't look human at all.

Eventually we ate all the leather in our clothes. We ate the leather belts we brought with us from Lhasa. And some lamas from Jang had thick leather soles on their shoes, so they ate their shoes. Some of us had skin coats so we would pluck the wool off and eat the skin. When you are that hungry, nothing else matters. You just want to eat whatever you can get your hands on. Many prisoners even ate their own shit, though I must say I was never able to do that.

We have the saying in Tibet, "The weight has gone to his neck." And, "His calves have gotten fat." We found out the real meaning of these expressions. When a person becomes really weak from lack of food there is no meat on him and the bones and veins stick out. In the morning when you wake up you can't hold your head up because your neck is too weak, there is no muscle. So you have to support your head with your hand and slowly lift it up. And on your legs, the calves are completely gone, only the shins are left.

So that was our situation after our first year at Jiuzhen. As we entered our second year, none of us was strong enough to make it to the toilet to take a pee. If you had to go to the toilet you crawled along leaning against the wall. The toilet was a distance of about one hundred feet from our hut. But to get there and back leaning against the wall would take half an hour. You had to move very slowly.

But even when we were that weak, we could still talk to each other, and our minds were still functioning. The hunger caused a very powerful pain deep down in our stomachs. But despite so much physical pain we didn't feel great mental anguish because we realized that the sufferings we were experiencing were due to our past karma, due to negative actions we had committed in this and previous lives. And we also knew that we were going through this ordeal for our country. We would say to each other, "We ourselves may have lost everything. We may lose our lives. But it doesn't matter because Tibet is like a tree. She has had her branches cut off, but the roots are still alive because His Holiness is the root of our people and he is safe in India. And one day he will return again, to shine like the sun."

During that second year our people began to die. The first to die was Tzedrung Tenzing Phuntsok. But it wasn't any great surprise. We were all so weak and hungry by then. We all thought, "We will never return from this place. We can only die here."

Dying from hunger can actually be an easy way to die. Not very painful. People would be sitting, and then fall over and die. No moans of agony. At night, while we were sleeping in rows crowded next to each other, you would hear some sort of noise and you would stretch out your hand to feel your neighbor. If he was cold you knew he was dead. It was no big deal. You just had to lie there beside the corpse for the night. In the morning we would take the body out into the passageway. Some would sleep with their clothes off under the blankets. When they died their bodies would just freeze naked in the corridor.

Under these circumstances we had a discussion. These people died naturally, we did not kill them. Their minds have left their bodies, so the flesh left on their body is just the same as meat. So with that thought some of us would go and try to eat the flesh on a corpse, what we called "the crops of Jiuzhen." I also have been to eat these crops.

But when I went to try, I couldn't even get a piece off the

body. First of all I was very weak, and the corpse was stiff and frozen. We didn't have any knives. I tried to pull off an ear but couldn't. You just had to put your mouth down and try to bite a piece off. But when I was about to bite, in my mind I felt this strong feeling, I felt that I could not possibly eat this. I tried twice but in the end I was not able to eat anything.

Of the seventy-six of us, fifty-three died during our second and third years at Jiuzhen. But only one died from disease. All the rest died of starvation. I developed the theory that people actually get sick from eating good food. Penpa Choedak was the fellow who died from disease. His stomach got very swollen, he couldn't pass any waste and he suffered terrible pain. He just lay in his bunk, but you were not allowed to miss work, so the guards ordered him out. Of course he couldn't move, so they dragged him out to the work site. There was nothing he could do there, he couldn't even stand up. We felt helpless, there was nothing we could do to help him. We took off our shirts and wrapped him up and left him lying there all day. He was crying out from the pain, and kept begging us, "Please hit me on the head with a stone and kill me!" That evening he died.

But the saddest scene, the most poignant memory I have from those days, was the elder prisoners offering the younger ones their meager share of food. "I know that even if I eat my share I cannot survive," they would say. "But you young men must go on living. And if fortune favors you and someday you return to Tibet, you tell the story of how we suffered to your children." But we couldn't take their food, and we would push it back to them, because we wanted them to live too, our elders, our teachers, one generation sacrificing itself for the next.

In the autumn, at harvest time, we were all eager to go to work. In fact it was assumed that if you couldn't get to work during the harvest you were going to die. There was a hospital in the prison and usually we felt lucky if we could get in there with some complaint or other, because you could get a rest from work. But when harvest time came around, everyone made sure that they were not sick, and if they were sick they pulled themselves together so they didn't seem sick. If you were in the hospital you told the doctor, "Now I am all better. I can go."

The reason it was so important to get to the harvest was of course the wheat grain and the opportunities we made to steal and eat it. Even though we could only eat a little bit, it had great benefit for our bodies. It helped us to survive.

The harvest was in August. But months before that we divided ourselves up into teams of three for working the harvest. Two people would move quickly through the rows cutting the grain. One person followed slowly behind; he would collect fallen grain and put it in his shirt. When an opportunity arose, we would thresh it under foot and then winnow it in our straw hats. One of the team would stand as lookout, continuously singing a tune. If the lookout suddenly changed his melody it was a signal that a Chinese guard was approaching, so we would quickly hide the grain and carry on with work. If the lookout kept singing we would gobble up the grain and stuff some in our pockets for our partners. Even though we could only eat a little bit of grain in this way, it had a very good effect on our health.

After the harvest came the threshing, but the authorities were careful about who they assigned to this work. It didn't require as much labor as the harvest, and they would only call those prisoners they trusted. If we got the opportunity to work on the threshing we would wear big shoes, shoes that were several sizes too big. We would walk back and forth among the piles of loose grain and a lot of it would fall into the shoes. Eventually we would take a break to go out into the fields to pee, and there we would eat the grain. Then we came back and started all over again.

So, eating a little bit in this way you would feel a little better. But if you eat raw grain you shouldn't drink water afterward. If you do you get tremendous cramps in your stomach. After we ate this grain we would try to lie down in the sunshine with our stomachs soaking up the sun, and this would help us to digest it.

As we moved into our third year at Jiuzhen they began to

give a tiny bit more food than before. With this little extra nutrition people got just enough strength to sit up. Among us there was one fellow named Rindo who played the *damyan*, the Tibetan lute. He had brought one with him and one day, after we recovered enough to sit up in our beds, he began to play and sing a traditional Tibetan song. When he sang and played that beautiful Tibetan melody, all of us began to cry. And then Rindo himself began to weep and his tears rolled down his face onto the damyan.

During the winter, for about four months, we had what they called "Winter Studies." In the morning we went out to work but in the evening from sunset until midnight we were kept up studying. Actually, there wasn't any real study as such. They just held the usual meetings to interrogate us and find out who had spoken against the Chinese Communist Party. They asked things like, "What are your ideas about communism? What mistaken things have you said against the Chinese? What has anyone else said?" Everyone would have to answer. If you didn't speak up for yourself then someone else would accuse you. So in this way we were pressured to inform on each other. So the cross-questioning and accusations would go on like that every night until midnight. If they were not satisfied with your responses you got thamzing.

Sometimes the Chinese would ask us, "What wishes do you have? What are your aspirations?" We all had the same answer, "Just to go back to a Tibetan place. To go to a place where we can eat tsampa and where we understand the language. Aside from that we have no other hopes or desires."

The Chinese guards had their favorites among the prisoners and also their scapegoats. If they didn't like someone they would hide his tools outside and then accuse him of losing his tools. On this pretext they would beat him up. This kind of thing they did quite often.

We Tibetans were a small minority at Jiuzhen. When we first arrived the Chinese prisoners gave us a very hard time. We all had basically peaceful attitudes and we were not actually criminals. Because of our meekness the tougher Chinese prisoners took advantage of us, and even stole the few tiny momos we had to eat. But eventually we learned the ropes and the Tibetans became quite tough. For one thing we had no hope of ever returning home, so there was nothing to fear. We stuck together and when a Chinese prisoner made any trouble for one of us we got together and beat him up. Acting together we managed to subdue the Chinese prisoners and gained such a fierce reputation that the prison officials would threaten Chinese prisoners, "If you don't behave we will throw you to the Tibetans."

Before we learned the ways of the prison other prisoners would reach in through the windows of our hut and steal our clothes. A lot of this kind of thieving went on until we started baiting the windows and waiting there with a rope. When a thief stuck his hand in we snared it and tied him up and held him all night with his arm stuck through our window. In Jiuzhen, aside from work hours, when the guards were around, there was virtually no control or discipline. So our snared thieves could cry out and moan all night and no one would pay any attention.

Some of the thieves were ingenious. Once a thief snuck into our room in the middle of the night. He came naked. One by one he stole all the different articles of clothing, a shirt, trousers, shoes. Suddenly one of us woke up and called out, "It's a thief! It's a thief!" We all leaped out of bed and captured him, but we couldn't find anything on him. We figured he hadn't actually stolen anything so we let him go. In the morning, when we got up to dress, someone said, "Hey, my shirt is gone." Another said, "I can't find my shoes." It dawned on us, the intruder we let go had left wearing our clothes. Then we went and found him and tied him up and held him all night. We taught him a lesson and left him tied up and crying all night. But even if we had killed him no one would have done anything. That was the degenerate state of discipline at Jiuzhen Prison.

We Tibetans were able to bring a lot of good warm clothes with us, things our families had brought for us the night before we left. The poor Chinese prisoners didn't have much in the way of clothes for the cold weather. They would come around to trade their few momos for our warm clothes. They would sell one momo for one chuba or ten yuan. They could do a good business in selling their food, but it was senseless. One of these Chinese traders died with wads of money around his waist; he had made a fortune selling his momos, only to die of starvation.

There was this kind of black market in momos and clothes and we did a little business. But we didn't handle much money. If the authorities caught us handling money there would be a lot of trouble. The warden's office kept all the prisoner's cash and we were not allowed to keep money in the prison.

Nearly every week I got a letter from my family in Lhasa. They were not allowed to send food or money, but they sent many letters. When these letters arrived they made me very sad, and by the time I recovered from the depression of the last letter, the next letter would arrive. I would try to forget, but each letter was a reminder of the life I had left behind. I had already determined that I was going to die, that I would never go back to Tibet or meet my family again.

Eventually these constant painful reminders began to really trouble me, and finally I wrote to my parents and said, "I have been carried away from my homeland, and I do not have to tell you the reason. You are well aware of the circumstances of my arrest. It was not because I committed theft or murdered someone. You know the reason, so you should be able to judge the situation. So please, from now on do not write to me and I will not write to you."

But this plea from me only worried them more and they started sending me telegrams! First one telegram, and then another telegram, and then another. In these telegrams they said, "Don't go thinking these wild thoughts!" They thought I was planning to do something drastic. The whole thing caused me a lot of frustration.

So in brief, this was our life in Jiuzhen Prison. I don't remember every detail, but this will give you an idea of how it was. In October, 1962, some soldiers arrived. Among these soldiers there were a couple of Tibetans. We saw them and we talked among ourselves and agreed that these soldiers must have come from Tibet.

Then a Chinese officer came and told us, "Now you Tibetans don't have to go to work anymore. You are going back to Tibet, so get yourselves ready to go." He told us that amazing news, but he didn't say exactly when we were going to go.

We were all completely overjoyed. It was as if there had never been a happier time in our lives. We got so excited we couldn't even sleep. We just sat up all night and even though we really didn't know where they were going to take us, we were happy. We tried to sleep, but one person would sit up to smoke a cigarette, then another would sit up and they would start talking, and then the rest of us would get up. And like that we sat up all night discussing what the future held in store. Before dawn we would start cleaning the room and packing up our things, getting ready to go to Tibet. We ended up spending a week ready and waiting to leave at any moment.

Finally they announced we would be leaving tomorrow, and they gave us our food for the journey. It was bread and it was supposed to last us for the entire trip. They said, "This bread has to last you until Lhasa. Do not eat it all at once." They emphasized this to us. But everybody was so hungry we could not resist it, and within three days all the bread was gone.

But this time the travelling conditions were better, and when we finished our bread on the road our soldier escorts gave us food from their own rations. We travelled by truck and the pace was not so brutal. We travelled for a few days and then rested for a day, and like that we had a relatively easy journey for the ten days that it took us to reach Lhasa.

How many of us were left? We used to say this: There were twenty-two and a half who returned to Tibet. Twenty-two of us were alive, and the half person was Yuthog Shar's chandzoe. The reason we designated him as "a half person" was that he was only half alive. He had developed T.B. and was confined to the hospital. He was very weak and couldn't go to the toilet. We thought he was likely to die on the road, so we said that twenty-two and a half of us were returning to Tibet. We had arrived at Jiuzhen as a group of seventy-six, and twenty-two and a half were going to return.

But it was Yuthog Shar's chandzoe who really deepened my faith in religion. It was an incident in our second year at Jiuzhen. I was sent out to haul manure to the local villages. He had the notion that while I was out on these trips I would be able to buy some food. Of course this was ridiculous, we just sat in the truck, unloaded the manure, and we were constantly under guard. One day when I was about to leave on one of these jobs he asked me, "While you are out there won't you please buy me some bread or something to eat? Couldn't you manage that?"

I replied, "What are you talking about? What are you going to do with something to eat? You are lying there sick in bed. I am supposed to be the healthy one, but even I am likely to die at any time. It is for sure that I am going to die. We are all about to die. Out of seventy-six of us twenty-two are left standing and you are lying there sick. So what is the use of getting you food?"

Then he said this, "We are definitely going to get back to Lhasa. It is absolutely definite."

"How can you be so sure you will return to Lhasa?" I said. "You can't even get up to piss. Why do you think you will make it to Lhasa?"

"Once, before the Uprising, I went to Lake Lhamo Lhatso to look for signs. There I saw a vivid picture. I saw the Lhasa Uprising. Then I saw myself put into the Lhasa prison, then arriving here at Jiuzhen Prison. I saw everything. I saw it all just as it has happened. But that is not all. After all of this I saw a vivid picture of Ri Gya, the mountain in Lhasa. This I saw very clearly in the lake and everything I saw in the lake has come true. But I haven't come to see the mountain yet. Ri Gya is still in our future. I saw it in the lake, and I know I will see Ri Gya in Lhasa again."

Frankly, when I heard all this I didn't believe it. But eventually we piled into the truck and we travelled back to Lhasa. And this old man, this half person, lay in the truck with us. At Lhasa they put us into Drabchi Prison. There, from the windows of Drabchi Prison, rising up directly in front of these windows, stands the mountain Ri Gya. You don't have to make any effort to look for it. If you are in the prison, and you look out the windows, it is there, right before your eyes. You only have to open your eyes to see it.

Chandzoe-la was still alive when we reached Drabchi Prison. He stayed one night there. When he looked out the window he saw Ri Gya. The next morning they took him off to a hospital. On the way to the hospital he passed away.

So the prophecy in the lake had come true. He saw his Ri Gya, just as he had seen it in Lake Lhamo Lhatso. And from then on I developed a much deeper faith in our religion.

4

We arrived in Lhasa on the night of October 19, 1962. They didn't tell us that they were taking us to Drabchi but the Tibetan soldiers who were guarding us had already given us hints. In the truck they would talk to each other and say, "Those Drabchi prisoners are tough. They give the guards there a hard time."

In Drabchi Prison they put us into two empty cells, fifteen or sixteen of us in one cell and the rest in another smaller room.

The night we arrived they didn't give us anything to eat. They put us in the cell, brought in a slop bucket, closed the door, and we went to sleep.

The next morning an official came round. He told us, "You are not allowed to talk to other prisoners outside this cell. You are not to have any relationship with them."

There were about fifteen cells in our wing. We would peek through the hole in our door to see who was out there and we could see that all the other prisoners were Tibetans. Each cell had about fifteen prisoners. At first we were not assigned to any work. We just sat in our cells, and each day for one half hour we were taken out for some sun. One cell at a time they took us outside where they had a little area marked out by a line. We sat inside that area for half an hour, soaked up the sunshine, and were taken back and locked up. Then the next cell would be brought out.

Our families found out that we were back in Lhasa and soon they began sending us food parcels. But when we began receiving these wonderful packages we discovered that we were physically so damaged by starvation that we could not tolerate decent food. When they sent meat, if we ate just one piece of meat, we got diarrhea. It was too rich for us. We just couldn't digest it.

Before we left Jiuzhen the food there had improved slightly, in quantity if not in quality. With this increase our condition had also improved a bit. We were still in a bad way but at least we had the strength to get up and walk to the toilet without leaning against the wall. We were just strong enough to do a little work.

The biggest difference between Jiuzhen and Drabchi was that at Jiuzhen the discipline was loose. At night the doors were not locked, you could wander back and forth and talk to each other. At Drabchi you were not even allowed out of your cell. If you happened to meet a prisoner you knew you were not allowed to speak. The food of course was better at Drabchi, but the discipline was very strict.

At Drabchi the food ration was twenty gyama – about ten

kilos – per month. This was a lot better than the starvation diet
we got in China, but it was not enough to fill your stomach, not
enough to stop you from feeling hungry. The prisoners who
were at Drabchi while we were out in China also suffered terribly during those years from 1960 to 1962. We heard that they
were eating beans, and they distributed the food to the prisoners by counting out the beans one by one. In Drabchi too,
many died of starvation.

The ceiling of the cell was covered with Chinese newspapers. To pass the time we would stand and read this "wallpa-
per." We read one article which said that the Tibetan refugees
in India had formed a Government-in-Exile and under His
Holiness they had drawn up a draft democratic constitution.
When we discovered this it made us very happy. This was the
first encouraging news we had had in a long time.

The prison officials would also give us recent newspapers
which we were supposed to "study." One person read out the
news and the rest would sit there and listen. There wasn't anything else to do.

From the newspapers we learned about the border war between China and India. The articles discussed the different
battles and where the fighting was going on. The news that
India had gone to war against China was exciting for us and
gave us high hopes.

Inspired with the hope that events on the border might
eventually change the circumstances inside Tibet and China
itself, the prisoners began to pull themselves together with a
new discipline and began to form secret resistance cells, making plans to capitalize on whatever opportunities might arise.
It was agreed among the resistance members that if conditions
changed sufficiently, we should be prepared to break out of
the prison and fight.

I participated in discussions along these lines with three or
four of my most trusted cellmates. Our plans began by hiding
the civilian clothes that our families had been sending to us. In
the prison we had to wear a standard black uniform. If we escaped there was no chance of getting very far dressed in pris-

oners' black. If an upheaval developed on the outside our idea was to change into our civilian clothes, kill the guards, break out and fight.

But these hopes soon faded. Within a matter of days India had lost the war. And their loss was a loss for us as well. Not only the loss of our dreams of an organized resistance, but eventually information about our secret plans leaked out. Once the intensity of the planning and expectation faded, people got careless and took things lightly. They talked to each other, to people they didn't know well enough, word got around, and of course eventually the Chinese got hold of the information.

Many people were eventually executed for these plots. But the reprisals were not carried out right away. It was a few years later, during the Cultural Revolution, after 1966 – it was during these years that they carried out the executions. Their method was to build up a file on every prisoner. They kept detailed records of a prisoner's work habits, how he responded in study sessions, and of course any suspected involvement in resistance plots would be included in his file. When the Cultural Revolution came around, anyone whose file looked a little too negative was executed. At that time it didn't take much, a small transgression would get you killed.

In the summer of 1963 they had a big shake-up in Drabchi. It began with an intense security check of the prisoners' quarters. Then one segment of the population was transferred to Sangyip, another major prison in Lhasa. Those of us who remained at Drabchi were shuffled around to different sections and different cells.

I was moved into a small and dark cell. All the windows were sealed up by bricks. The only opening was one small hole in the door through which you could pass a small mug. There was no light, it was dark and the door was always locked. There was a slop bucket inside; other than that there was nothing. Every morning two people would carry out the bucket. The others were not allowed out. We just stayed in the cell all day long.

It turned out that this crackdown was connected with the arrest of the Panchen Lama. The Chinese were planning to arrest him and in order to prevent any reaction by political prisoners they tightened security and put us into extended lockup. They arrested the Panchen Lama in 1964.

When you are trapped for such a long time in darkness, day and night, you become thin and sickly and your complexion turns very pale, white like a skeleton. I discovered then just how important sun and fresh air are to our health.

Every once in a while they would call one of us out for questioning. When you first stepped outside it was difficult to adjust your eyes to the daylight. And if there was a cool breeze you would gasp for breath and shiver. You felt so cold deep down inside that it was difficult to talk.

We were confined to our cell twenty-four hours a day for ten or eleven months. Then, in 1964, at the end of the year, we were let out of our dark hole. They moved us to a cell in a newly built wing in Drabchi. A few days after the move we were sent to work carrying stones for building projects. It was a long haul, perhaps six or seven kilometers out to the quarry and then back again, carrying stones on our backs.

Our health at this time was still very poor – especially after almost a year in a dark cell. Even without a load it was difficult for us to make the trip out to the quarry, to say nothing of the return trip loaded down with heavy stones. But if you didn't keep moving the guards came up behind you and beat you with their rifle butts.

When you arrived back at the prison they would weigh your load of stones, checking to see how much you had carried. You were supposed to carry one hundred gyama on each trip – that's fifty kilos, or 110 pounds. And each day we made two trips. If you didn't carry that much they would berate you. If you failed to meet the quota several times in a row they sent you for thamzing.

Doing this kind of hard labor, if we had to survive only on the prison food rations it would have been very hard on us. These rations were never enough to fill our stomachs. What kept us going was the extra food that our families brought to the prison. We shared this food with each other, and with this extra nutrition we were able to bear up under the hard labor. Slowly we became accustomed to the work, our bodies got stronger and the labor seemed a little easier.

In 1965 the Chinese organized an extensive campaign of political education, and our reeducation classes resumed. In these classes they started telling us that the Third World War was about to begin. They asked, "What do we need to do to prepare for this great war? What are your ideas about this conflict? When it breaks out, where will you stand?" This was the "education" they were giving us. We did not know it at the time, but these developments actually marked the formative phases of the Cultural Revolution.

In retrospect it seems that they were probing, to see how the Tibetans were going to react to the coming turmoil. The clouds of the Cultural Revolution were gathering, and they must have suspected that there was still a lot of resistance dormant among the Tibetan people. So in order to probe and prod this resistance, and to intimidate and push the Tibetans to cooperate, they initiated this political education campaign. Though they talked about a Third World War, this was just a cover, an excuse to prepare the minds of the people for the storm that was about to break.

I don't remember all the topics that were discussed at these classes, but in general they would lay out talking points, questions like, "Which is better, the old feudal system in Tibet or the Chinese Communist system? Are you in favor of capitalism, or do you prefer communism in a people's republic?"

I don't remember how I answered all these questions, but when they asked whether the old system or the new system was better, I remember saying, "Under our old system we didn't have to measure out our tsampa. We could eat as much as we wanted, we had as much food as we needed. Now, under the Communist system, each person has a specific ration, and you aren't allowed any more food than that. Nowadays, everything is in terms of weight, your quota, what you are entitled to. And on a larger scale, in the old days, if you wanted to go from the city to a small village, or from your village to the city, you didn't have to ask anyone's permission. Nowadays, if you want to go anywhere, you have to get permission. In those days, not only did you not need a pass to travel freely inside Tibet, but you didn't even need passports to cross the border to go outside the country. You didn't need the government's permission to go abroad. Everyone was free to go wherever they pleased."

This loss of freedom of movement really struck home for me. My sister lived in our native village, about fifty kilometers from Lhasa, while my parents stayed in Lhasa; and of course I was in prison in Lhasa. My sister loved her family and wanted very much to visit us, and naturally my parents and I always wanted to see her. But she couldn't go anywhere without permission. She wanted to see us, but they never allowed her to go. Even until this day, I have not seen my sister since before the Lhasa Uprising. So when they asked their questions, this was one of the concepts that I expressed.

Another argument I made was this, "You claim that the power is in the hands of the people. Of course we are only prisoners, the prisons are all we know. But in the prisons here in Tibet all the senior officers are Chinese, while all the low-level workers are Tibetans. So what kind of popular system is that? All the political power is in the hands of the Chinese. The Tibetan masses do not have any power."

Most of these meetings were in small groups, just the fifteen or so inmates from a cell, or they would bring two or three cells together. Occasionally they would hold large assemblies with all the prisoners. It varied according to their whims and according to the importance of the topic. The staff of the prison would operate and supervise the meetings. Senior officers would make the rounds, checking in on the different groups.

When I made these speeches the head warden of the prison

was there. It really seemed to wound the Chinese officers who were leading the meeting. They were shocked and angry. They made me repeat things and then told me I had to write everything down. They said, "It is not enough that it comes out of your mouth, you have to write this down. Put it in writing and submit it to the office!"

So I did as they told me and wrote it all down. I didn't have any hope of ever being freed from prison. It was already settled that my sentence was twenty years. With a sentence like that I had no hope of getting out. I assumed I would die there. So I really wasn't concerned for my life, for the consequences of my actions. This kind of thinking made us bold, and some of us just said the most damaging things we could think of.

Another point of discussion they raised at a reeducation session was this: "Is the Dalai Lama the source of all the crimes of Tibet or not? If so, tell us why this is true." There were about twenty of us at that meeting and we all sat and thought a long time. For a long time no one said anything. But we couldn't just sit there in silence forever. For one thing, silence was not permitted. You had to speak.

Finally Dreru Shabdrung, a lama, spoke up. "If His Holiness the Dalai Lama is the root of all the crimes of Tibet, then the root of the Dalai Lama's crimes is China. It was China that made him do whatever he did."

Then I spoke up. "I cannot personally agree that His Holiness the Dalai Lama is the root of all the crimes in Tibet. The reason I cannot agree with this is based on the education that I have received from the Chinese. During my prison life I have been studying with the guidance of the Chinese reform education. In these studies I have been told that the Dalai Lama was abducted by foreign counter-revolutionary agents and carried away to India. How they abducted him I do not know. But this is what you have taught me and I believe it. It is clear that since he did not flee of his own free will, but was abducted, he has not been acting against the Chinese.

"Furthermore, the Dalai Lama did not come to his position by means of heredity – it is not an aristocratic position based on bloodlines. Nor did he appoint himself. His Holiness was born in Amdo. He was recognized as the Dalai Lama by the people of Tibet. He was brought to Lhasa, recognized and enthroned and given the reverence that he deserves. This recognition came from the public. It was not that His Holiness declared himself a king: 'I came from the race of the Thirteenth Dalai Lama and I have a right to this throne.' It was the people of Tibet who chose him.

"In the old system the Dalai Lama selected the village heads and government officials. When he appointed these officials he always advised them, 'When you go to your post always remember that your responsibility is to look after the people. Your job is to serve the people.' His Holiness never told anyone to be cruel or to deceive or to mislead the citizens. In every case he advised government servants to look after the welfare of the public.

"Now it is true that these government officials did not always do the right thing. It did happen that they abused their authority or collected excessive taxes. The nobles did make mistakes and did sometimes take advantage of the people. But this was never on the authority of the Dalai Lama. These were the crimes of the officials themselves. His Holiness always told them, 'You have to do your job properly, and your job is to benefit the public.'

"And during the uprising in Lhasa, during the protests that started at the Norbulinka, I was there. His Holiness said at that time, 'It is not right to use violent means. The people must try to find a peaceful solution.' He himself always used peaceful means. He never encouraged the people to demonstrate and always told them not to use violent means. He always asked the people to be more patient and tolerant in their approach to difficult situations.

"His Holiness said that changes needed to be made in the old Tibetan system. He said that we need to introduce democracy, and he actually began to establish institutions for the development of democracy, such as the Reform Office where I worked, and where we had begun to make significant changes in the old system. His Holiness never ever said, 'We need to preserve feudalism in Tibet.'

"In light of all of these reasons, I cannot agree with your statement that the Dalai Lama is the root of all the crimes in Tibet."

Only two or three people spoke at that meeting. Of those who spoke up, not one agreed that His Holiness the Dalai Lama was to blame for the problems of Tibet. The meeting was adjourned. The Chinese did not react immediately; they did not punish us on the spot. They made notes of our statements, they made their list of names, and the consequences were always out there waiting in the unforeseeable future.

So the reeducation program went on. All the meetings and political discussion coming from the Chinese side inspired us to reconstitute our underground organization, and once again to hold secret meetings and try to develop a disciplined resistance. At that time I worked together with Kasur Shewo Lobsang Dhargye, Shekar Lingpa, Ven. Jampa Tsultrim, and Thangpe Phuntsok Namgyal, all of whom are now safely in Dharamsala and once again working in various departments of the Tibetan Government.

The Chinese were telling us of the danger of a new world war. We had no way of evaluating this information, but we felt it could only be good if it destabilized China and loosened their grip on Tibet. We came to the conclusion that if the conditions on the outside changed sufficiently, to the point where real resistance seemed possible, then the Tibetans on the outside would have to provide sixty percent of the resistance effort, and we prisoners had to be ready to deliver the other forty percent. So we began to make what preparations we could for the day when we could challenge the Chinese.

Again we started to gather civilian clothes. I had a little experience driving, so I was given the responsibility for driving an escape vehicle. They told me, "Even though you haven't driven for many years, now you must remember how to drive. One day you will have to do it for us." So the responsibilities were assigned in that way, as we planned and plotted.

In the end, of course, the Third World War didn't come. What came instead was the Cultural Revolution.

In 1965 they took us to see an exhibition they had set up, a kind of museum. What they had on display at this museum was the protest letter of the Panchen Lama, together with all kinds of items that were supposedly going to be used in an uprising against the Chinese, weapons, ammunition, and so forth. The museum was in a hall below Tze.

When we prisoners saw this display it did not turn us against Panchen Rinpoche. On the contrary, we felt pride and it deepened our respect for him. We saw that he was prepared to make this protest for the benefit of his own people and culture and religion. We were really proud of the Panchen Rinpoche, and I think the effect of this exhibit was only to bring the Tibetan people closer to him.

Basically, no one among us was opposed to Panchen Rinpoche or to His Holiness the Dalai Lama. There was a certain type of prisoner, a few who – in hopes of getting released sooner, getting better treatment, needing to be free of the great pressure of imprisonment – denounced our leaders. But these prisoners were ostracized by the rest of us, they were outcasts. No one would talk to them. Even though they were incarcerated together with us, we always regarded them as just like the Chinese.

In October 1965 I was called in to the office. It had been six and a half years since my arrest, but it was not until that day that I was informed of my sentence, twenty years of imprisonment. There was no public announcement, no ceremony, and certainly no trial. They just called you in and read you your sentence. Many of my colleagues got shorter sentences, fifteen years or less. I don't really know why I was given more time, but I suspect it was because of my involvement in the escape of His Holiness the Dalai Lama.

5

The Cultural Revolution began in earnest in the middle of 1966. As the treatment of prisoners increased in violence and cruelty, tensions on all sides were raised to a new pitch. The use of thamzing and harsh punishment became unrestrained.

At the study sessions they pressed us for answers to their questions, demanding to hear "our own ideas" on these issues. We faced a dilemma: If we told them what was really in our minds they would proclaim, "These reactionaries have not changed their minds at all!" and we would get thamzing. If we mouthed the words they wanted to hear and supported the Chinese point of view they accused us of lying and said, "If you really hold so many right ideas how did it happen that you ended up in prison? You are hiding your true thoughts." For that you got thamzing. If we didn't speak at all they said, "This one still harbors counter-revolutionary ideas in his heart." And once again you got thamzing.

As I said, the thamzing would not come immediately after you made a statement they did not like. They kept records of your statements, questioned you again and again. And at some unpredictable time in the future, at a time when it suited them, they would read out the charges against you and off you go to thamzing.

For example, one time they asked us, "What is your view of the Cultural Revolution?" When it came to my turn I knew I had to say something. So I answered, "In the Cultural Revolution Mao Zedong and Liu Shaoqi are struggling for power. Now I was imprisoned for saying, 'Tibet is independent.' And to tell you the truth, if Mao Zedong wins this struggle, I will remain in prison. If Liu Shaoqi is victorious, I will also remain in prison. They are both Chinese. They are both Communists. Either way, there will be no profit in it for me. So it really doesn't matter to me at all."

So I made this statement, and they took it all down. And later on they threw it back at me, and demanded to know, "What is the reason that you said that the Cultural Revolution makes no difference to you?" And on that basis they gave me thamzing.

The concept of thamzing is based on the Chinese claim that it is not they who are punishing the victim, but it is the people themselves who want to correct that person's behavior. Of course the authorities could easily take the "reactionaries" and just have the soldiers beat them up. And sometimes they did that. But if they did it too often it would make them look bad, it would undermine their stated position that the people support them and that these punishments are the will of the people. Thamzing gave the appearance that "the people are punishing the reactionary forces." And this way the victims were punished twice, once through imprisonment by the government, and again when the public beat them in thamzing.

Most of the people who were called out to perform the thamzing did not want to do it. They were actually coerced to do it because whoever stood back and did not actively participate was himself liable for thamzing. There was no way not to join in. If you didn't participate the Chinese would say, "You are not taking part in the thamzing of this person. You are the same as him." So the whole thing was a vicious cycle of fear.

Often, people from the crowd would actually protect the victim. They would jump on him, screaming and accusing him and calling him a reactionary, they would grab the victim's hair and knock him about, but actually, when others jumped up and tried to attack him, they would cover up the victim and protect him with their own bodies.

For example, there was Kalon Lhalu, who faced thamzing in front of a large public gathering. He was forced to bend over from the waist all day long, and of course it was very difficult. Then one of his old servants jumped out of the crowd and screamed at him, "You are the one who made us slave for you, who hit us with sticks and loaded us down with burdens. Now it is your turn to bend your back, to lean on sticks." And he shoved an old stick into the Kalon's hand. It looked like the servant was humiliating him, but actually he could lean on the stick, and it was much more comfortable. Then the servant screamed, "Now it is your turn to carry heavy loads." And he threw a dirty old sack on the man's back. It appeared to be degrading criticism, but inside, the sack was loaded with tsampa and butter.

When the victim was a lama, or an abbot, or a high government official, most Tibetans could not bring themselves to seriously attack or harm them. In general, thamzing for people of high status was not as bad as it was for the common people. In other prisons, where more lay people and peasants were held, the thamzing was more brutal. The worst cases were often situations where one man had a personal grudge against the victim – it had nothing to do with politics or wrong thinking, it was just a vendetta. They would really beat up the victim, and many were killed this way.

There were certain characteristic injuries from thamzing. The attackers would grab on to the victim's ears or hair. Many people had their ears ripped off. The hair might be pulled out in big clumps, tearing off the scalp, and often the sores that were opened on their heads would get infected. Or they would form big blood-blisters under the skin, with blood swelling up between the skull and the scalp. In 1970 I faced a thamzing in which my front teeth were knocked out. Many had their legs or hands broken. And some were simply beaten to death.

Along with the increased use of thamzing, the Cultural Revolution brought the extensive practice of "judicial executions." From 1966 until 1976, between sixty and seventy people were executed in Drabchi Prison. Many of these were prisoners in Drabchi, but others were brought from outside, or from other prisons, and executed in Drabchi. Among those who were killed were many women, including the rebel leader, Kundeling Kunsang. Many lamas were also executed.

During that time, it didn't take much to get yourself executed. You didn't have to do anything terrible. For example, there was a lama named Sersang Tulku, a lama from Ganden Monastery. He was executed for giving Dharma teachings – religious teachings – to the people. This was the work he was raised and trained to do. And for doing it, he was killed.

Then there was Dunwang Namgyal – his older brother is now in Dharamsala. He joined the NVDA in Lhoka, and became their secretary. We were in school together, but he was quite young. In prison he became mentally unbalanced and behaved erratically. One book we were allowed in prison was *The Quotations of Chairman Mao*. It was a small book with Mao's picture on it. One day Dunwang Namgyal said, "This person is not a lama! This book doesn't mean anything! I don't believe a word of it!" And with these words he chucked it into the piss pot. For throwing Chairman Mao's book in the toilet he was executed.

There was another mentally ill fellow from Kongbo. He would continuously sing. It was his habit. He would just sing because he was a little crazy. In 1976 Mao Zedong died. One day after Mao died, this fellow started singing as usual. Songs just naturally came out of his mouth. When the guards heard him they said, "He is singing after our great leader has died! He is happy that Mao Zedong has died!" So they executed him.

Actually, they would use incidents like these as excuses for execution. Usually they executed people who they felt were staunch reactionaries or troublemakers. They might want to kill someone for a long time, and then on some little pretext they would take him out and shoot him. At the end I will read you a list of names, the names I remember of those who were executed at Drabchi Prison.

Outside of prison, executions were often held just before important Chinese festivals, or when they were about to initiate new reforms. Then they would publicly execute a few prisoners just to discourage people from making trouble or opposing the reforms. They would call the Tibetan people to mass gatherings and one or two prisoners would be publicly shot. This gave a clear message that the functions and ceremonies should go peacefully and that there shouldn't be any demonstrations or disruptions.

On days when there were going to be executions in prison

they would wake us up before dawn. When the sun rose we could see platoons of soldiers out in the courtyard. This would be our first indication that there would be an execution that day. We were led out to the courtyard where they would hold a large meeting. There were lines drawn on the ground and we had to sit in very strict order.

As the meeting ended they would bring out the victims, however many there were, one, two, three, eight. By the time they brought them before the assembly they were already very badly beaten. They usually had broken ribs and bones when they were brought out. If they didn't beat them beforehand the condemned would shout slogans against the Chinese in front of the other prisoners. So in order to shut them up they were beaten into semi-consciousness.

They brought them out and made them kneel down. Each had his hands tied behind his back, and in front hung a plaque with a red cross stating their name and announcing their execution. Some would still try to stand up and shout, but the guards would pull the rope taught, their head would be yanked down, and they would almost lose consciousness. If they tried to stand again the same thing would happen. They couldn't do anything, but some of them were tough. They were hard to keep down. If they didn't beat them half-dead before they brought them out, those condemned prisoners would have been impossible to handle.

Officials announced to the assembly what the charges were, and the sentence. Then they took them away in a truck. Behind the prison there was a field; there they had dug a grave. They lined up the condemned people, made them kneel in front of the hole in the ground, and shot them from behind. The force of the shot would knock them into the grave. Then, without checking to see if they were dead, they covered the bodies with dirt.

The system was designed to intimidate the spectators, whether it was other prisoners or the general public. In the prisons, during the big meeting before an execution, we were surrounded by heavily armed soldiers. We were not allowed to utter a word, and we were told that if we so much as moved they would shoot us on the spot.

The ultimate intimidation was to the relatives of the condemned. They would be ordered to attend the execution and forced to sit up front to watch closely while their son or daughter or father or mother was tortured and killed. This practice was common throughout Tibet, and in Kham it was the rule that all children above eight years old had to attend the execution of their parents.

I remember a boy of about seventeen who worked in the tailor shop in the labor brigade where I was assigned after my release. He had served four years in prison for running away after his father had been executed, and now he was stuck in the labor brigade. He used to carry around a knife and was constantly sharpening and playing with it. One day I asked him, "What do you plan to do with that knife?"

"I am going to kill a Chinese with it," he said.

"Why do you want to do that?" I asked.

"My father was executed by the Chinese," he told me. "When they killed him they took me to see it. I stood there and watched it, and I felt horrible. But I couldn't do anything about it then. I was just a boy, what could I do? So I ran away, and they arrested me and put me in prison. But now I can do something. I won't rest until I have killed at least one Chinese."

I told him to put his knife away. "Even if you kill ten Chinese instead of one, what good will it do? You have to think in bigger terms than just killing some Chinese for revenge." And fortunately he listened to me.

So from 1966 to 1970 I saw between sixty and seventy Tibetans executed in this manner. This was the method in our prison. In other places there were other modes of execution. In some places the actual killing was public, directly in front of the spectators, but in our prison they didn't kill them right in front of us. They took them out back.

In Lhasa there was one public execution in which fifteen people were killed. There was an uprising in Nyemo in 1969.

The leader of the rebels was a nun named Kunsang Chodron. After the uprising was suppressed and the rebels were captured, fifteen, including Kunsang Chodron, were executed before a large public gathering in Lhasa.

In another incident they executed eight children in Lhasa, from the ages of seventeen to twenty. They had formed an underground organization, the Chinese found out and they were publicly executed. There were countless other times when they killed one or two individuals in public displays.

In 1967 the army took control of the political administration, and also took command of the prisons. During this period high officers, generals, and so forth, would come to give us lectures. We didn't know who they were, but I remember one of them told us, "You people are no more valuable than a carrot. It only costs us one bullet to take your lives. In fact, you are not even as valuable as a carrot, at least you can eat a carrot. So be careful. If you do not obey the rules it will only cost us one bullet to correct your behavior."

The Cultural Revolution grew more serious and conflict erupted in every direction. Inside the prison we were cut off from news, but at night we could hear the loudspeakers in Lhasa announcing that there was fighting in this area, or a battle in that place. We could also hear the fighting itself, rioting and gunfire. So it was clear to us that a real upheaval was under way outside the prison walls. Once again our hopes were raised that we might have an opportunity to join in a rebellion and take direct action against the Chinese.

But inside the prison conditions were increasingly rigorous. There were weekly shake-ups in which we were shifted from one cell to another and all of our belongings, bedding, and bodies were thoroughly searched. Commanding the yard in our wing of the prison the authorities built a fortified bunker from which they could shoot in every direction. This was discouraging for us. This new fortification made us feel like we were in the palm of their hands. It looked like it would be almost impossible to overcome this position.

Then the prison officials made an announcement. They said

that if a dangerous situation arose they would sound a siren, and then everyone had to immediately return to his cell. If you were found outside your cell you would be shot on the spot. Then they said that there was fighting on the border. Because of this fighting it was possible that a plane might come and drop bombs on Lhasa. If there was a bombing raid and the prison was hit, they told us to look after each other, and if anyone was wounded we should try to stop the bleeding until they could get medical attention.

They insisted to us, "If anything happens, we will not abandon you. Whatever emergency arises, we will not desert you. If we can no longer stay here, we will move you to another place. We have arranged for a safer place to move you."

So they were talking about fighting on the borders, but there were obvious signs of fighting internally as well. In fact, all of China was ablaze with civil strife. We took this as good news and began to make plans ourselves.

In my work unit there were about 150 prisoners. Once again we activated small secret underground cells of three, four, five members. One day when I went to the prison hospital I met Nyima Tenzing, someone I knew and trusted who was in a different work unit. We were waiting in line at the hospital. Generally we were not allowed to talk in this line, but I stood behind him and whispered when we were not watched. I told him that in our unit they announced that there was fighting at the borders and gave us special instructions. "They are also building a bunker in our yard. How are things on your side?" I asked.

He said, "In our barracks they are not building a bunker. But there is real tension."

I said, "If something happens they will not leave us, and they will not move us to a safer place. They will slaughter us all. It is better to die in a worthy way, fighting. Find out who are the trustworthy people in your section. That is what we are doing. Then we can all come out to fight together."

A little while after that conversation several prisoners were executed. At the same time Nyima Tenzing was accused of

involvement with these condemned men. He apparently confessed to involvement in underground activities and his sentence was extended for another twenty years.

When they announced his additional sentence he seemed
very frightened. We heard that he was being interrogated
heavily. Word spread that anyone who had a relationship with
him had better be careful because he was being grilled and he
would probably name all of us.

In September, 1970 they shook up the prison by mixing up
and moving everyone into different cells. In my new cell, out
of the sixteen inmates, most of us were known as the worst
offenders, because we were always speaking up against the
Chinese. Among the prisoners in that cell were Ven. Jampa
Tsultrim (who is now the Assistant Personal Secretary to His
Holiness) and Shekar Lingpa (who now works in the Kashag).
But three of the prisoners they put in with us were known
Chinese puppets.

Our friends told us, "You must all be very careful now. You
have been selected to be together in that cell and you are being watched." We could see that the situation was serious.
They were focusing their attention on us. They had placed
spies in our cell, and, needless to say, we were concerned.

After living under this tension for some time, one day
Shekar Lingpa said, "This is an impossible situation. I am going to go and test the waters, try to find out what is going on."

It was standing procedure that prisoners could go up to the
office to speak their mind; the door was always open for con-
fessions or information. So Shekar Lingpa went to do this. He
told them whatever, something that they wanted to hear, and
they answered him, "It is easy for you to say these things in
words. But you have to demonstrate your change of heart in
actions as well. We want hard proof of the crimes you have
committed. And we want to know who your co-conspirators
are." This reinforced our concern that we were suspected as
leading plotters in the underground resistance.

I knew that I had particular reason to be concerned. Nyima
Tenzing was being questioned, and I had good reason to be-

lieve that he would reveal the conversation we had had in the hospital line. I decided to go to the authorities, try to convince them of my sincerity, and find out just how much they knew. I went up to the prison office and told them, "I have done many things wrong up to now. I have had a lot of delusions. I confess that the idea that the old Tibet will someday return has been very strong in my thoughts. I was yearning for an independent Tibet. Because I harbored this hope I have not taken seriously the process of reeducation. And at work I have not really made an effort. But finally I have come to realize that I was wrong. These were dreams. In reality, there is no hope for these things. So from now on I will do my best."

The Chinese officer replied, "You say that in your mind you harbored hopes for the return of old Tibet. This is true. But it is not sufficient to tell us what you had in your mind. You have to tell us what you did to bring this about. Who did you contact? What connections have you made? These are the things you have to tell us."

"Aside from thinking these thoughts, I have not talked about my ideas to anyone," I told them. "I haven't discussed it. I never took any actions to bring it about, and I can tell you why: In the days of our old government we had an army, we had weapons, we had money, we had everything, but still we could not defeat you Chinese. Now, we have lost everything. I am in prison. In these circumstances, how could I possibly hope to gain any advantage against you? So of course I never said anything to anyone, I didn't have any relationship with anyone, I didn't do anything about it. Yes, these thoughts came to my mind because the Dalai Lama is in India – so the thoughts come to your mind. Definitely I have had such thoughts. But I never did anything about them."

"You are not talking straight," he said. "You say you were thinking but you were not acting. Now you need to think some more. You will no longer go to work. Now you will just sit and think."

They put me back in the cell and I was left to think things over. For seven months I was held in the cell, under guard, while my cell-mates went out to work. When they returned in the evening they were not allowed to talk to me. It was virtually solitary confinement, and the conditions were very strict. I was not allowed out for exercise. There were two guards posted outside, and if I did the slightest thing wrong they would come in and beat me.

We were all in a constant state of tension, waiting for whatever consequences were going to fall. One night during a study session, one of my cell-mates, a friend named Lhakpa Tsering, got up to piss. We had a silent system of communication: I casually put my second finger on my lips – meaning that he should not confess to any charges. He winked at me – signifying his acknowledgment.

Then at about ten that night a squad of soldiers appeared and two guards came into the cell. They told Lhakpa Tsering, "You have to come with us immediately." As they did this one official kept his eyes on me to see my reaction, and whether any signals passed between us. I just sat there and ignored the whole thing. Then they took him away, and I never saw him again. I found out later that he was transferred to another prison, and he died there. I don't know how; some said he died of natural causes, but I also heard that he was poisoned.

At night they took me up to the office for interrogation. And at every interrogation they asked me the same questions: "What secret plans did you make? Who are your contacts? What have you done?" I was very stubborn and I continued to insist that I never discussed or planned any kind of revolt. I told them that I never even spoke against the Communists.

But they accused me, "You not only formed an underground group within your own unit, but you also made contacts with other work units." I kept insisting that I didn't do anything like that.

After a month of this they got more explicit and accused me of having connections with the Fourth Brigade – which was Nyima Tenzing's unit. I told them, "I only know one person in the Fourth Brigade. His name is Chogyal." He was a known Chinese spy, so I gave them his name. "We were together on the trip to China with the Dalai Lama. So now if I see him on the way to work or something, I say hello. Besides him I have no connections in the Fourth Brigade."

Then they said, "You are not telling the truth. We are going to execute you." They told me to sign a bunch of documents and I just signed them. I figured they were going to kill me anyway.

At last they accused me of having connections with Nyima Tenzing. "What was your connection to Nyima Tenzing?" they asked.

"I don't even know the name," I said.

Then they repeated statements to me, words that I had said to Nyima Tenzing. "I don't know any Nyima Tenzing, but there is one fellow I know as Jola Jola. Maybe it is the same person." This made them furious. They screamed at me, "Look how big a liar you are! Pretending you don't even know the name. We already know everything you said to him!"

That night as I slept in the cell, beside me was Shekar Lingpa. He reached out his hand and poked me. I stretched out my own hand and he slipped a bit of paper into my palm. The light was on in the cell so I could read his note under the blankets. The message read: "Nyima Tenzing committed suicide."

I felt hugely relieved. At my next interrogation I absolutely denied that I knew Nyima Tenzing. Very confidently I told them, "If this Nyima Tenzing said this about me, please let me see him face to face. We can sort this out. Whoever he is, he is trying to frame me. He is telling you lies and I can prove it if you bring him here."

They began praising Nyima Tenzing to the sky. "Nyima Tenzing has told us everything. He will be released very soon, but you are going to be executed."

Boldly I answered, "Okay. I don't mind facing execution. But let me see this Nyima Tenzing. Bring him here and I will prove that I had no such talk with him. He is just trying to put the blame on my shoulders."

After that I felt completely relieved. For myself there was

nothing else to worry about and only one thing concerned my mind: One day, I thought, they will shoot me. When that day comes, what inspiring words should I cry out to the assembled prisoners? How should I put it? This became my main concern. I was worried that the right words would not come.

Actually there was another, more serious concern, and this was the condition of my compatriots. In the underground we had contacts with many different people. How much of these relationships had come out? How much did they know? This worried me greatly, because it affected many other lives.

At that time they executed one Drikung Kagyu lama. As usual we attended the execution. When I came back from the killing the Chinese asked me, "Now what do you think? Do you want to go down that same road? Do you want the same fate? Or do you want to talk to us? What do you want to do?"

"You are perfectly right," I agreed. "If someone has kept anything from the Chinese Government they should be executed. But if one sincerely confesses one's deeds, there shouldn't be any punishment. This is what you say, and I have faith that is what you practice. Since I haven't done anything, how could I say that I did? And even if I said I did something that I didn't do, how could I prove it?"

After that, every day for fifteen consecutive days I was given thamzing. It was during these thamzings that I lost my teeth. I believe the guy who knocked my teeth out was Ringzin Namgyal – he was called Khungrun. The others were clamoring round me, but not really punching, just pretending to beat me. But I think he hit me from below. Afterward I could feel that two teeth had been knocked inward. I pushed at them with my tongue and one fell out. The other stayed in, but you can see now how it was bent back.

But mentally, that thamzing made me very happy. I had connections with so many other prisoners in the underground, I carried around with me so much incriminating information, and these people must have suspected that under interrogation I had revealed all of our plans and all of their names. We were not able to talk to each other, but when I passed my confederates in the prison I could see the worry on their faces. If everything had come out a lot of people would have been killed. It was a very dangerous situation.

But when someone is brought out for thamzing they announce the charges against him. And they ask the same kind of questions they asked in the interrogation sessions, only now all the other prisoners can hear your responses. I was getting thamzing for not telling the truth, for not revealing information, and I continued to maintain that I was just a scapegoat. So it was immediately clear to everyone that I had not confessed, and I had not compromised them. I could see the relief on the faces of my fellow prisoners. I also felt relieved, because any mistrust was cleared away between me and my friends. So, although I felt the physical pain, mentally I was satisfied, I had mental peace.

As for Nyima Tenzing, I don't know for sure why he killed himself, but I have an idea. They were interrogating him very intensively. He told them of my involvement, but I continued to deny everything. This would have thrown the pressure of the interrogation back onto him. This was their procedure: after they elicited accusations from someone, they would confront the accused. But if the accused person doesn't admit to anything, then they go back to the accuser. So Nyima Tenzing was under this terrible pressure; he must have been terribly frightened of the renewed questioning.

The way he killed himself was that he tied a rope around his neck, and the other end around his foot, and then straightened his leg and hanged himself like that. For a rope he probably used his belt; we had cloth belts. If you want to kill yourself, they can't stop you. Some prisoners made ropes out of their blankets to hang themselves.

As it turned out, I was benefitted by two policy changes that were instituted by Beijing beginning in October of 1970. Chou En Lai had stated that, "Those who have committed crimes should also be treated as human beings. Those who have made a mistake should be given a chance to rectify themselves." And on that basis changes were under way in the treatment of prisoners in Tibet as well as China.

Furthermore, although we did not know it at the time, a rule had come from Beijing that officials in the Tibetan Autonomous Region were not authorized to execute former officials of the old Tibetan Government without approval. All such sentences had to be referred to Beijing. I now believe it was this rule, which we discovered much later, that saved my life.

After the two weeks of thamzing I was again thrown into the top security cell and spent the rest of the seven months in virtual solitary confinement – that was from October 1970 when they began my interrogation, until May 15, 1971, when I was returned to the general population, back in a standard cell, and given a work assignment as a tailor. After that, there was never any more mention of my "crime." My life returned to the usual prison routine: In the morning I went to work as a tailor, and in the evening I returned to my cell.

6

Many prisoners who were arrested after the uprising in 1959 were given sentences of fifteen years. So between 1974 and 1975 about seventy-five percent of the prisoners in my work unit were released. My sentence was twenty years, so I was one of those left behind.

What we saw happening to those who were released – those who had not been cooperative in prison, who had bad records – was that even after they got out, life was very difficult for them. They would not stay out for very long before they were thrown back into prison on one pretext or another. They were constantly harassed by the security forces.

I had five more years to serve and I began to give my situation some serious thought: Up until now I have been a tough, resistant prisoner. The Chinese consider me uncooperative. If I stay very negative, as soon as I get out I will have a lot of problems. Now, with only five more years to serve, I had real hopes that I would live to be released. I decided to become a more cooperative prisoner, I began to do my work with discipline and followed the rules.

Once I began to behave a little better, they began to treat me a little better. With so many being released, a lot of the responsible jobs held by prisoners became available. I was selected as the head of an agricultural unit where they grew vegetables for the prison. While I held this position I was happy to be able to be of some benefit to my fellow prisoners.

The gardens supplied vegetables to the prison kitchens, but we also sold excess produce to Chinese staff. They would give us a chit – we were not allowed to handle money – then we would weigh out the order and send the vegetables to be delivered.

We had no control over how much produce went to feed the prisoners, as the prison officials just told us to send a certain amount. But we were the ones who selected and divided up the vegetables and we were able to pick out the best and send it to the prisoners, and deliver the lower grade of produce to the Chinese.

I worked in the gardens like this for three years. Then I was assigned as a tailor to a shop where they made tents. It was difficult work, sewing thick canvas, and generally it was given to uncooperative prisoners. These machines were not electric, but were driven by foot. You had to use a lot of force pedalling those old machines, and they were always breaking down.

In the tailor shops we had a big problem due to a lack of skilled repairmen. There were many very old sewing machines but there were only two mechanics. Even a small fault in the machine meant a tailor had to stop work, and then he couldn't fulfill his quota. He would have to plead again and again to get the mechanics to fix his machine.

I began watching how the mechanics worked, and then doing a little fixing up of this or that machine. When prisoners couldn't get any attention from the regular repairmen they would ask me to fix their machines. Eventually the other tailors asked the prison authorities, "Now Tenpa Soepa knows how to repair these machines. Can't you assign him to be a mechanic in our section?" So in this way I came to be a sewing machine repairman.

For a repairman there was no quota, no fixed amount of work. If a machine was in trouble then you fixed it. Sometimes we were busy, but we didn't have the pressure of the quotas hanging over us. And while working on the machines, we also had a chance to do a little bit of sabotage against the Chinese.

The guards and prison staff didn't understand these machines at all. Every machine had a small adjusting screw. If it was too loose or too tight, the machine would not run properly. You had to adjust this screw just right. So when a machine began running poorly, instead of simply adjusting the screw we would say that a part had broken and we needed a replacement. "Without the part, it won't run," we told them. The officials would order completely unnecessary spare parts, we would install the new parts, or throw them away, and then move on to the next machine with a misadjusted screw.

Of course the prison staff had no idea of the names of the different parts. If we asked them for something, they didn't know what we were talking about. They would tell us to go along with them to the storehouse and we would take the most expensive parts and waste them by putting them into perfectly good machines.

There was another unit in our shop that sewed the heavy paper bags that hold cement. There were only four of these special machines, and they were only available in China – it was impossible to find parts in Tibet. About one hundred people worked in this shop, cutting the paper, stacking the bags, and sewing them. Every day each tailor sewed between five and six thousand paper bags. The machines were old, were in constant use, and were always breaking down. Although we could usually fix them with our tools, we would tell the officials we needed new parts, knowing they had to send all the way to China for the parts. This caused delays and the workers would have to sit around and take it easy. Sometimes they gave us a week to fix some machines, or else, they said, we would be punished. When the officials came around we would make a great show of working on the machines. And by the end of the week we would get the machines running, but in such a way that they would only run for a couple of days, and then break down again.

One idle machine would put many prisoners out of work, and it was a financial loss to the Chinese. But this kind of sabotage actually hurt the prisoners too, because at the end of each year there was an accounting to see if the prison had lived up to its annual quotas. If not, then both the prison officials and the prisoners would get into trouble. So in the tailor shop, if the machines didn't work during the day the staff would make the prisoners work at night, to be sure they met their quota. So our strategy became to fix up the machines just well enough to keep them running for a few days at a time.

In the tailor shop where they made clothes, the machines were electric, and there were about seventy of them. These seventy machines were expected to produce 210,000 garments – shirts and trousers – in one year. That was the annual quota for seventy machines. I also worked there for six years as a tailor. I sewed the seats of Chinese army trousers. In one day I had to sew four hundred of these. That was my work quota. Every day they noted down how many trousers were sewn, and if the shop turned out fewer than its quota they would find out who was holding up the line, and he would be punished. We were treated as if we were machines, not humans.

The attitude of the Chinese to the Tibetan prisoners was demonstrated by the complete absence of vocational training programs for Tibetans. We were in prison for so many years and did so many different kinds of work, but there was no effort whatsoever to give us any real training. If you had a skill before you came to prison you would be assigned to practice that trade, but you would not be taught anything new. Whatever we learned we had to learn ourselves. It was my own initiative that enabled me to become a sewing machine mechanic. I was a tailor for six years. All I ever learned was how to sew one patch on the seat of a pair of trousers. It was the perfect opportunity to train us to be proper tailors. But there was no thought of that. The only ones who learned a trade in those prisons were Chinese prisoners. But the Tibetans – they never even attempted to teach us anything.

While we were in prison we were free labor. They didn't have to pay us anything. Once we got out, if we were trained as proper tailors we would be able to find our own work. But if we didn't have a trade we would be forced to work in their labor brigades, where they paid us very little and worked us very hard. So the intention was always to keep the Tibetans as a body of free or very cheap unskilled labor. There was never any intention to retrain us, to make us more productive citizens.

There were many different types of work that the prisoners did. There was the tailoring, vegetable gardening, tire retreading, and construction work like carpentry, masonry, iron work, and so forth. Those who had to go outside the prison walls to work – like the stone carriers and gardeners – worked from dawn until sunset. There was concern that they might escape if they were outside in the dark, so their workday consisted of all the daylight hours. Those who worked inside the prison – tailors and such – worked from five in the morning until ten at night. We had a twenty-five-minute break for lunch.

In the tailor shop, we were locked in from the outside, and sometimes a guard would come in to check on us. There was no time to go to the toilet because we worked as an assembly line, the garment passing along and each worker doing one job. If one man left the whole system would stop. And if you didn't work fast enough the work would pile up with the man before you.

At night, after dinner, those who worked outside the prison had to go to study sessions where they reviewed the newspapers. Prisoners who worked inside did not have study sessions because they worked right through the evening until they went to sleep.

The main intention of keeping us on such a busy schedule

was so that we had no time to think. If you have leisure time you begin to think about your situation, and that could mean trouble for them. So after work someone would read out the newspapers and the other prisoners would have to listen. Officials would appear and point at a prisoner and ask, "What did you learn today? What is in today's newspaper?" If you weren't listening and couldn't answer, you got a beating.

If there had been some accurate information in these newspapers it wouldn't have been so bad. But it was all lies. Chinese propaganda. We knew it was full of lies. They would say things about Tibet that we knew from our own experience were not true. But every night we had to study their lies.

They had stories about the outside world in which they said that America is a "paper tiger": It looks very fierce but if you hit it, it crumples. They said that in America and Russia the people had nothing to eat. There was tremendous anti-government agitation by the workers, and the government could not control the people. The sun is about to set for America and Russia. They are two countries on the verge of drowning.

If you heard that would you believe it? We read these things, but we had no interest in it at all.

But China! They talked about how China was always progressing, how mighty they are, how many friends they have. China is developing greatly. We have no external debt, no debt to other countries. And internally our people have no debt. We are very rich. China, which has followed the Socialist path, is like the dawn, with the sun about to rise.

This is the kind of thing they put in their newspapers. They would explain each point very thoroughly and precisely, even though it was a complete lie. Although we didn't have very much experience of the outside world, we knew Tibet, and we knew very well the lies they told about old Tibet. And it was plain to see that they were lying about everything else.

For the stonecutters, the work quota was one *khung pang* per day. That would be about fifty slabs of stone, each measuring approximately twelve by eight inches. They would walk out each day at dawn and quarry the stone. They were lowered on ropes down the quarry walls, then they cut small holes, poured in the explosives, and blew out great chunks of stone. All the work was done with hammer and chisel; there was no automatic equipment.

It was a very dangerous job. The explosive charges were laid during the day, and in the evening five or six people would be sent to light the fuses. Then they had to run like hell because the fuses burned quickly, and they would hide under nearby trucks. The blasts would go off, rocks would fly everywhere. Sometimes the dynamite would not detonate. Then the next day, when there were people around, it would go off. Many people died that way.

But as dangerous as it was, from the prisoners' point of view, you would rather be a stonecutter than a tailor. Tailoring was not considered a good job. All year round you had to sit in one room and do the same job over and over. Every day all day sitting indoors with the incessant sound of the machines. You got no exercise so your body became weak. But stonecutting or building construction, though it was risky and hard work, you got outside, sunshine and fresh air, you could see things, and seeing the outside gave you a will to survive.

Every job had a work quota. The quota was always very high, and it always went up. If this year your quota was ten, next year it would be fifteen, and the next year twenty. The quotas would just get higher and higher, because, they said, from doing so much work you have gained experience, so you should be able to produce more.

If you couldn't fulfill your quota, some would get thamzing right away, that night. Some would have their names listed and at the end of the year, during the Winter Studies, they held a big meeting and read out a list of those who had failed to fill their quotas, and these prisoners would have their prison sentences extended.

The Winter Studies took place in the cold months when work was curtailed. The ground and the water were frozen and they couldn't build, so there was no work for the construction laborers. The tailors, however, might have completed their

quota for the year, and there would be a break before they
started the new year's work. So for two or three months in the
winter they held these study sessions.

This was supposed to be a process of self-examination and
evaluation of your own work during the year. They would tell
each prisoner, "You have to examine yourself. Have you developed new ideas? Have you changed your old ideas? Did
you say anything against the People's Republic of China?
What are your hopes and expectations for the future?" In this
way you had to evaluate yourself. First we had to discuss it
among ourselves, then the officials would come around and
accuse certain prisoners of not being honest.

Finally they held a big closing meeting. There they would
announce that they had decided to increase the sentences of
certain prisoners, or to punish or give thamzing to other prisoners. During the Winter Studies there would be thamzing going
on regularly, and there were periodic executions. In theory the
Winter Studies were called political reform study groups or
Communist study groups, but in fact they were just devices to
increase work output or to punish prisoners.

The recalcitrant prisoners, those who refused to submit to
the Chinese ideas, who refused to pay lip service to the Communist propaganda, these prisoners would be transferred to do
the most dangerous work. They would be sent to do blasting
at the rock quarries, or sent off to work in the mines.

They called it education. They said, "We are going to make
you into a new person!" But their purpose was not to make a
new person. Their purpose was to squeeze the Tibetans for
their hard labor, and when they were finished, to eradicate the
Tibetan race.

It didn't take much to get yourself thrown into prison. It was
easy. If you uttered the slightest word against the Communist
Party you were put in prison. In fact, the more prisoners they
got, the better. They were happy to have more prisoners because it meant more free labor. In Tibet, the main source of
production for the Chinese was Tibetan prisoners. Coal mining, other types of mining, all kinds of life-endangering work

was given to the prisoners. They could not refuse to go. They did not have to be paid. Only food had to be given, and what food! If they did not have the prisoners they would have had to pay the general public high salaries to do these jobs.

The Chinese really went out of their way to create prisoners. Everyone who showed sympathy for the Tibetan people, anyone concerned with the public welfare, was rounded up and thrown into prison. For example, there was the chandzoe – the manager – of Tsang Tanag Gompa, a monastery in Tsang. In 1958 he performed a special religious ritual, called a *Tor Gya*, which was intended to eliminate negative conditions for his local community. He had no political involvement, and he had no involvement at all in the 1959 uprising. But he was the type of person who cared about the welfare of the people, and he was widely respected and looked to as a leader of the community. The Chinese had nothing to accuse him of, but they arrested him anyway, and the charge was, "In 1958 that Tor Gya you performed was in order to aid the reactionaries. That is proof that you are working for the reactionaries." For that "crime" he was sentenced to twenty years. We were both released from prison at the same time.

After the initial wave of arrests, right after the uprising, the Chinese continued to hunt down and pick up individuals who were still living in society. Anyone who had anything to do with the Reform Office or any new institutions was rounded up. In general anyone who seemed to have a social awareness and progressive attitude was put in prison.

Once everyone was imprisoned, selections were made. Those who held on to their ideas, their nationalist feelings, their sympathy for the Tibetan people, those who did not readily submit to Chinese reeducation, they were sent to do the most dangerous work. The intention was gradually to eliminate these people.

There were several stages in the process of destroying the Tibetan people. First of all, in 1959, many people were killed in the fighting. When the fighting was over the survivors were rounded up and imprisoned. They were not all shot right away; rather they were killed gradually by the momo gun – feeding the prisoners only one momo a day. Starvation. Of those who survived the years of famine, many were eventually executed or died in thamzing.

The Chinese have always claimed that we were put in prison because we fought against the Chinese. But there were many people in prison who did not fight, who were put in prison merely because they cared about their own race. And that is why I feel that the real Chinese intention was to eliminate the Tibetan identity.

7

My twenty-year sentence was due to end on March 20, 1979, but to demonstrate their generosity of spirit the Chinese authorities released me seven days early. I was released with six others who were serving twenty-year sentences. It was one day before Losar – Tibetan New Year.

On the day of our release we were summoned to the office where they told us, "Today you will be released. Those of you who have family to stay with, you can spend Losar with your families. You can stay for three days, then you come back. Those without families can go into town during the day, but you have to come back in the evenings."

We gathered up our bedding and belongings and everything was thoroughly inspected. It was serious business, these final inspections. You were not allowed to take anything out of the prison with you. We remembered Lobsang Gyaltsen, a retired civil servant who wasn't even in the government at the time of the uprising. He was imprisoned in Drabchi until 1974. While serving his time he began writing a detailed account of the life and conditions and events in the prison. He wrote it in tiny letters on whatever bits and scraps of paper he could scrounge. He captured every detail, even making notes of when an airplane passed over the prison. And this chronicle he hid inside his mattress. In 1974 he was released. On his way out, in his last inspection, they found his papers. He was immediately rearrested and we never saw him again. We heard later that he was executed for this crime.

I passed through the prison gates and immediately walked over to the labor brigade that was just beside the prison. I had a number of friends staying there, Kasur Shewo and others who had served fifteen-year sentences. I left my baggage with them, and I headed down to Lhasa. I had not been in Lhasa for twenty years, so there was a lot to see. So much had changed I could hardly find my way. But from my memory and navigating by the landscape I was able to estimate where things should be, and found my way to my family's house.

When I left the prison I was still wearing my black prison uniform, the only clothes I had. My friends in the labor brigade said it wasn't auspicious for me to go into Lhasa in these ragged old clothes. I told them, "I don't feel at all inauspicious wearing these clothes. This uniform was provided to me because I was working for my country and people. I didn't get it for committing a crime. I am not ashamed of these clothes." But they refused to let me go out looking like that. They brought their own clothes and loaned me something respectable to wear.

So, slowly I made my way through to Lhasa. My father had told me in his letters that he was staying at the home of my younger sister. Their place is on an upper floor. When I reached the courtyard I found a boy of about fifteen. My father was called Pa Lungta-la, so I asked this boy, "Where is Pa Lungta-la's house?" The boy led me up the stairs. It turned out that this boy was my nephew, the son of my younger sister, but he was born while I was in prison so I had never seen him. A whole generation had come of age while I spent my lifetime in prison.

I entered the house and I called out to my father, "Pa-la!" He was ill and lying in bed. He said, "Who are you? Who is it?"

"I am Tenpa Soepa. Your son."

Father answered, "Why have you come? What are you doing here?"

"I was released. I was released. I am coming back," I said.

"If you were released from prison, where is your bedding?" he asked me.

"I left my bedding with some people at the labor brigade," I told him.

With this my father's doubts – his worries that I might have escaped from prison – were relieved. He started to cry. "My only wish was to see you again," he said. "I hoped so very much to see you once again before I died. Now my hopes have come true." And he cried.

That night we talked and talked until finally it was time to go to bed. My niece – my elder sister's daughter – was looking after my father. She was twenty-five years old. When I was arrested she was five. I didn't recognize her and she didn't recognize me. During the day she worked as a cook at a construction site, and at night she took care of my father.

Before we went to bed my father told her, "My son has come back. Tomorrow is the first day of Losar, the New Year. Inside that cabinet is a little bit of rice. Let's cook that. Make that rice for the first day of Losar."

She began searching in the cabinet just behind my father, which held his altar. She looked and looked but she couldn't find the rice. She asked me to help her find it. We found piles of old clothes and rags and junk. Underneath all this, wrapped in black rags, we found about a half kilo of rice.

Father said, "Someone gave this to me. Four or five years ago. I have kept it until the day you returned. I wanted to eat this rice with my son."

Then he told his granddaughter, "Tomorrow is Losar, so make *chemar*." Chemar is a special arrangement of tsampa and barley and butter in a decorated container, and the grain is offered to all the guests who come to visit your house on the New Year. When we were about to go to sleep the girl quietly asked me, "How do you make chemar?" She was twenty-five years old but she did not know how to make chemar, which is one of our most honored and well-known customs. The Chinese had so suppressed all these traditions since 1959 that they had wiped out our cultural traditions. So I prepared chemar, putting in a little tsampa, and then a bit of butter.

My niece was very worried, "If we make chemar like that, won't the Chinese come?" I reassured her that there was nothing to worry about, nobody would come.

Traditionally in Tibet, for a whole month before Losar we begin to make preparations. We start making new clothes and preparing foods for the occasion. Here, I arrived one day before Losar and they had not begun any preparations at all. They were not allowed to make the traditional preparations. They were not allowed to celebrate Losar, the most important traditional festival in Tibet.

And as for this rice, this half kilo of rice, normally people couldn't get rice. It had become a precious commodity. So father had kept this precious gift for all this time, to celebrate when I returned. So the next morning we cooked it. We ate the rice, we drank some tea. Aside from this rice all they had to eat in the house was about two kilos of tsampa. Since the rice was not enough to fill us up my father said, "If you are still hungry, you can have pak. Make some pak." When I saw that there were only two kilos I thought, if I eat enough to fill myself up, these two will end up with nothing to eat. With that thought it was hard for me to eat anything. I ate a little bit of pak, but not enough to fill me up.

All this was quite shocking to me, to see how Tibetans were reduced to "celebrating" Losar under Chinese rule. But later in the morning it became more cheerful, as many old friends, former prisoners and relatives began to stop by for traditional New Year greetings, and especially to see me after so many years in prison. They brought gifts of various foods, the fried pastry called *kapsey* and many delicious things like that. And so we ended up having a lovely Losar together, with plenty to eat.

In fact, it turned out to be a bit too much. It is considered impolite not to take at least a little bit of the food that your guests bring as gifts. So whatever our friends brought, I had to taste. For twenty years I had been eating the most basic prison food, and now all in one day I was overwhelmed with a rich variety – sweet tea, Tibetan butter tea, barley beer (called *chang*), kapsey, and so forth. I had a little bit of each thing, and I ate so many different things that the next day I got sick.

On the evening of my third day of freedom, I had to return to the prison.

On March 17th they assembled all the prisoners who were about to be released, at the office of the Tibetan Autonomous Region. They made a formal announcement that we were free, and gave each of us a pass certifying that we were no longer prisoners. There were 114 of us from Drabchi Prison.

Formally, we were free men. But we were not free to return to our lives like normal civilians. We had to go to live and work in a labor brigade. I was assigned to work in the labor brigade of Drabchi Prison, repairing sewing machines. We were free to leave only on Sundays, and we always had to return by Sunday night. We were never allowed to stay outside the labor brigade overnight. I remained there from March until December of 1979.

Actually, we continued to work together with prisoners. The main difference was that in prison at night the cell door was locked. And when you went to work a guard escorted you. In the labor brigade the doors were not locked, there were no guards, and on Sunday you could go to Lhasa. Otherwise, the life was not much different from prison. We still slept in rows on the floor, with simple mats for bedding. We had five or six people to a room. They paid us a salary of – I think it was forty-one *yuan* per month. From that salary you had to buy your own clothes and you had to pay for your food and all your personal needs. Everything had to come out of that small amount.

On December 1, 1979 there was a big transfer. Some from our labor brigade were sent to Lhoka to do agricultural work. I was sent with another group to a labor brigade at Uti Tod in Sangyip Prison, another large prison complex in Lhasa. There I was assigned to work as an automobile mechanic, I suppose because I knew how to repair sewing machines. Of course I didn't know anything at all about auto mechanics, but my job was to assist Chinese mechanics who worked in the shop.

Once again this job afforded some opportunities to do a little sabotage. One of our jobs was to reassemble engines after they had been overhauled. We would drop tiny slivers of metal into the cylinders, and then close up the engine. If you did this the vehicle would not run for more than a week. Then they would have to bring it back to the shop again for more major repairs. We caused quite a bit of damage this way.

All of us Tibetans, we were constantly thinking about ways in which we could harm the Chinese. We all had this motivation and we always looked for opportunities.

I spent about eight months in this job, and then I was given permission to leave the labor brigade and go home. This came about as a result of the changing policy of the Chinese in Tibet. In 1979 they announced that they were opening the doors of Tibet. Tibetans living abroad would be free to visit their homeland, and Tibetans inside would be allowed to visit relatives in other countries. Announcements of the new policy were broadcast on the radio and they included lists of names of people who had been released from prison. These broadcasts were monitored in Dharamsala and the names circulated among the refugee community in India and Nepal. Tibet had been so completely sealed off that the fate of many of these survivors was unknown to their relatives abroad.

The former Kalon, Kundeling, who now lives in Rajpur, India, was a relative of mine and he heard that my name was mentioned on the radio and that I was probably still alive in Tibet. In October, 1979 the first Delegation of representatives of His Holiness made their fact-finding tour of Tibet. Kundeling sent a letter for me with the Delegation and asked them to try to find me.

This was not an easy task. I was still living in the labor brigade and they were not able to locate me. I had a friend, a fellow prisoner, who also had a letter waiting for him with the Delegation and he was given permission to go and collect his letter. One of the representatives, Tashi Topgyal, showed this fellow an album full of photographs of old Tibet, of old government officials, and asked him if he knew any of the people. My friend said, "Yes, I know some of them."

"Who do you know?"

"I know this one, Kundeling," he said.

"Oh that's good," said Tashi Topgyal. "He has a relative here, Tenpa Soepa, and we have a letter for him. But we haven't been able to locate him. Can you find him?"

"Yes, I can find him. We are mates," my friend said.

So he came back very excited and told me, "The Delegation brought a letter for you. They are looking for you."

I decided I'd better go and speak to the Chinese security officers. I couldn't just go to visit the Delegation openly, without permission, and I couldn't go secretly because other prisoners had heard us talking about it. I went to see the Chinese officials and told them, "There is a letter for me with the Delegation, from my relatives in India. Is it alright if I go to collect it?"

They told me to come back tomorrow for an answer. The next day I returned and they said, "Who is this relative? What is your relation? How can you prove that this is really your uncle who sent this letter?" They knew everything about my family and background. It was all there in my file, and I had told them these things so many times, in so many interrogations, but they pretended they still did not know. But once again I gave them the information. And then they gave me permission to go and collect the letter.

Two or three days later a Chinese official at my work place came over to have a chat with me. "Did your letter arrive?" he asked.

"It arrived," I said.

"What did it say?"

"It said, 'We heard from the radio that you were released, but we do not know where you are. We are fine here. This place is fine. Is there any chance that you could come to visit us here in India? Please write to us.' That's what the letter said," I told him.

A few days after that two people from the Chinese Security Office came to see me. They said, "Now that you are released, how are things? Is everything fine with you? Are things alright with your work? Do you have any problems in your life? Do you have any special needs or anything you want to tell us?"

"Right now I don't have any problems," I told them. "I just have my work. If I need any help from you I will definitely let you know."

"If you were to go back to Lhasa, is there anyone there who could support you?" they asked.

"I only have my old father who is sick, and I would have to look after him. I have nephews and nieces, but they are young and doing construction work. They can hardly make ends meet now, so I don't think they could take me on."

Then they asked, "Don't you have relatives abroad?"

"Yes, I have." And I told them who my relatives were.

"And didn't you get a letter from them?"

"Yes, a letter arrived."

"And what was in the letter?"

Again I repeated the message in the letter.

"And the person who gave you this letter, what did he say?" they asked.

"He said that my relatives wanted me to know that if it was possible, it would be very nice if I could come to India for a visit."

"And how did you reply?" they asked.

"I told him I didn't know if I would be able to come. I don't know if people are allowed to go. I told him to tell my relatives that I am fine. I am working in a labor brigade. That is all I said."

"Do you have the wish to go?" they inquired.

"Yes, I have the wish to go," I said.

"If you have the desire to go, you can go," they told me.

"How can I go?" I said. "I am not allowed to go, am I?"

"It is okay. We will help you to arrange it." This is what the two security men told me. "But before that," they said, "while you are still staying here, don't you have any problems? What are your hopes and aspirations? We want to help you." They kept pressing me on this. I insisted that I had no problems but if I did face any problems I would let them know.

A month later they visited me again. After some idle conversation they asked, "Did you receive another letter?"

"Yes, I got a second letter," I said.

"Did you send a reply?"

"Am I permitted to send a reply?" I asked.

"How dare you say that!" They acted offended. "People are going back and forth to India now. Why shouldn't you be able to send a letter. You should answer their letter. Go on and send a reply."

I said, "If I send a letter, what should I say? Should I tell them I am coming there or not?"

"If you want to go, that's fine. We will help you to go. So you can tell them that you are coming. Go on and write to them."

"How do I do this? What are the procedures if I want to go for a visit?" I asked them. They told me to make an application through my work place. It would then work its way through the proper channels.

I went ahead and put in an application requesting permission to visit my relatives in India. That was around January, 1980. Then I waited a long time but heard no more about it. I went to enquire many times about my application but I got no reply.

By then the Second Delegation was on its way. I searched out the Chinese security people and told them I had put in my application. I explained that, "I am getting letters from my relatives in which they say they have invited me to visit but they have had no reply. 'Don't you have any concern for your relatives?' they are saying. 'Please send us a clear reply.' Should I tell them that I have requested permission but I am not being permitted to go? I don't want to say to them that I don't wish to go. They will think I have no feeling for them. I don't know how to reply. And soon the Second Delegation will be here. The First Delegation brought the letter, so the Second Delegation will surely ask for me. What should I do?"

The security officers told me, "You tell them you will be leaving very soon. Don't worry."

On June 25, 1980 I received formal permission to go to India for six months, and I received a loan from my work place to cover expenses. But it was another month before I could arrange transport to the border. On the night of July 24th the Second Fact-finding Delegation arrived in Lhasa. The next morning I set off from Lhasa for the Nepalese border.

Just before I left the two security officers came to see me. They said, "When you arrive in India, you shouldn't get the notion that this is a free country, now I can say anything I like. You must report the facts: That here in Tibet we are giving freedom to the people and improving the situation. Besides reporting these facts you shouldn't say anything else. Otherwise it won't be very good for you when you return. If you just go and visit your relatives and then come back without making a nuisance of yourself, then when you come back you will be treated in accordance with your behavior."

Throughout this process many of my old friends from prison urged me not to request a pass to leave Tibet. They told me the story of the Kuomintang who disappeared. When the Communists took over China many Kuomintang were arrested. Years later, when they were released, the same question was asked of them – did they want to go visit their relatives in Taiwan? Many of these former soldiers said yes, and they were given permission to go. But these people never reached Taiwan. Nor were they ever seen again in China. They were lost somewhere in between. Their whereabouts were never traced. So, my friends advised me, I too might disappear if I asked to visit my relatives in India.

We knew very well the Chinese technique in which they would release a prisoner, treat him well, then send him off somewhere. They used this method if they wanted to flush out some document or hidden treasure that the prisoner had not revealed. When he left on a journey he would collect the treasure and take it with him. Then the Chinese would suddenly seize him on the way and he would disappear.

I knew all this, and I was constantly worried that they would catch me if I carried any secret messages or documents. But I had made up my mind. I thought, whatever happens I want to go, and I am going to apply for permission. I wasn't that confident that I would ever reach India, but I was determined to try.

But before I left I found a good knife and put it in my pocket. I thought, if they seize me on the road I will defend myself, and if necessary I will kill whoever comes to take me. This was my only thought, I took this knife and didn't show it to anyone. As I travelled, when I lay down at night on the road, I never took my clothes off. I just kept this knife with me and ready at all times.

I travelled from Lhasa by bus, down to Dram, on the border with Nepal. When I arrived at Dram I had a terrible scare. I was staying at the house of an acquaintance I had. I was sitting there when suddenly, from outside, someone started calling my name, asking me to come out. When I heard my name being called, here in a place where I knew hardly anyone, I became very suspicious. I immediately thought there is something wrong here and I got very frightened. I gave no reply and just sat there.

Then the person who was calling my name opened the door and came in. He said, "You strange man. Why didn't you come out when I called you?" I recognized him. It was a fellow prisoner, a man who had also been released recently. He told me that he had been sent there to study the conditions of the Sherpa people who lived along the border. He had just heard that I had arrived in town and so he came to see me.

I didn't believe his story. I thought, the Chinese have sent someone I know in order to trick me, and now they will try to seize me. I held the knife inside my chuba. Normally, when this fellow and I used to meet we had a habit of jostling each other, kind of wrestling playfully. Fortunately, on that day he didn't try to grab me or play our usual game. Because if he had come near me, if he had tried to touch me, I was ready to use my knife. But since I was not acting very friendly, in fact I was looking downright hostile, he didn't try to play with me. Finally I asked him, "Why have you come?"

He said, "I came to invite you to stay with me, the food is better and it is more comfortable."

"I don't wish to move," I told him. "I will stay here." And that was the end of it.

Later on I found out that there was nothing wrong with this guy. That he just happened to be working there, as he said. But if he had come toward me, to joke around, I would have used my knife.

The next day I boarded a bus down to the Friendship Bridge that marks the border between Tibet and Nepal. My mind was clouded with fear. It was the same dark terror I had felt twenty years earlier when they loaded us on trucks and drove us out of Lhasa to meet our fates in the unimagined prisons of China. But this time it was not the destination I feared, it was the lurking suspicion that I would never reach it.

Halfway across the bridge there is a red line, the far side of that line is Nepal, the near side is Chinese-occupied Tibet. At the bridge gate everyone gets out of the bus and all the luggage is unloaded. So many people had asked me to carry gifts to their relatives abroad that my luggage had become impossibly heavy. All the other passengers were carrying their luggage toward the red line, but mine was too heavy, I couldn't manage it. I asked someone to help me get it up on my back and I struggled along with it. But just before I reached the red line I couldn't go any further. I collapsed. Then two other travellers came over to help me. Together we lifted the heavy bags and proceeded across the line.

When I crossed the bridge I stood in Nepal and I looked back at the Chinese border guards. I felt so relieved and light and happy. I watched the Chinese soldiers on the other side and I thought, "Eat shit!"

I reached Kathmandu on August 1, 1980. In Kathmandu my mind was flooded with the images and impressions and discoveries of a whole new world. It was all so peculiar: Wherever you went, in the bazaar, on the streets, the people walked very slowly. Whatever they were doing, they were taking it easy. Everywhere you saw women just sitting in the windows of their houses watching the world go by. It seemed as if no one had any work to do. In Lhasa, under the Chinese, you saw people in the markets very early in the morning, or again in the evening. But in the middle of the day there was hardly anyone on the streets because people were working. In Kathmandu at all hours there were people shopping, women strolling majestically along the streets, and I wondered, what do these people do? How do they live?

Also, the clothes they wore were so different. The women wore these long skirts – saris – that drag on the ground, and the men wore such tight trousers. How do these people work in clothes like that? I wondered. If we wore such clothes in Lhasa we wouldn't be able to work. Our pants would split open.

I stayed with relatives in Kathmandu. We would go out for walks together, and whenever we went out I was always the first to reach our destination. I always ended up walking way out in front of them, because I walked so fast. They would stroll along at a leisurely pace, while I was racing off, and they would tell me, "Tenpa-la, calm down. Don't be in such a hurry. Take it easy. There is no rush."

Even smoking a cigarette, I would finish a whole cigarette in the time it would take them to smoke one quarter. They smoked so slowly. But in Tibet, we were always working, and our breaks were so short that there was no time for a proper smoke, we had to quickly consume a cigarette and go back to work. I realized then how much of our behavior is determined by the habits and customs of our society.

My relatives and friends in Kathmandu were extremely kind and hospitable to me. I hadn't seen them in so many years, and they would invite me to their houses and serve me their very best food. I would sit at the table and look at this delicious food, but I never felt comfortable eating. I would think about all the people who were hungry in Tibet, the people living on one meal a day, the people in prison who couldn't even get enough food to fill their stomachs.

I had an urgent desire to get to India to meet His Holiness the Dalai Lama, but arranging the Indian visa was going to take a long time. Now that I was so close, I could not bear one extra day, even one extra hour's delay. So I decided to stay in Nepal only one week, and then, with a friend, I left for India without a visa.

On the Nepalese side we arranged for a car to take us across the border in the middle of the night. At two A.M. the driver picked us up and he began driving through all kinds of obscure back roads. We had been warned with stories of dishonest drivers who might deliver us into the hands of thieves, so I was quite worried. My friend knew a bit about the roads, so we agreed that if the driver took us in the wrong direction, or tried to rob us, we would stab him. Then I would drive the car and my friend would navigate us across the border. But there was no problem, and by dawn we were at the bus station on the Indian side of the border.

We travelled by bus and then train to Dharamsala, but when we arrived we discovered that His Holiness had gone on a visit to Ladakh. So I left Dharamsala and went to Rajpur to meet my relative, Kundeling. He was very happy to see me, but also extremely anxious because I didn't have any papers. "Without papers they will arrest you," he warned me. So for a week I stayed in an inner room of their house and didn't go outside. And then I returned to Nepal to organize my residential permit to live in India.

Crossing back into Nepal was easy. They didn't care about passports or visas, they just treated me as a Tibetan refugee living in India and all we had to do was give the border guard a little *bakshish* and they let us through.

It took about three months to get my Indian permit in Kathmandu. Once again I crossed the border, this time with proper papers, and on November 10, 1980 I was able to have an audience with His Holiness the Dalai Lama. For twenty-one years I had dreamt of this day, and now this prayer that I had held in my heart, day and night, for all those years, was being fulfilled.

My first audience with His Holiness lasted for three hours. But in those three hours I could hardly speak. I was so overwhelmed with emotion. His Holiness was showing so much concern for me. It was a strange feeling, a flood of great happiness blended with tremendous sadness, a feeling I can't describe.

His Holiness, seeing that it was difficult for me to speak, said, "We will meet again tomorrow. It will be more relaxed." And so the next day after lunch I had a second audience for three hours. Even then, I was only able to express perhaps ten percent of the things I had on my mind. Although I had thought so many times of the things I wanted to say, when I got there it was as if my mind was shattered with emotion. It was difficult to collect my thoughts, and even when I could think it was hard to speak.

Finally His Holiness asked me, "Will you stay here or will you return to Tibet?"

I replied, "Whatever you wish me to do. If you tell me to stay I will stay. If you tell me to go back I will go."

My father was eighty years old when the letters began arriving from India. I asked my father whether I should seek permission to go to India or not. I told him, "You are my father, you brought me up. I will follow your advice, whatever you say. If you tell me to stay here in Tibet, I will stay. If you think I should leave, I will go. Right now, I don't know if I will get the permission, but you tell me what you think I should do."

At first my father did not reply. He took a week to think it over, and then he told me, "It would be better if you go."

I told him, "If you think I should go I will apply for permission. If I get permission, I will go. But once I reach there, I cannot promise that I will come back. When I was a young man you put me into government service. You trained me to serve the government and the people of Tibet. Our leader is His Holiness the Dalai Lama, and as a government servant I will have to follow his wish. If he tells me to stay in India, I will stay there. If he tells me to come back here, I will come back. I will follow his decision, which will be the most beneficial for all of our people."

"That is fine," my father said. "You apply for permission."

In this way, I had left with the understanding of my father. He knew that we might never meet again. I was able to tell His Holiness, with a sincere heart, that I had come to serve the Tibetan people, in whatever way he thought best.

His Holiness said, "So, if that is the situation, then you should stay here and work." Since then I have been here, in Dharamsala, and now in Mundgod, working for the Tibetan Government-in-Exile in different capacities.

Some time after I arrived in India I heard that my father passed away. But I felt at peace with this news. It was alright. He died in Tibet. And he died knowing that I was once again working for the Tibetan Government, doing the work that he raised me to do. And I knew that he was happy.

From the beginning I faced many difficulties in this work. First of all, the climate is very hot. Secondly, I don't know the language. Even if I wanted to do something simple, buy something from a store, order food in a restaurant, I needed an interpreter. Because of these problems, for a while I wondered if I would be of any use here. I thought I might die just from the climate, and perhaps I should return to Tibet.

But there was a particular reason why I felt I had to do my best to stay on. When I was in Tibet we were hearing rumors that the Tibetan Government-in-Exile was dismissing all the old officials who had previously served in Tibet before the Chinese invasion. When I left Tibet many old-timers told me there was no point in going to India. "They won't take care of you and you won't be able to work for the government there," they said. Now I was in India, and I had been given work with the government. I knew that if I went back it would confirm the rumors that old-time officials were being neglected, and it might do great harm. So I put all my effort into staying here and making it work.

I was the first among the old Tibetan officials who came out in the second wave of refugees, in the early 1980s. When I was

242   *A Strange Liberation*

able to get a position in the Tibetan Government, my success encouraged others who were still in Tibet, and after me, many others have come and are now working here.

Today we can honestly say that we have a government combined of the old and the new. We have Tibetans who have lived in India for over thirty years, young people who were born and raised in India, working together with those who came out in the 1980s, and even recent escapees, people who escaped from Tibet very recently, working together in the Tibetan Government.

8

I have given you a basic account of what happened to me personally in Tibet. Now I would like to discuss the events that took place in our country in more general terms.

First of all, it is important to realize that Drabchi Prison, where I served most of my time, was not like other prisons in Tibet. It was in the capital of the Tibetan Autonomous Region, it was the most visible prison in the country. It was known as "Prison Number One." Most of the government officials and high lamas were imprisoned there. The officials who ran it were high-ranking officers and it was under the watchful eye of even higher Chinese Government or Party officials. It was one prison where the jailers actually had to follow regulations and couldn't treat the prisoners according to their whim. For these reasons the conditions were a bit better than at other prisons. Although the rules were very strict, we did not suffer the same kind of brutality that was common in prisons that were situated in less visible places. In general, the more remote a prison was, the more brutal the practices were. In most of Tibet's prisons jailers were free to use whatever kind of torture and cruelty they could imagine, and there was no end to the variety of tortures that were used.

In Drabchi, the government-mandated food rations included special consideration for former government officials, abbots of major monasteries, and important lamas. These special categories were allowed a slightly larger ration than the common prisoner. It was fifteen kilos of tsampa, one kilo of butter, and one kilo of meat per month.

Now, this was the official ration on paper. Of course the prison staff who actually measured out the food were Chinese, not Tibetans. We were never sure how much they were giving us, and how much they were keeping for their own profit. If you think about it now, on paper the ration seems like it should be enough, at least enough to fill your belly. But our bellies were never full. One problem was that we were doing hard work, putting out a lot of energy and so we required more food. The other problem was that we simply were not getting the stated ration.

Another drain on the prison food supplies was the livestock that they were raising at the prison. There were two hundred pigs, one hundred chickens and about five hundred rabbits. The meat from these animals went to the prison staff, not to the prisoners, but the food that the animals ate was taken from the prisoners' food. It was not leftovers; it came from the main storeroom for the prisoners' food.

During the Cultural Revolution this preferential system was turned upside down. From 1966 to 1976 the rations declined for everyone in Prison Number One, and the ordinary prisoners were given better treatment than the VIPs. The normal ration for general prisoners was supposed to be eleven and a half kilos of tsampa, one half kilo of butter, and one half kilo of meat per month. In the years of the Cultural Revolution the ordinary prisoners were not even getting this, and the officials and lamas were getting still less. And to make matters worse, during those years we were not allowed to receive food packages from our families. We were allowed no contact whatsoever. For ten years we could not even write letters back and forth.

But regardless of what the Tibetan prisoners were getting at

Drabchi, the Chinese prisoners were getting better food because they had a completely separate kitchen. From the Chinese kitchen they served rice, meat, and vegetables, which we did not get. The excuse for this was that the Chinese prisoners were not used to eating tsampa. Needless to say, when we were at Jiuzhen the authorities did not give us Tibetans the consideration of serving our traditional foods – meat, butter and tsampa.

We were hungry. But you were not allowed to say you were hungry. If you said out loud that you were hungry you got thamzing. They said, "You have dishonored the Communist system by saying that our prisoners are hungry. You are prisoners, you have no right to say such a thing."

Now, during all those years that I was in prison, what were the conditions among the general public? After the 1959 uprising the Chinese instituted radical land reform with a policy called *Su Dab-De Thob*, which means "harvest to the tiller." They confiscated all the large estates and for some time there was chaos; no one was cultivating the fields at all. Then they began redistributing the land to the peasant farmers.

In 1961 they instituted the program of "The Three Cleanlinesses," to eradicate three evils of Tibetan society: the feudalistic system, reactionary forces, and tax and compulsory labor. The main object of this campaign was to flush out those who had been involved in the 1959 uprising but had escaped arrest. They wanted to catch and put away all the sympathizers that they didn't know about, all those with relationships to politically active people. This program stalled in 1962 when war broke out with India and the Chinese had to focus all their attention on that.

The years 1964 and 1965 were taken up with "Evaluation and Education," which was an attempt to root out the connections and sources of the Panchen Rinpoche's "70,000 Chinese character" memorandum concerning the independence of Tibet.

In 1966 the Cultural Revolution began, and from then until 1970, in the worst excesses of the Cultural Revolution, thousands of monasteries and statues were destroyed, and monks and nuns were disrobed, humiliated, and killed. The program was called "Demolish the Four Olds – Establish the Four News." The "Four Olds" were old ideology, old culture, old habits and old customs. The "Four News" were Maoist ideology, proletarian culture, communist customs and habits.

What this program amounted to was an effort to eliminate any evidence of an independent and distinct Tibet. All documents and monuments that demonstrated Tibetan independence were destroyed. Anything that suggested a relationship with China was protected.

For example, in Lhasa are the two most sacred Buddha images in Tibet. One is the Ramoche Jowo and the other is the Tsuglakhang Jowo. The latter was brought to Tibet by the Chinese princess bride of the Great King Songtsen Gampo. This image was protected and never damaged in the Cultural Revolution. The Ramoche Jowo was brought by Songtsen Gampo's other bride, a princess from Nepal. It was totally destroyed. This vividly illustrates the process that was under way in the Cultural Revolution of preserving all evidence that Tibet belonged to China, and destroying all evidence contradictory to that.

The destruction of Tibetan culture and habits was everywhere, and we did not escape it in prison. We had to destroy anything that was Tibetan – all our Tibetan clothes, chubas, Tibetan shoes, and we had to wear only Chinese clothes. Tibetan women traditionally wear their hair very long, Chinese women wear it short. The Tibetan women had to cut off their long braids and wear their hair short.

We even had to change the way we ate! Our custom is to eat while sitting cross-legged on a couch. But we were not allowed to do this. We either had to eat standing up, or sitting on a chair like the Chinese. In this way they tried to destroy every small detail of Tibetan identity.

Place names, city names, street names, were changed from

their ancient Tibetan names to Chinese. Even the Tibetans who worked for the Chinese Government made a show of sinicizing their names, adding an "-ee" sound to the end of their Tibetan names to make them sound Chinese.

The Cultural Revolution began as a struggle between two opposing political factions, both of which were instigated by the Chinese power structure itself. There was the Opposition Faction and the Cooperative Faction. But in Tibet the struggle evolved into a fight in which these two Chinese factions joined together against a third group – the Tibetans.

The Cooperative Faction was the Red Guard, which was terrorizing the whole country, demolishing monasteries, and so forth. The Opposition Faction evolved from the group of people who were opposed to such radical action and wanton destruction. This group naturally attracted the Tibetans' sympathy. It became bigger and bigger, until the situation shifted into a battle between the Tibetans and the Chinese.

At its peak, regions of Tibet were in open revolt, real civil war, and the Tibetans were successful in recapturing control of certain regions for a time. The peak of the rebellion was from 1967 to 1969. For example, there was the revolt I mentioned in Nyemo, where a nun called Kunsang Chodron led an uprising that killed all the Chinese cadres and gained control of the area in a very short time. The rebels were very strong and held control of the region for quite a while. Eventually heavy reinforcements were brought in from China and the Tibetans were suppressed. Forty or fifty key rebels were captured, and we heard that most of them were taken to a riverbank and shot, and their bodies floated down the river. But Ani Kunsang Chodron herself and about fifteen of her comrades were brought to Lhasa for a public execution.

Similarly in Kham, in the Driru and Phenpa regions, there was fierce fighting between Tibetan rebels and the Chinese faction. Finally the army came in and ruthlessly suppressed the rebellion. They massacred or arrested nearly the whole adult population. Not just the men but the grown women of the community were taken away as well. There weren't even old women left because they too had risen up against the Chinese. We heard that in Driru and Phenpa after the rebellion there was almost no one left but young girls. And for these girls, if they didn't grow food they wouldn't eat. So the young girls had to plow and plant and harvest the crops in order to survive.

We have already described how the prisoners died of starvation in the early 1960s. But the famine was not confined to the prisons – it also killed many thousands among the civilian population of Tibet. In Tibet, before the Chinese came, if someone said that farmers were dying of starvation no one would believe it. But once you know the facts it becomes understandable.

The Chinese agricultural reforms established a system where officers of the local commune would periodically check the crops and make an estimate of the anticipated yield of each field. They made these estimates when the grain was a few inches high; again when the crops grew to half their height; and finally, just before the harvest. Based on their estimates of a farmer's expected harvest they would estimate how much tax – in grain – the farmer had to pay that year.

At threshing time they would come around and tell the farmers, you have to give so many kilos as a "voluntary contribution" to the government, and a certain percentage you must sell as "voluntary sale" to the government, and another portion is your "voluntary contribution to defense." When all the obligations were complete, there was nothing left. The Tibetans had a saying in those days, "When the threshing starts, the pak stops."

Soon people were starving. People began to eat the grass and weeds at the edge of the fields. From starvation, or from eating weeds all the time, their bodies would swell up and they died. Many people died this way in prison, and they died the same way in the villages. First the body and face and hands swell up, and when the swelling starts to subside, you die.

There are many stories from the famine of those years. In Samye Monastery – Tibet's first monastery – there were huge prayer wheels which had leather coverings. The people there ate the leather from their prayer wheels.

So, many, many people died of starvation, some were executed, and many also committed suicide, driven to it by political persecution. For example, in Lhasa there was a man called Lha Dopa who worked as a teacher in a Chinese school. He was accused of consorting with reactionaries and subjected to extensive thamzing. One day he called together his four children and his wife. He killed them all so that they would not suffer at the Chinese hands, and then he cut his own throat. He died the next day at the hospital.

There were cases where whole families, father and mother and the children, would jump off cliffs together. These people just could not bear any more oppression from the Chinese. How could they kill their own children? It was not that they did not love them. But they saw their children in such a state of starvation they could not bear it. When the parents received thamzing the whole family would suffer, the parents might be killed and the children would become beggars. These parents simply could not bear to leave their children to such a fate, in such a society. They did these things out of love for their children, not because they did not care for them.

Many of the relatives of "reactionaries" were put into labor brigades. There were four categories – the parents and relatives of those who participated in the 1959 uprising; the families of refugees who fled to India; noble families; and wealthy business people, farmers, and nomads. These groups were given the hardest and the worst jobs. They had to get up before dawn to clean the streets and pick up garbage, for which they were not paid anything at all. Then at eight in the morning they would have to go to their regular jobs. In the evening they were kept up until midnight in political reeducation classes. They were given thamzing and constantly were under pressure to inform on each other. Some of these people didn't eat a hot meal for months because they had to work so hard they had no time to cook.

Another abuse imposed on "class enemies" was to shackle

their hands and feet, and leave the chains on for ten years. This was quite common. Some were chained so that they could not raise food to their mouths, so they had to crouch over and lap up their food like dogs. Or they would have to carry heavy loads of stone and brick with their legs in chains and would get terrible sores on their backs. On some, the shackles were so tight that their hands or feet would get infected, the sores would be filled with maggots and the open wounds would reach down to the bone. I myself saw wounds like this on prisoners. People died from these infections.

In some places people were put to work on utterly useless projects. Nomads were forced to build walls to divide their endless wild pastures. This disrupted grazing practices that had succeeded for thousands of years. Even in the winter they would force the nomads to try to dig the frozen ground in order to build useless walls. Similarly, farmers were forced to terrace fields in order to cultivate steep mountains where the land was no good. Tibet had never had a shortage of land. Before the Chinese came Tibet had always fed itself, and it was a land where the people and their environment maintained a harmonious ecological balance. These mindless projects served only two purposes – to oppress and intimidate the population, and to keep people occupied so they did not have time to think or energy to act on their own.

The Chinese introduced fierce restrictions on freedom of movement. If you lived on the north side of Lhasa you were not allowed to freely visit the south side. You had to get a permit, which was not easy to get, and you were not permitted to stay overnight. Similarly, travel between the villages and towns was restricted. I already told you how my sister, who lived in the village of Pagmo Shue, fifty kilometers from Lhasa, was not allowed to visit her family in the city for eighteen years. She applied many times for permission but she was told, "You are a counter-revolutionary family. You are not allowed to go."

The Chinese claim that they have brought much improvement to Tibet. They have built many factories and developed the economy. But before the Chinese came Tibet never had to borrow even one sack of grain from another country. It never had to buy one yard of material for clothing from another country. We were a self-sufficient nation. Before the Chinese came to Tibet starvation was unknown.

When we wanted to travel we never had to ask permission. We were able to go wherever we wanted. Never mind travel inside Tibet, we could even go to Nepal or India without asking anyone for permission. Tibet was a free country.

Now when I look back, I can see that Tibet was in some ways backwards. Certainly we did not have many things that other countries have. Because people were satisfied with their lives, because people had enough, and were happy, the society became complacent, people just took it easy. We didn't feel we needed any changes. Because we liked what we had, we did not strive for innovation. It was the contentment of the people that blocked political and social development in Tibet.

Here is an analogy: Before the Chinese came I never had to patch my clothes, I never had to sew and I didn't know how to sew. When I was in prison, after a few years my clothes were made up of nothing but patches, and sewing was a basic life necessity. When you are in a desperate state even sewing becomes easy. And it is the same for a society, it only changes and innovates when there is a need for change. In Tibet, people never felt the need.

It reminds me of another skill we learned in prison. We were not issued cups or bowls to hold our food. We would pick up old tins when we could find them to use as mugs. But they didn't last long – they got rusty and would start to leak. Then we would find empty toothpaste tubes, and we used that soft metal to patch the holes in our cups. Now, if utensils had been plentiful we wouldn't have learned such subtle skills of metal work. I discovered that when things are plentiful, you don't make advances. That is why Tibet was backwards. Because people were satisfied with their lives.

This was also one reason why Tibet was closed to the outside world. When you have all you need, you are not curious about what is on the other side of the mountain. People were ignorant of the outside world, and in the end we paid the price.

And it is also true that throughout this century the Chinese used their influence at the monasteries and in the Tibetan Government to subvert and forestall any kind of opening to the West or social innovations. Chinese spies, who were always active buying influence at these institutions, convinced some Tibetans that new schools or a Western-style hospital would undermine the traditional culture.

For example, the Thirteenth Dalai Lama established an English school, but it did not last long, and it was closed because a minority of influential people among the monasteries and nobles protested against it, and they were influenced by the Chinese spies.

These conservative pressures came naturally from some government officials who wanted to maintain their positions, but it was also influenced by the Chinese. Most of these Chinese spies entered through the three great monasteries in Lhasa, because there were no restrictions on who could enter as a monk. There was also Chinese involvement with certain nobles, but their influence was strongest in the monasteries.

Representatives of these three monasteries were involved in all governmental decisions, and in general they had great power. The Chinese spies would make large contributions to the monasteries to gain influence with the abbots, then they would persuade the abbots to oppose things like the English school, telling them that it would be bad for Buddhism. This kind of subversion was an important factor in preventing social innovation, especially during and after the reign of the Thirteenth Dalai Lama.

I personally discovered how many spies there were at the monasteries in 1959 when they rounded everybody up after the uprising. Many officials and abbots and monks were captured. We discovered then that there were spies from both the Kuomintang and from the Communists. It became obvious because the Communist spies were immediately given jobs with the Chinese administration. The spies from the

Kuomintang and other countries were charged and imprisoned. I found out in prison that some of these spies had been
geshes for many years. They would slowly influence and corrupt others in the monasteries, right up to the abbots. Then
the abbots would repeat whatever they said at government
meetings, and this would mould the entire national policy.

It was virtually impossible to stop this sort of thing because
anyone could come to study at these monasteries. It gave easy
access to Tibet. They would enroll as students, and some
studied hard and became good geshes, while others just made
a big offering to become geshes. Some might even have become abbots.

Unfortunately, all this corruption came to light only after the
damage had been done. But we learned a good lesson for the
future.

If we look at the big picture and try to understand the Chinese actions in Tibet, we see that their main intention is to
swallow up Tibet. It is a very big land with a lot of natural resources, resources which have yet to be exploited. Tibet also
represents a vast area with a small population, a natural temp-
tation to overpopulated China. The vast potential wealth of
the land, and the emptiness of it, were the main reasons they
invaded. There were also geopolitical reasons. Tibet is located at the center of Asia, between three great countries –
China, India and Russia. Its importance to Chinese military
strategy is evident.

The Chinese want to eliminate the Tibetans and have the
land of Tibet for themselves. The intention is apparent because they not only destroyed Tibetan culture, but they have
not taught the people new skills or offered Tibetans new opportunities. They do not want Tibetans to survive and prosper. Their intention is to slowly eliminate the Tibetan
identity until they have Tibet all to themselves. The cruelty
of their policies is designed to make the Tibetans submissive

to their masters. If any Tibetans survive this process, the Chinese want them only as their slaves.

The Chinese have treated the Tibetans as beasts of burden and even their name for Tibetans means "ox" – *Moniu*. Another name they call us is *Latseng*, which means "waste" or "garbage." They call us "Garbage Tibetans." These are not just curses uttered by prison guards. This is language you could hear from high Chinese leaders in large public meetings.

His Holiness the Dalai Lama was awarded the Nobel Peace Prize in 1989. It seems peculiar that the world would bestow such an honor on someone who is nothing more than "worthless garbage." But that is what the Chinese think of us. It seems that their view is quite different from that of the rest of the world. Perhaps the Chinese are actually living outside of our world community.

On a personal level, if you ask why I survived when so very many perished, there was no external factor that enabled me to get through. At Jiuzhen the conditions were the same for all seventy-six of us, but only twenty-two (and a half) survived. The hunger and the work and the cold were the same for all of us. But during those difficult times our religious faith became very strongly implanted in our hearts. Because we have always been a religious country and we were brought up in a religious system, we were always familiar with the ideas of Buddhism. But many of us never had a deep understanding or a direct personal experience of these ideas. From the time I was a child I was taught that there was a past life and there will be a future life. And the actions we take, our karma, depending on whether they are virtuous or non-virtuous, will determine the happiness or unhappiness of this life and future lives.

Although these concepts were imbued in our culture, there is no guarantee that you will believe in them or have faith in them. But during the Uprising and in its aftermath, we saw plainly how different people exposed to the same circumstances experienced very different results. Some were killed immediately in the fighting, some were wounded. Some stayed in prison in Lhasa, some were sent to Jiuzhen. Some survived Jiuzhen, some never came back. So it became clear to me that my particular fate, my own level of suffering, and my survival, were dependent on the subtle propensities, the storehouse of karma, of good and bad actions that I had committed throughout all of my previous lives. I had the karma to suffer these things, but I also had the karma to survive. Even when I wanted to die I could not make myself die.

In the midst of the violent storm of the Uprising, when shells were falling all around me like rain, when the ground was breaking up and the sky was black and the sun was just a red dull glow, in such critical circumstances, even though it seemed like certain death, I survived. Even though I was sent down to the prison camps of China and faced hardships there that could have killed anyone, I came back. And in Tibet, with all the cruelties of prison, the Cultural Revolution and the executions, I survived. And now, here I am, in India, working for the Tibetan Government. So, somehow I feel it was my karma to survive, to live in order to be able to serve the people once again.

Appendix to Tenpa Soepa's Story

1. THOSE WHO DIED AT JIUZHEN PRISON

Of the seventy-six who were deported to Jiuzhen, fifty-three died of starvation. I don't remember all the names. These are the thirty-six I remember.

    1. Chikhyab Khensur Ngawang Namgyal. The *Chikhyab Khenpo* was the ranking monk official in the Tibetan Government. *Khensur* means he was retired and had previously held that position. He was about seventy years old.
    2. Murja Tsewang Norbu. He was the general of the Murja Regiment. He fought against the Chinese on the Eastern border. He was also retired, about seventy years old.
    3. Donwang Kenchung Gyaltsen Dakpa. He was the Tibetan Ambassador to China, living in Beijing from 1952 to 1957.
    4. Tzedrung Lobsang Dhondup. He was an officer in the Tibetan Embassy in Beijing.
    5. Tzedrung Thubten Gaphel. He had served as a District Commissioner of the Lhoka region.
    6. Shudrung Rong Gadewa. He worked in the Research and Analysis Department of the government.
    7. Tzedrung Penpa Choedak. He was the one who died of the swollen stomach. He was the only one who died of ill-

ness. But of course the reason he got ill was that the food was so poor.

8. Tzedrung Ngawang Choephel. He worked in one district of Toe, "Upper Tibet," in the west, as a District Commissioner. During the uprising against the Chinese there were a lot of private underground organizations. He organized one of these.

9. Tzedrung Tenzin Phuntsok.

10. Thubten Oser. He was District Commissioner of Chushul District.

11. Tzedrung Yeshe Dhondup. He worked in the Reform Office along with me.

12. Thubten Lekshe. He was a teacher at one of the Chinese schools.

13. Nganchung Lobsang Tenzin. He worked as an assistant in the Kashag.

14. Rongdak Jamyang. A civil servant.

15. Dakar Kunga Lhakjung.

16. Kundeling Dejang Tenge. The principal secretary of Kundeling Labrang.

17. Kesang Chandzoe Yeshe. The manager-attendant of the lama Kesang Rinpoche.

18. Pekhong Chandzoe Pema Wangyal. One of the managers of the estate of Phala Dronyer Chenmo.

19. Dunyonsang Chontse. He was a bearded man. His daughter is in America. Her husband is Phondon-la.

20. Kumbeling Chontse. *Kumbeling* is the name of a monastery in Kham. He was their manager.

21. Liushar Chontse. Kalon Liushar's caretaker.

22. Gyabomgang Lama.

23. Tsewang Norbu. A great lama from Amdo.

24. Tseten Norbu.

25. Kunchok Namsum. These two were also lamas from Amdo.

26. Rupon Kunga. *Rupon* is an officer's rank in the army. He was stationed in Toe for many years.

27. Yabshi Takla Pen-la. The servant of His Holiness the

Dalai Lama's brother, Gyalo Dhondup.

28. Lhasa Jatsa Drungyig. A clerk in the Lhasa Tea and Salt Department.

29. Dorphan. He was from the Jang region.

30. Tsewang Jorgye.

31. Jinpa. These two were also from Jang.

32. Palden Lodro. From Medro.

33. Chusu Yeshe. He had learned boxing and martial arts in India.

34. Sopa Gyatso.

35. Khangar Bakdo. These two were from Ganden Monastery.

36. Ganden Abra. He was one of the representatives of Ganden Monastery at government meetings.

2. THE 22 ½ WHO RETURNED FROM JIUZHEN

1. Tzedrung Thubten Tsepak. He worked in one of His Holiness's offices. He died in Drabchi Prison, around 1976.

2. Sechung Sonam Topgye. He was imprisoned for eight years and then released. Now he is working for the Political Affairs Committee in Lhasa.

3. Shudkor Kunga Gyaltsen. He stayed in prison for fourteen years. Now he also works on the Political Affairs Committee in Lhasa.

4. Dr. Tenzing Choedak. He is now in Dharamsala, the physician to His Holiness the Dalai Lama.

5. Shewo Lobsang Dhargye. A former Kalon. He is now Secretary of the Department for the Reception of New Arrivals in Dharamsala.

6. Drotong Tsewang Rabgye. He served fifteen years in prison. He died in 1986 in Tibet.

7. Jampa Dhondup. In prison for fifteen years. Then he became the leader of some farming projects.

8. Tzedrung Thubten Legdrub. In prison for about eleven years. He is now working in Lhasa on the Political Affairs

Committee.

9. Tzedrung Thubten Tsondru. He was in prison for fifteen years. He is now a teacher at the Tibetan Children's Village School in lower Dharamsala.

10. Myself, Tenpa Soepa. In prison for twenty years. I am now the Representative of the Council for Home Affairs of H.H. the Dalai Lama at the Tibetan Settlement in Mundgod, Karnataka, South India.

11. Lha Gyari Lodoe Gyaltsen. He died in Drabchi Prison.

12. Lha Gyari Kesang Norbu. He is still in Lhasa. He works in a factory. He lost his right hand while working in a brick factory.

13. Kesang Choephel. He was sixteen years old when he was thrown in prison. His mind became unstable and he died around 1980.

14. Tsechar Rinzin Dorje. He died in Lhasa about 1980. He drowned himself, jumping in the river after his release.

15. Reting Labrang Tsongpa Jamyang Rigdun. He died around 1967, after his release.

16. Surkhang Nyerpa Tenzin. The storekeeper of the former Kalon Surkhang. He died in Drabchi Prison.

17. Yutog Chandzoe. He was the "half person" who returned from Jiuzhen and died the next day in Lhasa.

18. Thubten Kalden. In prison for fifteen years. He is now in Tibet.

19. Chamdo Chiso Bhulud. The manager of Chamdo Monastery.

20. Chamdo Chiso Tsinga. I have heard that he is still alive in Chamdo, but I can't say for sure.

21. Zikhyab Labrang Tashi Tsering. He stayed in Lhasa. Now he is working in a cement factory.

22. Garpon Pasang Dhondup. *Garpon* means "Master of Dance." He is in Lhasa, the head of the Tibetan School of the Arts.

23. Sothab Surpa Jampa Thinley. He was His Holiness's cook. He came to India after his release and died here.

Those are the twenty-three who returned from Jiuzhen. Of

those, ten have already died. Maybe now it is my turn.

It is perhaps ironic but many of my old comrades from prison were given government jobs in the administration of the TAR after their release. The Chinese were forced to acknowledge that there was no way to rule Tibet without the help of the nobles and government officials who worked in the old government. These were the only people that the Tibetan public trusted, the only ones they would listen to. Furthermore, they were the only Tibetans with the education and know-how to run a government. When the Chinese wanted to win the respect and confidence of the Tibetan people, and show that they had put reliable people into their administration, they had to turn to the very individuals who had been wasting away in prison for decades.

3. SOME OF THOSE WHO WERE EXECUTED IN DRABCHI PRISON

I can recollect a few of the names of people who were executed at Drabchi while I was there.

1. Kundeling Kunsang. The woman who founded the Tibetan Women's Association in Tibet. For her nationalist efforts she was executed in 1969.

2. Sersang Thubten Gonpo. A Ganden lama from Tsawa Kamtsen. He taught Dharma in prison in secret. They found out and they killed him.

3. Damdul Lhagyal. He was from Lhoka, a village head there. He was executed.

4. Sera Me Tsangpa Kamtsen Jampa Tenzing. A monk. I don't remember the reason for his execution.

5. Metrok Kunga Dzongtsab Lhakjung. The acting District Commissioner of Metrok.

6. Pema Donden.

7. Drikung Lama Kunchog Tenzin. When my long interrogation started, it was his execution that they used as an ex-

ample –"Is this the road you want to go down. . . ?"

8. Sangngag Chodren. A woman from Lhoka, an associate of Kundeling Kunsang.

9. Khamo Thachok Bhuti. A woman from Kham.

10. Ani Yeshe Nyima. A nun.

11. Dungang Namgyal. Executed because he threw *The Quotations of Chairman Mao* into the toilet.

12. Thubten Paljor.

13. Kunsang.

14. Kongpo Namgyal. Executed for singing after Mao's death.

15. Trinley Gyatso. He was a monk. He planned an escape from prison with some others. They found out and killed him.

16. Sham Namling Jampa Choephel.

17. Sonam Dorje. One night he tried to escape by climbing the roof. He was killed on the spot.

18. Kalsang Dolma.

19. Phusang.

20. Namgyal.

21. Tatoe Techung.

4. SOME OF THOSE WHO COMMITTED SUICIDE AT DRABCHI PRISON

1. Chadring Tsultrim.

2. Nyima Tenzing. My co-conspirator, who probably saved me from execution when he killed himself.

3. Tenzin Norgye.

4. Losang Choden. He mended bicycles in the prison. Together with a few shoemakers, who were all cripples with bad legs, he formed an underground cell. When he heard that the Chinese had discovered their secret he took a hammer and killed the shoemakers and then hanged himself. He thought that if he did not kill the shoemakers they would reveal the names of others.

5. Drepung Gomang Drungyig Gendun Wangchuk. He was an associate of Losang Choden. He worked in the prison kitchen. After Losang Choden killed himself he was called to the office from the kitchen. He decided that they had uncovered his relationship, so he took a kitchen knife and cut his own throat.

6. Thokme. He was from Dromo.

7. Lobsang Namgyal. He was from Lhasa.

Acknowledgments

Just prior to undertaking the interviews that culminated in this book I attended a conference on Tibetan translation sponsored by Tibet House in New Delhi. The problems engaged in those discussions centered on the translation of Tibetan religious literature, fixed texts built upon a technical vocabulary. In that context the challenge of translation is invariably to preserve accuracy and "literalness" without sacrificing lucidity, readability, and grace.

The challenges I discovered in dealing with contemporary oral histories were of a different order. The technical vocabulary is limited to Chinese propaganda-speak, and the grammar is conventional. But each speaker presents a distinctive voice, a personality, a regional dialect, and an emotional undertone that is unique. In the effort to capture these voices and transform them from oral Tibetan into written English I had the good fortune to work with three talented and tireless translators.

Ngawang Choephel from the Human Rights Desk of the Department of Information and International Relations in Dharamsala provided the translation of Ama Adhe's narrative, which, delivered in a thick Kham dialect, was inaccessible to me, and would be difficult even for many Tibetans. It was in fact Ngawang Choephel who introduced me to Mrs. Adhe and suggested her as a subject for this book.

In dealing with Tenpa Soepa's story I worked with two translators at different stages of the process: Chung Tsering, Secretary, Office of the Representative of the Council for Home Affairs of H.H. the Dalai Lama at the Tibetan Settlement in Mundgod; and Michael Lobsang Yeshe, a monk at Sera Je Monastery in Bylakuppe, and an old friend.

All three of these translators gave tirelessly of their time and their formidable skills, and were indispensable in bringing these stories into an English form.

I was directed to Tenpa Soepa's dramatic tale by his colleague, Tenpa Tsering, who has served the Tibetan Government in a number of important capacities and is currently the General Secretary of the Department of Information and International Relations in Dharamsala. For an account of Tenpa Tsering's own tragic and inspiring life story I refer the reader to John Avedon's *In Exile From the Land of Snows*, a book which provides the historical context of the lives that are recounted here.

I received helpful advice and criticism on the manuscript from a number of friends, including: Ngawangthondup Narkyid, Robbie Barnett, Canyon Sam, Geshe Thubten Tandhar, John Makransky, Roger Jackson, and finally Mary Christine Lauppe, who supported this project, from beginning to end, in innumerable ways. Susan Kyser, my editor at Snow Lion, made many perceptive suggestions as she turned the manuscript into a book.

In the final stages, Thubten Samphel, the editor of *News Tibet*, and Geshe Thubten Tandhar were most helpful in solving certain conundrums of Tibetan names, titles and spellings, and in the preparation of the glossary. James Seymour assisted me with the Chinese. And for his transcendental computer wizardry I am indebted to Mike Austin of Tower House.

Rackledown Farm
Bristol, Summer, 1991

Glossary

Ama (*A Ma*): Mother – a title applied to married women of middle age or older.

Avalokiteshvara: The bodhisattva of compassion; the patron deity of Tibet. The Dalai Lama is an incarnation of this deity.

Ba (*sBra*): A yak-hair tent.

Barkhor (*Bar sKor*): The inner circular road around the main cathedral of Lhasa; it circumscribes the commercial heart of the city.

Bodhisattva: A highly accomplished practitioner of the Mahayana path who has realized the altruistic mind to attain enlightenment in order to benefit all other sentient beings.

Chandzoe (*Phyag mDzod*): The steward or financial manager of an estate or monastic unit.

Chang (*Chang*): Tibetan beer, brewed from barley.

Chemar (*Phye Mar*): A special arrangement of tsampa, barley, and butter in a decorated box, offered to guests on the New Year.

Chikhyab Khenpo (*sPyi Khyab mKhan Po*): Highest ranking monk official, the head of the Dalai Lama's personal staff.

Chuba (*Phyu Pa*): Traditional Tibetan dress worn, in slightly different versions, by both men and women.

Dal: A staple food of India; lentils cooked to a thin soup with various spices.

Damyan (*sGra sNyan*): Tibetan lute.

Debon (*mDa' dPon*): Tibetan army commander.

Dri (*'Bri*): Female yak.

Dronyer Chenmo (*mGron gNyer Chen Mo*): An important monk official who arranges audiences and ceremonies for the Dalai Lama.

Dzo (*mDzo*): Cross between a yak and a cow. *Dzomo* is the female.

Geshe (*dGe bShes*): Literally "spiritual friend." A degree awarded on completion of the religious curriculum at one of the three great monasteries of the Gelugpa sect in Lhasa.

Gormo (*sGor mo*): A standard unit of Tibetan currency before the Chinese takeover.

Gyama (*rGya Ma*): A measure of weight, about one half kilo.

Jedrung (*rJe Drung*): Title for a son of a noble family who becomes a monk.

Jokhang (*Jo Khang*): The central cathedral of Lhasa. Also called Tsuglakhang.

Kalon (*bKa' bLon*): A minister of the Council (Kashag) which was the principal executive body of the Tibetan Government.

Kamtsen (*Khang mTsan*): A residential unit of a monastery, generally populated by monks from a particular region.

Kapsey (*Kha Zas*): Fried pastry, made especially for New Year.

Kashag (*bKa' Shag*): Literally "The Council." The principal executive body of the Tibetan Government. It usually consisted of three lay nobles and one high-ranking monk.

Khata (*Kha bTags*): A white scarf offered upon meeting or departing as a token of friendship or respect.

Khel (*Khal*): A measure of volume, commonly used for grain, equal to about twelve kilos.

Kungo (*sKu Ngo*): Respectful title of address for officials in Tibetan Government.

La (*Lags*): Honorific suffix added to names or titles to indicate respect or endearment.

Lemi ruka (*Las Mi Ru Khag*): Labor brigade.

Losar (*Lo gSar*): Tibetan New Year.

Mala: A rosary used for counting prayers and mantras.

Mani wheel: A prayer wheel.

Mo (*Mo*): A form of divination using special dice.

Momo (*Mog Mog*): Steamed dumpling, sometimes filled with meat. In the prisons it was a small lump of bread.

Mu: A measure of area, approximately one acre.

Norbulinka: "The Jewel Park." The summer palace of the Dalai Lama.

Om Mani Padme Hum: The mantra of Avalokiteshvara, the patron deity of Tibet.

Pak (*sPag*): The staple food of Tibet, consisting of roasted barley flour moistened – usually with butter tea – and rolled into balls. Other ingredients, such as dry cheese or meat, can be added.

Potala (*Po Ta La*): The residence of the Dalai Lama and seat of government in Lhasa.

Powa (*'Pho Ba*): A special technique for directing the consciousness to a particular rebirth at the time of death.

Puja: Offering ceremony or other religious ritual.

Rinpoche (*Rin Po Che*): "Precious One." Title of respect for lamas recognized as reincarnations of previous adepts.

Rupon (*Ru dPon*): Captain in the Tibetan army.

Sa ma drog (*Sa Ma 'Grog*): A class of semi-nomadic farmers.

Sangha: The community of ordained Buddhist monks and nuns.

Shamthab (*Sham Thabs*): The lower garment or skirt of a monk's habit.

Stupa: A reliquary or other ritual structure worshipped as a symbol of the Buddha or other holy being.

Thamzing (*'Thab 'Dzing*): Struggle session. Verbal criticism and physical punishment of individuals in a public gathering.

Thanka (*Thang Ka*): Painting of a deity or holy person.

Thukpa (*Thug Pa*): Noodle soup, or porridge made from any grain. In the prisons it was a generic term applied to the thin gruel that was served to the prisoners.

Tor Gya (*gTor rGyag*): Special ritual with a torma for dispelling adverse circumstances.

Torma (*gTor Ma*): A ritual cake, consecrated during a ceremony and offered to divine beings.

Tsampa (*rTzam Pa*): Roasted barley flour.

Tzechak Office (*rTze Phyag*): Tax and provision office.

Tzedrung (*rTze Drung*): Monk official of the Tibetan Government.

Tson srung (*mTson Srung*): A protection amulet containing various consecrated substances.

Tsuglakhang (*gTsug Lag Khang*): The central cathedral of Lhasa. Also called the Jokhang.

Tulku (*sPrul sKu*): A reincarnate lama.

Yuan: The standard unit of Chinese currency; a Chinese dollar.

Zung mag (*bZung dMag*): Prisoner of war.